TRUE LIVES
Cycling Ten Thousand Miles In Europe

TRUE LIVES

Cycling Ten Thousand Miles In Europe

by

PETER ALFRED PLEASE

A W A Y
publications

2000

First published in 2000
by Away Publications,
P.O. Box 2173, Bath BA2 3YN

Cover © Alan Peacock, 2000
Illustrations © Sean Borodale, 2000
Special thanks to Verona Bass and to all those open minds
and open doors who offered hospitality on the way.

British Library Cataloguing-in-Production Data

ISBN 09530330 3 1

Book production by Robert W. Palmer
at *Tuff Talk Press*, Bath

Printed and bound by Antony Rowe Ltd,
Bumper's Farm, Chippenham,
Wiltshire SN14 6LH
England.

'Neither have I been careful, in weaving the web of my story, to follow the order of time...I have rather studied to follow such an order as would string together facts of the same class and kind, although they may have taken place at different times.'

St Bonaventure, *Legenda Sancti Francisci*

For Ben, Michael and Elfie

PROLOGUE

**❝This is the road that no one's been down before
and no one knows where it goes to.❞**

Tell it to us like a story, she says, you know, at the beginning. But the beginning is such a long time ago. Who can remember that? And besides a beginning is always difficult even when you know how it starts. Take a deep breath. Tell it as it happened. Here we go. This is the road that no-one has been down before and no-one knows where it goes to. I started down it before I even knew I was on it and I needed that knock on the head to know that. There are all these roads and each one goes somewhere. The signposts say that: this goes to London, this is the Old Kent Road, this goes to heaven, watch out pinbrain you know where that one goes. This one leads to middle age, and who knows what's after that? At eight years old I wanted a road which led to a shop selling sweets, that's right, losing the odd fag or two, spreading gobstoppers about; being sick on chocolate was my idea of heaven. Then I was really sick and I changed my mind about heaven. I didn't like it. That was my first real thought that I wasn't spoon fed. Not that it did me any good and neither did it put me off chocolate.

Already I'm lost but that's all right. We're all lost really, though we pretend we're not. When we're not giggling we're hanging on by our fingertips. I never liked roads with signposts, especially signposts that other people put up. I didn't like school. There are pictures of me scowling out of school photographs, and I am always at the corner as if looking for a way out. I always preferred the unmarked trails, a bit of dirt under my feet or soft grass, something bumpy, awkward, not flat pavements and hard play-grounds where the only thing you trip over is your shoelace. I suppose I wanted adventure. Not dangerous adventure, for at heart I'm timid and fret when I'm tired, but adventure where you don't know what's around the corner. And who knows what's round the corner? As a friend says, you're a long time dead. And as I never had any dosh – what can anyone do on threepence-a-week pocket money? – I walked or cycled. I had to like what was free.

Now here's something strange. Walking was always a thing in my family. My father loved walking and so did his father. Every Saturday they walked from their Peabody Flats in Battersea along The Embankment counting the barges and imitating the horns. Grandpa could always do a doomy Thames barge sounding off under Waterloo Road Bridge. In fact he met his wife to be, my grandmother, while crossing that bridge. He had no money to buy her a meal and then he found half-a-crown by his feet, and so a little dream fell into place; and on through the City of London, by the Houses of Parliament and so on to St James's Park where he'd stop and hold a biscuit in his fingers, and the sparrows would land on his thumb to peck at the crumbs. Then onto Buckingham Palace Road and thereafter I forget. Roads were the only free thing that led out of the city, and I think grandpa dreamed about roads to the seaside in Kent and the cherry orchards and the land girls, and dad must have got it, too, for he studied all about roads: tarmacadam, skid resistant surfaces, and knew about bitumen and how sticky the stuff was. Then he did get out of the city and got a good job and deep pockets. I went back there once. The white poor have gone. It's the black poor now. Nothing changes. I ought to say there's an older sister called Sarah. She was there at the beginning. She's married and always working and has deep pockets too, but no time. Not like me. I've always preferred time to money, and time for Providence.

JUNO MONETA

I would like to make Time into a goddess along with Juno Moneta for Money. She would be in a temple made up from small things, plaster, little earthen bricks, cut stone and wood, pebbles, bits of coloured glass, the ephemeral beauty painted around her; metallic flying insects, mayflies and shadows would be her attendant deities; the flowers would be renewed each day. It would be on the side of the road, South-facing and sheltered to the North, where anyone could stop for a breather. We all inherit Time. She would remind us of this precious passing moment and that one day what's around us now will be found in a centimetre of rock. She would focus our minds wonderfully.

When I was a child I used to raid the cake in the larder, making sure to take a bit at a time so I wouldn't be noticed. When I was confronted with the nearly empty cake tin, I pleaded in my defence: 'But I only took small slices'. I think this is our attitude to time. If we give it away in little amounts then it doesn't matter. But strangely it's a commonplace to hear, 'I have no time'. Where does it all go?

Now to make things worse, imagine some Cosmic Authority has decreed that there will be even less time in the world, the supply will be reduced. What would this mean? We have to go faster to stay as we are. We will be driving in a fast-speed film, accepting stress and environmental degradation as normal. If China or India had the same consumption as Europe – and they are among the fastest growing economies in the world – the results would be catastrophic for everybody.

Here in the West, Time is Money. The dispossessed, the beggars, the deranged have plenty of time to watch the world go by but never the time to do what they want. On the other extreme, time for the rich is a paradise island, a limbo where you switch off Time – as long as you pay in hard currency.

I would like two currencies – Time and Money. I would like to be a techno-peasant (a catch-phrase of Frank Herbert). The techno solutions – networks, infrastructures, power – are as vital as the peasant mentality using time to give us roots in communities, to be producers, to grow culture as well as vegetables. Techno has time-saving gadgets (highly visible) and time debts (highly invisible). Cars are supposed to save us time, but how much time do we spend earning the money to buy the car, then money to service the car, maintain, clean, pay tolls to visit cities etc? Half our working lives can be accounted by it; we know where our time is going.

I would use Time to worship Juno Moneta. She understands the paradox that distances can be illusory, that New York can be closer than my neighbour. She understands my need, now and again, to buy time, to let her have her ways.

Let it be written over her portal:

Time is Money

Money is Time

JUST DO IT – WITHOUT NIKES

William van de Geer woke up one morning in 1989 thinking: 'I want to walk to Santiago de Compostela.'

'You're crazy,' said his wife, 'it's the other side of Europe.'

At that time he owned a successful electrical installation business in Rotterdam employing several dozen people. He had started it from nothing forty years before, when, as a dyslexic fifteen-year-old, he realised that conventional education was a road to nowhere for him. I met him on September 17, 1996, at Le Puy-en-Velay. He had walked from Rotterdam in four months and planned to be in Santiago de Compostela by Christmas. (He arrived in early December.) First impression: a big-jowled man with a voice that reaches into you and a barrel for a body, my comic idea of a burghermaster. Already he was in a box. 'I will tell you my story,' he said lowering his pince-nez glasses. 'Tell me when you get tired.' Well he kept thinking about Santiago, the urban pilgrim's destination in Galicia. He kept thinking about a snippet of conversation he had heard at a social party, 'There are 500 young people sleeping rough in Rotterdam each night'.

'In my business I was always chasing time and there seemed to be less and less of it in the world.' Then one day he decided: 'Just do it William.' It took some years to sell his business ('I had no right to burden my children with it') and at the end of this the doctor told him he had leukaemia. 'You need a new horizon,' he told him. 'Trust your body. When it is tired, rest; when you want to walk, then walk.' On May 5, 1996, he put a sign on his business door Ik ben even wandelin' *– 'Just popped out for a walk'.*

'I am walking to Santiago for the homeless. All my life I have used money to achieve things and now I want to do it another way, to use my positive thinking and time. If you only think about yourself you will be unhappy.' To everyone he meets he speaks about the homeless, his plans to start a community farm outside the city. 'When people are on the street they have nothing, but in a home base they can be helped.' He added my address to a long list. 'On February 15, 1997, I will write you a letter about my progress.' I believed him (and he did). He had the homeless children singing with him in the traveller's kitchen.

When I met him he had been given the all-clear with his leukaemia. 'This has become my life now. Perhaps I will see you when I go walking in England. Just do it, without Nikes.'   (Le Puy-en-Velay, France, September 17, 1996)

REFLECTIONS

Medard and Toots, the Togo boys, arrived at Dunsford farm, exiles from bluer skies. Both were dressed in grey suits, white shirts and ties, and with short, stylish hair. One carried a portable laptop, the other a briefcase. The English farm workers carried jembe drums, braided their long hair with beads and some wore batik shirts.

There's a good word for you, living on pennies and providence. That's me. Everyone thinks I'm well nutty but I've always thought that. What's wrong with nuts? They grow into trees. They say I'm always dreaming of far away places. I tell them they only dream of changing the wallpaper or getting a bigger TV. There you go. It takes all sorts. Sarah has a daughter called Chloë. I'm her godfather. She thinks the world of me. I think she's wonderful.

Already I am at a crossroads. If I go left I'll be looking backwards, and if I go straight forward I'll have to leave it all behind. This road is like that. Full of questions most of the time. And bones. I keep stepping over them. Some have names on them, people I have known or places where I lived. Sometimes I think it's all bones. I never know whether I'm right or wrong, whether it's a no-through road, and I still don't know. I used to want someone BIG to give me a sign, but I think BIG wants me to find out for myself. Your own mistakes are the only ones which count. You know, sometimes I'm shy and I smile when I speak. I don't know what to say and, if I did, I wouldn't know how to say it. I want to say that I've tried and failed, and that's not a crime. How else can we learn? I mean does BIG get it right all the time? He can't even get the weather right. I've lost count how many times I've told BIG only to do it at night, but it still rains in the day. That's the problem. We expect BIG to get things right. Perhaps BIG is struggling to make sense of it all. Perhaps BIG needs us in ways we can only dream about. Everything needs a little darkness before it can come into the light.

This story starts with the earliest thing I can remember, a picture of a child running down a grassy path and I had the feeling that it led to a garden. I saw that on a little black box. That's all. And the other thing is this: once sitting in the back of the car and seeing the water-colour sunset over the Thames Valley and thinking: It goes on and on. I wonder where it ends? And then: I want to go there when I'm big and find out. I can still see the black trees pencilled as far as my eye. This wanting to know and not knowing teases me for I know I will never get to the bottom of it. But for you, I'll try. I want you to understand.

I come here, I suppose, to try. On a busy day about four cars will pass this front door, but they have to know it's there to see it. It's covered in ivy like the rest of the cottage. My grandmother couldn't bear to cut it down when my parents bought it for them, a present for their old age, to make that dream of a road into the country come true. The best thing, I think, that they ever gave them. There is a path at the bottom of the railway track where Tugger, the Border terrier, is buried under the Yorkshire Hessle pear. That tree marks the grave because she said that it was like her dog: from the North, small and hardy, with sweet juicy fruit which melted in your mouth. Fruit to be eaten off the tree. It didn't travel well and neither did Tugger. He didn't live long, not like this tree which grows up like a pyramid. When I inherited the cottage I paid off Sarah, gave her most of the furniture (and that picture!) and boarded up the windows. I let the ivy grow onto the roof. They think I'm mad, but it's my house. I can do what I want with it. I wanted it to be like the simple signal box, two-up-and-two-down that it used to be, the house I knew best as a child. It's that long ago. I didn't want a stranger to rebuild and extend the walls, put in central heating and the rest of the gizmos which cost you an arm and a leg. It would be like walking on my grandparents' graves. My father scattered their ashes next to the oak and willow by the stream where it goes under the railway track. They had wanted to live in the country, I wanted them to remain there in peace.

It's important to see this cottage. It's down a long road which fords a stream and goes around orchards with small, bent apple trees. You don't see it until you are right on top of it – just past the old railway crossing – and then you look left and see a wall of ivy but really it's the front and side of the house. The ivy protects the bricks, that's what they say. I think a little owl nests there as it squawks half-an-hour before sunset. The long narrow garden runs beside the railway line but that's overgrown with brambles, hazel bushes and seedling ash trees. I like to stand there sometimes and see the fruit trees which grandpa had planted. He never picked the Victoria plums; that was left to me. Once steam trains painted gold and blue went along it every day to the seaside. That's amazing! People walk along it now, but not many. I wave to them if I'm here. I can see they think that I'm out of my depth, that I've pushed the boat out too far. Granny remembers waving to the passengers sitting in the carriages. The train used to go so slowly that if someone lost their hat leaning out of the window all they had to do was to get out and collect it and then walk back and climb back onto the train. You don't believe me but it's true. They called it The Slow and Dirty Railway, but everybody loved it. I love this cottage because it is in a jigsaw of small fields and corners of woods stretching to the top of the hill. The new road is on the other side but you can't see it. There are footpaths everywhere. I can lose myself without trying, and I like that.

ZALAEGERSZEG

I had an anxiety dream about Hungary months before I went there. I was lost down some back road and all the signs had the same unintelligible name. That's it, I thought, I'm lost. I will disappear. This base-line emotion of losing my way, not being able to read the signs, must have coloured my response to Hungary. The hay wagons appeared more antique, the abstract blues and creams and rose paints on the houses more strange (and intriguing); the little white roads with straggling gypsy women with silver bangles, bare feet and flimsy red dresses, more exotic. Then there were the rabies signs tacked to trees, a picture of a mad dog, and the furtive hours I passed eyeing swooping gnats, sneaking past cats, eyeing mistrustfully sparrows. In Kaposvár I stopped in the city centre, by the brass arrow on the ground. It said: 2088 kilometres to Bath. Kaposvár is twinned with Bath. In a bar in Zalaegerszeg all the locals were laughing at the 'Return of Mr Bean' dubbed into Hungarian. I watched Austria draw with Cameroon, and everyone thought it a fair score. They lost ten minutes of the World Cup to watch 'Return of Mr Bean'.

'And who are you?' said the proprietor in immaculate English.
'Ich bin Englander.'   (Zalaegerszeg)

This house is strange. It's far away down the lanes but I'm never lonely here. When I'm back in the city and I think about it, it's closer to me than your face. And when I come here, whatever the time of year, I feel I have never been away. As a child I thought it was the sort of place that had forgotten about people, but then I remembered the smoke coming out of the chimney. My grandmother always kept a coal fire going in the front room even when she wore straw hats outside. When grandpa first opened the front door he saw leaves flying up the stairs and then they flew back down over his shoulder. It wasn't the draught. They were bats but he never saw them again. She and grandpa had moved there to grow vegetables and suck sugar from little straws, or that's what he said. She stayed when he died. She said that there were no more trains leaving this station, and where would she go anyway. Not back to the Peabody Flats, not in a million light years. And she wouldn't live that long. She was a brave and kind woman and took her secret with her. She lived alone and always had things to do. She was also stubborn, especially with Tugger. She wouldn't let him out of her sight. It was no use saying anything different. That's what happens when you get old, I suppose. It's hard to change. I see a bit of myself in granny, this stubbornness, this holding on. Yet without it where would I be? I have to taste things for them to grow. No-one ever told me that. Well they may have done but sometimes I'm duck-headed and it slides off my back.

This road that no-one has ever been down before starts here. Once the children used to come with me but they prefer the bright lights on the screens. I tell you, you are on your own. There's no easy way into this story, even getting into this house is tricky. The special trap door is still here hidden in the outhouse. You have to pull up the two planks and crawl into the hole, feel your way through the darkness under the wall and then push up another board to stand in the hallway. It gets harder each time, that's older age for you, and my heart beats a little faster and I wonder what I'm doing here alone, why I come back. I have my reasons. One hundred reasons and as many pieces of paper. I have spread them on the floor. Each one tells a story, brings back a face, a moment, a meeting. I never looked for them. They came to me. I want to make sense of cycling ten thousand miles in Europe. I'm interested in what I don't know, and there's plenty of that. Yet all these roads lead back to you and this cottage, and the Christmas with the big snow. How long is a road? How long is a life? Perhaps I

15

am well nutty. I've always thought that real things are strange one-offs. I'm certainly not all good, and I'm all right. If I want to be here, that's okay. I'm harming no-one.

I never think of this cottage as empty. Here I can open and close doors, and this one opens at Christmas. I have to begin at Christmas. I made a fire in the old signal room, that's below the attic, once our childhood bedroom. The levers controlling the signals have long gone, except one, and the ivy is back on the inside of the windows. I like it that way. That was here at the beginning. A queen wasp is overwintering there, and she flew into my dreams last night waking me up. I sat up in the dark. For a split second I didn't know where I was. Beginnings are like that, this panic of losing my way. I hung the blankets off the picture rails and made myself a kitchen with the shelf: a few boxes, a spoon, a fork, and a knife. I am not expecting visitors. Here I am like that tramp who is going nowhere. I travel best that way. I let silence brush me with her fingers. I tingle. I remember my question: Where is the beginning?

LILAC DROPS

I need to go back to nature, to the little things within my touch, what is here in this moment. This freedom to respond without pre-judgement is what I am after. This discovery of raindrops sliding on the underside of cracked lilac boughs. There is this screen between us, a glass pane smudged with golden raindrops. It protects me from the elements outside. I am comfortable with this screen. I reach out but I cannot touch the lilac or press my nose against its bark. I can only see through this glass, and it's blurred. From the inside the lilac is flat, all in a line. It is a closed book. It is not part of me. I am a stranger, the lilac is a stranger. I am used to seeing through screens, showing only bits of myself. What does it feel like? Vacuum seal, airless, touch limited...I am skinny with this screen between me and the lilac, skinny on the inside. This is a ragged spring, and I want to change that. I will contradict this.

There's a wind cooling my nose and cheeks, shooting holes in the lilac. These raindrops splash the white of this page, upsetting the symmetry of what? I notice a single petal embraced by a lilac leaf, a veined mauve, an exotic from who knows where? Yet they are here together, clasped. And these tears are answering what? That I have shut myself away this winter, been caught in the right angles of fixed points and ends. I want to come back to this beginner's place, to this messy beginning, this idiosyncratic moment. The noise of roller blades, the metallic tracking of a scooter. Olga appears and we notice the bulbs from her bottom drawer are opening at last. This is what happens when I put myself here. Let every spot of rain adorn these moments, be the pattern for this

day. I return to the embrace of the leaf and the petal, this unsought for union.
I am touched by this, by this hope. (Bath, March, 1998)

BIKE CRAZY
'Going far?'
'Frederikshavn.'
'Frederikshavn! By bike? You must be joking.'
'I'm not.'
'Hedvig! Hear this.'
'What?'
'He's going to Frederikshavn by bike.'
'It's not that far. All you got to do...'
They nod knowingly. 'You got to be fit.'
'That's a well cherished myth. If you walk you can cycle.'
'Many punctures?'
'Only in your mind.' They giggle.
'You adjust a little screw here and away you go. I meet grannies doing it.'
Something heavy presses down their furrows. 'Where have you come from?'
'From Århus.' Their eyes balloon up.
'But that's... '
'Not far...'
Silence seals their mouths. 'You're stopping in Frederikshavn?'
'I'm going to Oslo.'
Their eyes glaze over. 'To Oslo.'
'Via Sweden.'
They lean on each other for support.
'To Oslo via Sweden.'
'And back.'
Some vital muscle wobbles their legs. 'Back from where?'
'England, of course.'
They fight for air. 'To England...' They slide to the ground. The air hisses
out as helpless laughter. The gigantic thought is punctured.

(Varde, Denmark, June 19, 1997)

* * *

'Bonjour!'
'Are you mad?' says the French cyclist. 'Can't you see I'm busy.'
'Bonjour!' I say again.
The man stares at me.
'Mon cher petit,' says his mother. 'Tu as peur? Qu'as-tu vu?'

'Un homme orange...'

'Olala.'

'Comme le vent...'

'Olala.'

'Avec les yeux rouge...'

'Olala.'

'Avec une tête métallique...comme un insect grotesque.'

'Pas peur mon petit. C'est un cyclo-tourist Anglais.'

* * *

'Bonjour.'

'You are not a pilgrim. Where did you get this shell?'

'But...'

'Where did you get this hat? Where did you get this passbook?'

'But, but...'

'I thought so! A cycling T-shirt. On your knees and pray. We were given feet to walk as pilgrims and not wheels. So on yours and sin no more.'

CAMARADERIE OF CYCLING (Portsmouth Ferry Terminal)

'I've seen your face before.'

'Sustrans. Welsh Tour?'

'It's a small world.'

'Going far?'

'Oslo.'

'You have to be a happy person to go cycling by yourself.'

'I bet those two cyclists took the train. They look so fresh.'

'That's my baby, the Moulton. Will you guard it while I get some food?'

'We're off to Brittany twinning with a cycling club. They're dead keen, reception tonight, picnic tomorrow...'

'So we got to the end of Wales. I was feeling proud of myself. Then I saw these tall people cycling...'

'Where are the other two? I told them to be on time.'

'They were on pennyfarthings, dressed in breeches and what not. They had cycled from Northampton to Bristol.'

'They're in the pub, aren't they? I'm not going to wait.'

'Did you catch the train?'

'A hundred miles to get here. We started on the back roads but it's like this, up and down. I'm the oldest and they stuck me in front. My knees hurt.'

'No brakes or gears. Dead hard work.'

18

'I said to the Breton, they'll be six coming. "And vere's ze car for zee luggage?"
We carry our own luggage - there was silence.
"I zee." They do things differently there.'

'We got five minutes.'

'I see that smug git. I'll spill a drink over him. You've got a little car. I've got
a big lorry at home.'

'Christ, it's Piccadilly Station here. Can you guard my bike mate?'

'I love the coming and going.'

'My wife doesn't like cycling. She thinks it's a bit below her.'

'Did you know they've got someone in the French mountain bike team. Shit!
My knees are wobbling.'

'He's going to Oslo.'

'By yourself? I'm a truck driver in my other life. Let's see: Italy, Germany,
Sweden...yes, June 15. See you there.'

'I'm off to Cherbourg for four days, peace and quiet. It's how I clear my mind.'

'Nice bike Dawes.'

'£20 from a mate. I'm a copper see. Gotta watch the pennies. I'd retire now but
it's the mortgage. Going far?"

'Oslo.'

'Jesus, that sounds like paradise. I've put in for early retirement in 2004. They
know you're swinging it.'

'What's that?'

'**Danish bike. I'm psychiatrically disabled but they still give me enough
buttons to get this.**'

'The things I could write about. It's not cosy like The Bill. All careers. They
promote someone to get them out the way.'

'**That's a wide-flanged hub. Spreads the tension. The wheel died three
times before.**'

'If we had no Force, make no difference to the crime figures.'

'**I'm off for a month down the Loire, then Ireland...**'

'When I retire I'll do a couple of local charity rides, then I'll limber up for a big one
around Britain.'

'Everywhere I go, my Moulton goes too.'

'It's a small world. You must know Tony Ambrose. He's got an allotment with
fruit trees.'

'He lives down my road!'

'People don't want to work more hours to earn more money so they can shop
at Sainsburys. They'd rather have more time and grow it themselves.'

'I'm doing bits and pieces, and really enjoying myself.'

'I'm putting all my energy into one thing, and it's great.'
'I must check out what they did with the Pegasus bridge. By the way, Blair walked it.'   *(Route d'Aizier, Normandy, May 2, 1997)*

AKUBRA SKAWAY

'I came in at 7.10. Got a taxi.'
'Hi lads. Name's Philip.'
'I was thinking of going to Frisco, Fiji and back home. World tour, £1200.'
'These friends landed on the coast in Greenland and skied with a kite. 20-30mph. They came to a ball on the horizon, a US early warning system.'
'To fly from Perth will cost you £700.'
'They'd taken all the sensitive stuff out. They camped inside. Spooky!'
'Problem with going away for a year you have to take stuff for all weathers.'
'I checked the temperature in Oslo two days ago 14C – bloody heatwave ever since.'
'They got shellac in their food. They ate 250gms of margarine with every meal. Highest energy value.'
'Got my pills to take, anti-malarial pills for SE Asia.'
'I got my typhoid shot travelling to Turkey. Doctor said I might feel a bit sick. I was permanently sweating and freezing for three days.'
'Doctor told me that you tank up on vitamin B and garlic you can't go wrong.'
'It's serious. I only bought 18 kilos of gear. Then I'm not travelling all round the world.'
'This hat is typical Australian – akubra. It keeps your head cool.'
'I was working from a temp agency – Moorgate, Bank, Baker Street, The Angel. All the business areas.'
'Did you go to The Mean Fiddler Pub? You get a 263 bus from Willesdon Green tube station.'
'Did you ever find The Greyhound pub in Fulham? Sunday morning, that's a mad Australian pub. All they drink are cases of Fosters. A great crack.'
'Horrible stuff!'
'You can get Tasmanian beer in London. £4 a stubby.'
'There's no point in having big glasses in Australia. The beer will be hot before you finish it.'
'I did a tour of Heineken in Amsterdam. They put you in a drinking hall for 45 minutes. If you're any good you could walk out blotto.'
'He shows me the still. There's a way of testing it. If it turns clear it's all right; with blue it's got impurities.'

'It doesn't really feel like 23.05.'
'You go to Andorra and keep going. We were in the dip.'
'I met this guy in Italy who spoke 13 languages...'
'Gaelic is becoming popular all over Ireland.'
'In Skaway in Alaska the hostel lady said she found mammoths in the glacier.
They ate the mammoth steaks, 2000 years old. Imagine.'
'In Hobart you can walk out into the bush and see nobody for days.'
'The Indians in Alaska are wealthy — £1000 a foot to carve a totem. They
had work for years ahead. They ship the totems out.'
'My father built dams in central Wales. Met my mother in a pub.'
'They're wild in those bays. Straight in from the woods.'
'You know McAlpine? I worked for them renovating the harbour in
Wexford.'
'When the wind comes down from the glaciers everything stops for days. Down
to -70F.'
'The English had a sweep and shot the aborigines. It was easier than
shooting sheep. They didn't move.'
'The mosquitoes in Alaska are like bumble bees.'
'They're babies in Sweden but I still woke up with half my face
swollen up.'
'I didn't actually see the mosquitoes. I left before the eggs hatched.'
(Oslo YHA, June 14, 1997)

I should put you in the picture. I discovered my cycle brain when I sold
my car, and I discovered time again. I just had to press another button. I
planned these six journeys as a whole -10,000 miles between 1995-1999. All
those years I had a car I never travelled anywhere, not properly; there was
always glass in the way. I wanted to go somewhere under my own steam, in
my own skin; stop when I wanted to, on a city street or a back-road, step
out of the clothes which I wore every day, lose myself for a month or two. I
wanted to go somewhere I had never been before. Now here's a thing. I was
looking for something but I had no name for it, and because I had no name
it was always behind me. Like the ivy behind me I know it's there but I
can't see it. The whole of Central Europe is a hinterland for me. Several
thousand miles down the roads I realised that I had known this fascination
before, this looking for something — mice under logs, stamps off postcards,
old cigarette boxes from the wayside. All things I found by myself. These
cycle journeys were like the stamps I collected as a child, a way of travelling
on threepence-a-week pocket money. Always the strange names and lands
were familiar, as if I had known them from before...

TRANSDANUBIAN CHILDHOOD

I did not see the cowboys — the Ciskos — herding up the cattle, or discover bottles of vintage Tokay dusty in village shops and going for pennies; nor did I see the bustards roaming the prairie plains; or the peasants in their ethnic costumes (only old timers in shawls and floral shirts and hefty arms to wield their mattocks). I did not see the red paprikas (it was the wrong season) or find old copper coins still in circulation. But I did see ribbons of azure blue on the wayside, the larkspurs (Delphinium ajacis). They lived up to my expectations. The faces of these larkspur toughing it out beneath Gleditsia, the honey locusts, I found strangely comforting. They seemed to smile back at me, and so did the red poppies.

I cycled along the pencil-line roads. I was wrapped in calico against 40 degrees of sun. The land, flat as a pancake, was ankle deep in haze, the fields stretching on forever, a world without end it seemed. Where did it go? Has anyone been there before? Vague questions, and I had no answers. I was alone with nature and dreaming. Of what? It did not matter. I knew I was happy. The intense blue sky, the steam-rolling heat reduced everything to pure sensation until it seemed time stood still. I belonged to this picture. I accepted it as a child does. The faces became bigger and so did the bustard, and I heard the shout of the Cisko Kid, the drumming of horses' hooves. I saw the waving lasso, and before I knew it he was riding on the great bird's back. They were in some special time zone and so were the elder trees, the swallows, the great-crested lark, the wall barley among the ancient peach groves — all dimly remembered, but from where?

Whirling, pot-bellied and iridescent green beetles flew beside me, and I fancied I could see their smiling faces and big green eyes. Then I saw two dancing together, a sort of rag-time and they held canes in their hands. Then gone! The blackcap sitting on a thistle nodded at me, or so I thought. I saw the perfection of little flowers against vast horizons. I could see lizards basking on dry walls. I stared at one marvelling at its pulsing heart and little giveaway tongue. I pushed my finger slowly towards it. It dived away but not before a bubbling laughter erupted from me. The crested lark evoked from me an exclamation. I had never knowingly seen one before. But I had. Where? I cycled for hours. Then I understood. Instantly! They were pictures from my earliest nursery books of wayside flowers and fairies, and from the stamps I collected, those marvellous windows on the world.

Here in Transdanubia I found glittering pieces of my earliest childhood. I was alone with nature and dreaming of what? I have no idea.

(Pécs, Hungary, June 8, 1998)

* * *

When the train comes, I'll know
When I hear the train
I'll know I am happy.
I'll intone the base notes, the high-pitched ones
Coming down the track,
The Transdanubian express, all safely aboard
The two-tone horns
mmmmmmmmmmmmOOOOOOOOOOOOOOOOOO
The pilot sees the night ahead
Safe together over the plains we mustn't be late,

                                       we mustn't be late

All together
Somewhere here we mustn't be late,
Transdanubia is a long way
Over the plains
To my heart, I'll know.

This signal box is a wayside. I have always loved this edge, not this, not that. Maybe it's a failing in me this Celtic fascination with border zones: not mist nor rain, not night or day, not sky or earth; this glamour of change. Everything you throw away is here: insects, rubbish, broken dreams, native flowers... Everyone comes here at some time. It's the end bag, the loose ends nobody wants, the discarded lives. It's what's left behind. If I had a God, she would live here and give every one their due, the time they needed to mend. This edge is a wild line, and the people on the roads are going somewhere, and the fields are going somewhere. Perhaps they'll meet over breakfast. But you can lose yourself here; a ruby-tailed wasp may dazzle you from nowhere; a minute is a gap, is a possibility.

THE WHITE ORCHID

I stopped immediately when I saw the single white spire two feet from the tarmac. I dropped down beside an albino orchid, trestled white and playful out of sheathed green leaves – unique among thousands of royal purples and liquid chocolate of its cousins, the early-spotted orchid (Orchis maculatum). They colonised the spaces between the cowslips, an unforgettable picture on this back lane in Perche, Normandy. Closeby is St Mark's fly with its long legs tucked neatly down the grass blade. It is sitting out the dreary weather, but for me the sun is shining. I could not continue onto Mondoubleau; something made me pause. I crossed to the opposite verge. Behind the white orchid is an ocean of mustard and beyond that another ocean of silage grass.

The natives grow only along this uncultivated strip. I don't have a problem with that. These fields mirror the vast cities; half of the world's population are due to be living in cities in the 21st century. But I do want to honour this wayside ground, a wild line left in this landscape. I want to honour this uniqueness, this fertile ground. I bowed to the white orchid and pressed my hands together. I walked away pushing my bike and kept looking back over my shoulders. (St Agit, France, April 30, 1998)

KORNBLOMPST

On the sandy soils of West Jutland where glacial boulders guard farm entrances, where sticky catchfly spells doom to flies, where pines in ranks hold together the fragile soils — it's here you will see the cornflowers, sky-blue strips along the boundaries of wheat fields. That's as far as the herbicides reach. In Danish the flowers are called Kornblompst, and that's also the name of the dairy farms marketing organic cheese. One of them belongs to Steyn and Ann Dissing, about 40 hectares of undulating glacial soils, grass and cereals. They are in their thirties, handsome people with three children; Steyn's golden pigtail is pinned to the notice board. I am amazed by their commitment, their days and minds full of the farm and their three children, birthday parties and playgroups and the rows of sugarbeet still to be hand-weeded, and the twice-daily milking of 40 Jersey cows. But they are glad of company and a reason to rest. The farm belonged to Steyn's parents, pioneer teachers of organic farming.

A modern, open-plan house overlooks the undulating land, pastoral and unremarkable. The history is in the land. Steyn knows every field, where the glacial soils change; black medick on gravel, wood rush on clay pockets, tall ryes and clover on the mixed soils; they will make the best hay. The red clay is buried by the glacial dumps; perhaps the old pottery rim he picks off the field is from this source. In the fodder beet he picks slivers of flint in his strangely old and gnarled hands. He makes me see the low-lying land before us which was a lake in prehistoric times. This field was the shoreline, and by my feet is where they worked the flint to make axe heads, knives and scrapers, arrow heads for birds and fish. Everywhere are flakes with the characteristic compression mark from the blow and their secondary ripples. 'Every time I pick one up,' he says, 'I think of the person who flaked it off.' I find part of a stone sickle which cut corn here 3000 years ago. Only time separates our hands — but I needed someone to show me. The continuity is like the cornflowers; the natives are on the edges. (Struer, Jutland, June 11, 1997)

Why Europe? In my daydreams other European countries appeared in the night-time, or they were like distant cousins or lost aunts and uncles whom I had never met but knew of their existence. We were linked but how? I met a Hungarian woman who dreamt of buying a cottage in Cornwall so she could walk beside a rocky coastline with white waves and shifting blues. In a Polish shop-cum-cafe a Polish woman touched my shoulder and kept smiling at me. She bought me tea and orangeade and a plate of chocolate biscuits and polished every inch of the table, lifting my plate and cup, placing them back slowly, so tenderly. I was amazed. She wouldn't let me pay one złóty. 'My brother, Bedford, Bedford.' At last I understood. This tenderness was the tip of an iceberg.

All our different languages and national borders amazes people from North America. In Canada you can travel for five days and hear the same news, speak the same language, spend the same currency. What's all the fuss about? A man from Cameroon has no problem recognising us: English, Scottish, Irish, Serbian, Belfast, Greek, Danish, Hungarian. It makes no difference. She's from Europe, welfare, power, infrastructure; fortress Europe keeping out the displaced North African hordes. That's one view, Europe as a reservation for the privileged. Yet ask anyone from France or Britain or Denmark if they think of themselves as a European and, almost without exception, we are out of our depth. Chernobyl reminded us that we're all in this together. If we are in a room with Japanese, Brazilians and Venezuelans, we have no problem thinking of ourselves as Europeans. Or are we Westerners? I am tongue-tied by the complexity, the contradiction of simple things: in Ottoman days many Albanian husbands were Muslims, their wives Christians, in order to protect their rights; in Carinthia they use only the seeds from the pumpkins to make the much prized *Kurbiskernol* oil; in England we throw them away.

Nearly everyone I met who could say they were European, also felt stateless, part refugee, as if they had no home, as if they were on their own. There were gaps in their world, in their words, spaces in their minds. That's why I loved Pécs in Southern Hungary. It was the first place I felt instantly at home. Everybody was so different from me – Magyars, Germans, Gypsies, Turks, Croatians – and that's why I could belong. I could see out of different windows. I discovered some of my lost aunts and uncles. I wanted to give these Europeans gifts: I would give water to the Spanish; sensitive fingers to the English; I would read love stories to the Germans; I would give fruitcake to the Danes; time to the Hungarians (and Czechs); laughter to the Swedes (and cheap beer); cycle lanes to the Norwegians (and Britain and Spain and Hungary); dollars to the Albanians; lovable insects to the French; mixed marriages to the Serbs; real dairy ice-cream to the Poles. It was as if there were these new ties linking us, cutting across what I expected to see or to think. And, naturally, out came the demons.

PREJUDICES

What you think before you think. I collected them, word for word. The nationality refers to the source.

'You can always tell where the Dutch are on a campsite from the noise.' *(Belgium)*

'The Germans make so much noise.' *(English)*

'The Dutch talk and talk and talk but they never show their true feelings.' *(Belgium)*

'The French make so much noise. Always going one way, then another, clicking their tongues, elbowing each other.' *(English)*

'The Hollanders are too direct.' *(Belgium)*

'The Belgians build their houses twice as big as they need to, that's why they work twice as hard.' *(Dutch)*

'The English are so polite you never know what they are really thinking.' *(Dutch)*

'The Dutch restaurants are very expensive but the food quality is low. Calvinist thinking: you need a reason to eat out, and then it must be expensive.' *(German)*

'The Germans have a provincial mind; if this is what they think, then you must think the same too.' *(Dutch)*

'Denmark is a rather dull country.' *(Dutch)*

'The Germans wear yellow plastic raincoats and drive their Mercedes onto the beach.' *(Danish)*

'The Scots are mean. They even recycle their loo paper.' *(English)*

'Good morning Mr Hollander.'

'Good morning? Vot is dat? Ah! Good business!' *(English)*

'The Spanish drink a lot of wine and don't like to work too much.' *(German)*

'The English are heavy drinkers.' *(German)*

'The Danes are heavy drinkers.' *(French)*

'The Germans are heavy drinkers.' *(English)*

'The Finns are often drunk.' *(Sweden)*

'The Swedes in Denmark drink like swine.' *(Danish)*

'Nobody believes in God in Denmark.' *(Danish)*

'The English are prudes.' *(German)*

'Sausage krauts!' *(Danish)*

'The Finns are fast with their knives.' *(Danish)*

'The Danes are quite fat, a bit German like in appearance.' *(Sweden)*

'The Swedes are so polite when they travel, not polite at home.' *(Danish)*

'The Germans are obedient to authority.' *(Danish)*

'The warden at the German youth hostel switched off the World Cup game ten minutes before the end because the rule said all lights had to be off by ten. The Germans went to bed.' (Dutch)

'The French lorry drivers blockade, their fishermen blockade, the farmers blockade, and the government always gives into them.' (English)

'The church bells are upside down in England so you can ring them. In Germany they are fixed: you are not allowed to ring for fun.' (German)

'Watch out in Norway and Sweden, the women drag the men off into caves.' (Danish)

'You have to tell the Germans to stop for a tea-break, the French stop when they think they have done enough.' (English)

'The Italians you cannot rely on.' (German)

'The Hungarians are capitalists.' (Slovak)

'The Czechs are calculating.' (Slovak)

'The Slovaks are emotional, more simple.' (Czech)

'The British clean their cars on Saturday mornings. If you make friends with one they are friends with you forever.' (German)

'The Poles have problems with everybody.' (Czech)

'It's all horse-carts and tractors on Polish motorways.' (Czech)

I'm lost again. Time keeps going backwards and I can't stop it. I only have an inkling of where I am. I am with you now and the snow and the black-outs and the white-outs and the road which stopped outside this signal box. Is that why I come back, to pump up the tilly lamp, to see by half-lights? I need to find my way, the way you wanted me to when your back was turned and when Tugger cocked his ears at a falling leaf. I would like this to be a piece of string with a beginning and an ending. But here I go round and round. I will lose my way, I will find myself. It's a true life, you see, your life and mine. That's why it's such a mess.

Your letter arrived a week before Christmas: black, spindly writing as if a spider had crawled through an ink stain then dragged its feet off lost. Someone had printed our address beside it, so I suppose that's something to thank her for. My mother, too quickly, said that it was from a distant friend of the family and held it over our heads so we couldn't read it. But we had to. Inside was a card with giraffes, elephants and birds cut out of some picture book. They were flying across the sky and under it was a steam train with Father Christmas waving from the end of a carriage. He was going somewhere but it was out of the picture. This was the first time we had heard from you. To our questions mother said that his proper name was J.P.

Tomas. He lived in the country in a big house with rose gardens all the way round, and behind that was an orchard and two ponds with big carp fish which took bread from your fingers, and sometimes they rolled over like battleships so you could tickle them. That's what she said. He must be rich to live there and have people do everything for him. He was one of God's children, she said, but he wasn't a child. We didn't know what she meant. 'We're all God's children,' said Sarah. 'That's what they tell us at school.' She said it stamping her foot. You have to listen to my sister.

This signal box is a listening place too.

FINCA LA MOHEA

I start with the macaw: several clear fluty notes after a rain-burst then a swift gaggling laughter vanishing into the treetops. What is a tropical bird doing in the Serrania de Ronda? I have no answer.

This road from Malaga to Ronda outdistanced my expectations; half-strange and half-familiar; prickly pears for hedges; massive American agaves (originally imported as a soap to wash grandmother's black clothes) are sentinels on rocky outcrops; Bermuda buttercups instead of daisies. I could hardly name a flower and I liked that. I cycled past orchards of five-starred almonds, blossom against ruined crags and each one an imagination of fortresses and crenellated castles; past groves of oranges lit with fairytale lanterns. I listened to the sing-song of small birds. I could hardly name one and I liked that. The blue sky, the empty roads and everything unknown drew from me a longing to sing back – and out came carols. 'O little town of Bethlehem' I sang several times.

The arrangement had been made by letter: go to Genalguacil, follow the dirt track for six kilometres, cross a river, then look out for the big chestnuts. Finca La Mohea is a tiny white-washed house halfway up a mountain. Pines and more pines (Pinus pyraster) hug the steep slopes while below are millennium-old terraces, the heart of this permaculture farm. The trees dripped, every bucket splashed, a posse of cats sheltered under the roof-eaves staring at me. I knocked and waited. No answer. I turned the fist-sized key in the door. First impression: I am in the stone age! The simple oblong room is a temple to the hearth dominating one end; the walls are dedicated to the fruits and nuts and bottled preserves; bags of edibles hang from nails. Outside, the clouds curled below the treeline; up the valley the wind had shunted a black reef-line. I listened, mainly to my beating heart.

The night surrounded the cottage and I and the cats hugged the glowing fire. I made a big stew and laid the plates on the table. I waited. And I waited. I locked the door. I went back and bolted it. The thoughts arrived: I had never met these people. I had come a long way to be alone. I listened to the wind. I had been set up, I knew it. I could hear a troll side-stepping quietly down the

*path; an annual sacrifice they had to pay, a rent. That's why they were away.
That's why I was here alone! I checked the bolts. I could not sleep. At
midnight I heard squeaking voices, something louder, indecipherable, and
coming down the mountain. I could hear it outside. I stared at the door. The
cats did the same. A fist banged the door. The troll asked in German to be let
in. They were a family lost on the mountain. I gave them my potato stew.*

*Ruth Bond said she had dreamed of a macaw the night before, fleeting and
tantalising like my song. It's a mystery. Ruth is broad-faced, fair and freckling
with ginger hair touching her shoulders. She is a biologist from South
Yorkshire. Rory is Irish, a long time-traveller with and without money. He
used to build and change scenery for the Welsh National Opera, but it was
while teaching English at Estepona that he trailed these mountains by motorbike and spotted this deserted farm. The previous owner had bought it for
£250. His own life was going round and round paying bills to stand still, so
he bought it. With his old donkey jacket, tousled hair and black rolling tobacco
he could be out of the Boglands; his broken nose is set in a long-boned face,
his words street-wise and pithy. 'It's only because some buggers eat meat that
we can be vegetarians.' Yet this changes too, and another person I will call
Dieter emerges, especially when he talks about their fruit trees: apricots, plums,
persimmons, oranges, mandarins… Dieter is a doctor and every little graft has
its history; their futures are already in his eyes. Many of them he will never see
on this earth. I am amazed. I have never thought of this before: why dwarfing
stocks are like battery hens, prolific at first and then discarded; how an old tree
can be rejuvenated ('Plant a nursery tree beside an old one and the veteran will
fight back'); letting wild plums sucker to graft onto them choice varieties.*

*For them, each day is a new day in the biodynamic calendar: a root day, a bud
day, a leaf day; whether to fell pines for the new apricot terrace; cut posts from
logs and fire the tips; root out the New Zealand spinach; paint dung and horse-
tail preparations on fruit trees to protect the bark or twist off mandarins for the
health clinic on the coast. And if it rains there is always marmalade to make
on the open fire, separating the juice from the rind, cutting the rind thin and
boiling the lot as fast as possible and adding thirty percent sugar. Whenever it
rains, both go out with mattocks to channel the water along the contours, make
deltas to break its force and drop sediment in places where they want new
terraces or to plant a tree. They work with gravity: the compost loo overhangs a
lower fruit terrace; the scraps from the washing sink are dropped into the
wormery directly below. I waver between timidity at their spartan life and
admiration at their ingenuity; the pig fat from a neighbour could be dubbin for
their shoes; the old vegetable oil can be boiled into soap with caustic soda; even
the fine clay can make a hair shampoo.*

29

Once or twice I see them huddled around the fire and feeding in sticks. I wonder what this has to do with the 21st century. Then I remember the olive groves on rafts of roots, the earth scissored by floodwater, the slopes and summits of mountains denuded of native firs by goats. These mountains are a defenceless land. Permaculture could bring back diversity, buffer it from extremes, bring back young people to these abandoned farms; the biodynamic philosophy is the home-grown magic of these future techno-peasants. 'This only works because of the affluent society around us,' says a sober Rory. 'We are not all chasing the crumbs.'

For several days the sky deluged these mountains leaving squelchy tracks, dripping roofs, and puddles everywhere. Ruth hadn't seen rain like this since Venezuela and Peru where she had worked as a field biologist. Every day she walked up the same mountain, walked with the giant blue butterflies drifting before her and macaws flying out of their roosts sounding like melodic crows. Every afternoon she walked back down the mountain and the macaws came back with her. 'I never forgot the jungle,' she said. 'Life and death was there every minute. You never knew what was around the corner. When I came back to England I only had to hear a rustle in a bramble and I felt my heart pumping.' That rain broke the drought that has plagued Andalucia for the past five years. 'This summer is going to be tropical,' says Ruth.

Perhaps the macaw is coming to Andalucia.

(Zahara de los Atunes, January 27, 1996)

This wasp will keep me awake. I'm scared of wasps, the menacing bands of colour, that in-your-face humming noise pricking my fear and timidity. They like the rubbish bags, find something in the juicy odds and ends. They're wayside hunters like me, finding sustenance in what is discarded. I dreamt once of a rubbish bag covered in wasps but when I looked inside I found a beautiful, naked woman. What was she doing there? Who threw her away? I'm ashamed to say, I did. I'm always throwing things away. You see I'm scared of gaps and silences, my voice, of having nothing to say, of touch, of having to feel my way in the dark.

FOR ME

I awake in the night my stomach telling me to get up and find the toilet. I am in a strange house and don't know where the lights are. I find the bedside light then fumble by the kitchen door, nature wanting her exit, I wanting mine. I find the kitchen light and move as quietly as I can to the far door without precipitating the ominous rumbles going on below. I cannot find the passage light. I stumble down two stone steps tracing my fingers along the wooden panelling. There is no time to unlock the back door. I pull myself into the bathroom, but the light switch eludes me. One hand feels the wall, the other cradles my bum. The loo is not there. I don't believe it! I surrender. The shit instantly fills my hand then splatters onto the tile floor. At that moment I find the toilet seat. I stand in the midnight darkness. I step in the shit and out of it, then in it. I find the light. It's everywhere, on the carpet, my knees and hands, shirt, all over and in the sink. I want to howl with frustration – but that will only wake everybody up. Then I notice the bathroom mural, an ethereal naked lady crowned with the glory of the waters and the radiance of the moon. One of her hands is raised in salutation. I undress, scrub my body, the floor, the sink, my shirt. It's 1.30 am. I am naked, wet and very alone. I'm humbled before this Goddess. I am always looking for lights to switch on, wanting to know my way instead of trusting in this darkness. I feel ashamed, but why? Of this mess? Of my fear of failure in work and relationships? Of being alone in another country? Of the nameless fears of falling apart and having nothing to hold on to?

So very human this shit.

I would have liked to have offered it to the Goddess and to have seen her favourite pig devour it. Down into the shit, come up smelling like roses. I'm not hundred per cent sure about that at this moment, but it's all right.

(La Cellete, Limousin)

MAX'S WALK

The lights went out for Max 20 years ago. The experiment in the chemistry laboratory went wrong and the explosion shattered his right hand and blinded him. Here in Dijon I am his guest along with his friends Mireille and Martine at a small roadside restaurant; nothing grand, it's an intimate local. He smiles tenderly when she speaks. She is like his moon. There is lightness about him, in his clothes and informality, in his questions and folded arms, his teasing tongue and listening ears. All creams and greys. A quiet face behind his lightly-shaded glasses until he smiles and talks of love. He is rarely without a woman, I am told. Yes there is tranquillity and laughter with his words. He says he dreams of himself as he is, with his handicap. 'It means I accept myself.'

Sometimes he takes off his shades and rubs his watery eyes. His English and my French allow us to speak slowly. I enjoy the gaps to choose my words. He listens with his whole body, still and intent on every word. Somewhere there must be a geography of faces which go with words. When I close my eyes I have to stay with myself. He looks to whom is talking. Everyone knows him at the restaurant, even Holly the tiny dog, the burly lorry drivers, the Mormons all buttoned-up and official as traffic cops shake his hands. His questions are considered and to the point. 'Are the English youth more free than the French? Are you political?' We discover we are all divorced. 'Twice,' chirps in Max. He knows I'm cycling. Once he cycled for 95 days through France to the top of Sweden and down through Norway and the Low Countries to Spain and North Africa. He was 20. He says he can close his eyes and see long stretches of these roads. And in his dreams they are in colour. His subsequent blindness never stopped him: he cycled the Tour-de-France for the handicapped. 'That was hard! It's impossible to find a pilot now.'

These days he concentrates on body-building. His friend spoons up the remains on his plate and feeds it to him. He enjoys this. 'I'm in love,' he tells us and says it again. 'I'm in love. For six weeks.' He loves women, his friend tells me. 'In Blackpool (at a special holiday for the blind) I was so much tired from all the love-making.' His friends pretend to be shocked. 'Why do you talk like that?' I laugh, not quite believing him. He hated the English food. 'Dégueulasse!' Later he softens. 'The breakfasts were good.'

Now Max is retired with a pension and teaches (voluntarily) chemistry to some students, and he is writing about his life. In 1980 he fulfilled a promise to himself that he would not live in the shadows, that he would be boss. How? He would walk alone from Dijon to his home town Trugny, a distance of 48 kilometres. He planned the route with his father and set off on the D966 at 7am. He walked by the side of the road next to the traffic and, whenever he wandered off his route, he listened for the cars. He reached home safely at 18.30 hours. I said I would remember that on my travels whenever I was losing my way.

It is a small world. His parents live closeby. We say goodbye on the road. Max hugs his moons. He swings his stick before him up the gravel drive.

(Dijon, May 3, 1998)

OSLO BOTANICS

The Indian mother sat by the waterfall. Her black glossy hair trailed down her back and over her khaki shorts. Her daughter sat beside her in a purple hat, a matching skirt and a red blouse. They were happy together, and I noticed that. Later I saw them walking along a woodland path, the girl skipping ahead of her mother and singing to herself. I saw them seated like statues under a willow, the daughter on her mother's lap. I wanted to say hello, be part of this happiness but I would only spoil it. They were exotic butterflies and would fly away if I came too close. I sat by myself in a herbal chessboard with a dozen parallel paths. Halfway down one, they passed me on the next path walking the other way. We smiled. We passed each other perhaps six times during the next twenty minutes, and twice talked about cooking herbs.

(Oslo, June 14, 1997)

AT LAST!

One evening in Orgiva there was a power cut in the restaurant. The owner brought out a candle, shaking her head sadly at the storm and apologising. 'No *importa,' I said. Behind the door they pulled switches, banged tables and all the time they clicked their tongues. It took awhile to realise the difference; no non-stop beat from the cassette, no continuous television football commentary or drumming feet, just candle-light and voices burbling in the adjoining bar. I breathed a sigh of relief.*   (Orgiva, February 6, 1996)

IN PRAISE OF SOFT COCKS

In Andalucia I thought of soft cocks, small and undemanding, and minding their own business. Mine was dozing curled on a little forest floor. I have always wanted an outstanding cock (a Fifties and Sixties dream), to bulge in the right places, to give out the right signals that here is the home of a tiger: to be sensitive to praise or a pretty face, in a word: responsive. I am reminded of this in Andalucia, the strong silent types in leather jackets, restless and working their hips while watching television in a bar. I admired and emulated them when I was a teenager – this directness – and I mistook it for sexuality. I liked the Andalusian girls, not afraid of themselves or showing their feminine charms. They are like tropical flowers to see but not to pick. Sometimes I lusted, impossibly of course – I'm not made of wood – yet each time I fondled a fantasy there appeared another figure, not hard and erect, but wanting something other; touch, words, some eye contact. Each time I went too far, figuratively tying a condom to a woman's body – an impossible thing – I encountered insecurity, a sinking feeling of losing contact. This wanting too much connected them both. I like my soft cock, not going anywhere, happy to be still, knowing well its best interest; like some sleepy dog it cocks its ear at things I know nothing about. I can get it by the throat and say 'Give' and it will, but it will be hard and quick and silent. And some aperture in me will grow smaller. This gentle touch it likes, this connection.

(Orgiva, February, 1996)

I liked your picture of the animals flying in the sky. It was so fantastic. We drew you a card of a bear walking under a rainbow, such a sweet bear and flicking its legs out as if it were dancing. It was a happy picture, one for another. Christmas came and went and then another squiggly letter arrived with our address printed beside it. This time there was a picture of a train in a red desert and Father Christmas was waving from the last carriage. But there was no snow, only sand. Sarah pointed to something she thought really horrid, a monster with hair sticking up like rats' tails, and it had two eyes on one side and three arms sticking out like whips. He was leaning backwards balanced on a tail, and its eyes stared at us. You could move the card around and they followed you, as if they knew what you were thinking inside. They were not hard eyes but were big and soft as if they were seeing

33

something we couldn't see. He had stringy hair, hairy ears and sharp fingers; that's why I called him Pincha. Nothing was growing in this desert except red stones. Sarah saw it first, the tiny earwig standing between Pincha's toes. I thought it was a twig with eyes but in the end I agreed it was an earwig. It had a golden helmet on.

Straightaway, I don't know why, I thought that J.P. Thomas (but we called him Jo) must be a traveller to see all these things. You may laugh but I pictured you with a suitcase and standing at a station checking your watch with the clock. I saw you well-dressed in a suit, with round glasses, slightly old-fashioned like my great uncle Edmund who couldn't go anywhere unless he had planned the route backwards and forwards and bought the tickets three month's in advance. Yet he was always in a hurry or late, or something was slightly wrong, a shirt-tail was sticking out or he was wearing odd socks or his glasses were at a funny angle or stuck together with sticky tape. Sarah sent Jo a picture of the seaside with the train puffing beside a beach with ice-cream sellers, sand castles and an island with a tree on it. Instead of Father Christmas, I stuck onto it three cut-out paper figures holding hands. He sent us a really quick card with the same black writing leaning backwards but this time they did not trip over themselves, they stood up so we could read them.

This picture showed a wood with a see-through house and coloured birds crawling over it. There was also a path concealed by tree roots. No-one had been down there for a long time. Sarah's sharp eyes saw it first. She always sees things. She pointed to where two branches crossed except one of them was not a branch. It was the side of a man but shaded so it was hard to see him. He wore a funny black hat, round and with a rim, and his trousers, shoes and coat were black. He had a big white beard. Sarah thought he was Father Christmas, but he's never drawn in black. 'He may have run out of red crayons', she said. We stared at him and then I saw the bird perched on his shoulders looking straight at us. You had to know it was there to see it. It was drawn beautifully small as if it were very close. We could see every detail of the beak and wing and straight tail feathers. I knew by the pear shape that it was a Little Owl. But who's ever heard of Father Christmas and a Little Owl? Not I.

Then I had a question. The most important thing is this question. It knocked one day at my brain door. I had it nearly in my mind but it was Sarah who said it. Is Jo lonely? And this led to another question: Does he want something? It had never occurred to me that I had anything to give.

You have to remember I was nine and Sarah eleven. It's as obvious as day-light now. They didn't want to take us at first. They said it was an old people's home and old people had their routines, the signposts throughout the day. My father said it was too far away and he said it turning his back to me which meant no. They talked about him as if he lived in another country and that was always in the dark. He was 41. They hadn't seen him for years. What would we say to each other? The only thing he liked were parakeets, canaries and finches. He lived for his little birds and nothing else. Then why did he send us pictures without parakeets and canaries in them? Sarah's good at saying the obvious. When that didn't work we showed them Jo's present, a picture history of the Great Western Railway we had bought with our pocket money.

They said that he had never been out of the grounds alone, then suddenly we had the answer to our first question. Nothing, nothing would stop us now. We nagged them until they had to say yes.

How many ways can you say *yes*?

THE FARTHEST SHORE

They are at the jungle edge of the roadside – a spinning wheel of clicking sounds.

'Shall we do it? It's now or never.' I whizz by. They don't blink an eye. They are bright-green things brooding with antennae and poised on six spring-loaded legs. They stroke the metallic shields of their cheeks, but something holds them back. Not the sight of their squashed companions in front of them or the heat radiating from the tarmac. They like that. Perhaps they can't see the other side of the road.

It's all the same,' I shout. 'Rocks and lavender. You've seen it before. Why risk your lives?' Something in the stone-clear air, the glowing, autumnal colours, contradicts this caution. They walk up and down the white line, the edge of their known world. Every minute from the maquis, a bush cricket steps over it and into my cycle tracks.

'You fools!'

'We must.'

'But why?'

'It's on the other side.'

Onwards they march, each on their own way. I think of my autumnal journey to another shore. 'You fool,' I say to myself. 'Why? I must. It's now or never.'

(Estella, Spain, October 3, 1996)

ON THE SPOT

A little pluck has its own rewards. At first light I use the cover of snorers to creep down the stairs. I do not want the others to see me dance. I choose the stage – this refugio on the Camino Francés is an old theatre – for the space. All goes well until I hear footsteps coming down. I am on the spot and my devils are with me.

'What makes you so special?'

'Bog off.' I continue with my Tai Chi-style dance.

'You're embarrassing them. Think about others for a change.'

I refuse to be shamed. He is sitting at the table below me. I finish in my own time, my heart bumping a little.

Ole Vicente Nielson is happy with the world at breakfast and shows it, a 63-year-old trim figure with silver hair and inquisitive eyes behind quartz glasses. This is his second pilgrimage. He talks easily. 'I love my wife and my big family. I have been a busy busy headmaster in Denmark. To be alone for me is joy, with nature, the birds, their songs.' Yesterday he had seen a fat gypsy woman steal underwear from a clothes line. 'She ran off like a boy.' He laughs showing his little pink tongue. He peers at me over his glasses. 'I was watching you dance and it reminded me of Pamplona. One evening I sat in the park with perhaps a dozen Spanish men, in their forties. You know, too much money, too much fast cars, too many women. Then an elderly Japanese man comes along with two younger Japanese men, perhaps his grandsons. Without embarrassment they practise Tai Chi in front of us. The old man is so beautiful and peaceful in his face. The Spanish men stopped their chattering. They stared, and then one of them got up and copied the movement; he put his feet shoulder-width apart and pushed out with his hands. One by one the others joined in. The Japanese man carried on until the end.' Ole smiled again. He lingered a moment by the open door. 'I will practise that Tai Chi when I get back.' Then he was gone.

(Santo Domingo de Silos, October 5, 1996)

FREEDOM

I had wanted to go to Burgos. Everyone goes to Burgos. You have to go to Burgos. I was going to Burgos. I walked through Belorado to telephone my hotel confirmation. Then the ominous tip-tapping came at the small little door. Tigger the badger, peering at the world under my seat, alerted me with the squitz. The symptoms disappeared halfway back. I decided there and then I was NOT going to Burgos. I was sick of the Meseta. I was sick of the lorries on the Nl20. I would cycle the mountain road from Belorado to Santo Domingo de Silos – twenty miles at 4,000 feet across the Sierra de la Demanda.

The rain curtains opened. I cycled in sunshine, just me, the mountains and a golden leaf floating out of the blue sky. I bristled with exquisite sensation. I had overcome my timidity. Six hours later at Salas de los Infantes the late afternoon sunlight painted the rocky badlands red, ochre and yellow. Fortress mountains encircled my senses: fantastic jagged edges towered over me; San Carlos appeared, dotted black with junipers; storm-bringing clouds floated over my head. I had never seen this before. I pedalled faster.

I was unprepared for the last ten kilometres. The gorge swallowed me up, twisting down as the sides reared up, monumentally smooth and bulging, the remnants of an ancient river bed. They were stained with mineral reds, creams and blacks. Single pines, groves of cupressus clung to the sides as if they were prehistoric too. I was frightened by this elemental beauty. I pedalled faster. CRACK! I glanced back. CRACK! A huge bird followed me and then another. Their wings appeared to span the sides of that confined gorge. Panic shot me forward with its arrows. Seconds later I slammed on the brakes. I forced myself to look round. Black vultures sailed over my head, stacked one over the other. I sensed they too were desperately trying to get out of the gorge, to escape from my flapping day-glo jacket. They soared to the highest ridge and shrank into patrolling specks.

I had had enough excitement for one day.

An hour later I stood inside the cloisters at Santo Domingo de Silos. I understood why the monks had chosen this remote place as a hermitage. Everything breathed serenity, especially this quadrangle of turf and the finest Romanesque carvings in Spain. No revolution had desecrated Christ dressed as a Santiago pilgrim on the road to Emmaus. Then I saw the long-necked birds carved on the capitals (flamingos or black vultures? I could not tell), now entwined in the Islamic-Christian dance, the Mudéjar style. The artist had repeated this motif several times. Had he come through that gorge a thousand years ago and marvelled at these birds, the same colony perhaps? At vespers, along with the well-heeled and pious Spanish families from Burgos, the colony of monks soothed us with Gregorian chants. I kept thinking of the vultures. I wanted them to be here, along with the Asturian bears, the Smyrna kingfisher, the ruby-tailed wasp, the snake's-head fritillary, the little golden pig...

(Santo Domingo de Silos, October 5, 1996)

That's it! The real signposts have always been questions. Everyone wanted to give me answers. If you do this such and such will happen, if you go down this road you will get grief or happiness. But they were always somebody else's road, somebody else's questions.

WHY DO MULES LISTEN TO FROGS?

In Bath Small School, by chance, I saw a poster for Granada: a composition of stylised buildings (mostly ancient) set one on top of each other as if they were stones in a terraced wall, and soaring above that was the crown – the Alhambra palace, the kal'-at al hamra – and the snowfields of the Sierra Nevada. It was a pretty poster; no noisy, fuming cars or clashing modern architecture or hordes of people or anything to show the tenacity of the past, the hybrid nature of culture. The poster exuded tranquillity, a static peace of former days when the pace was set by donkeys, perhaps early 19th century when Washington Irving wrote his romantic recollections of the palace or when Prosper Mérimée penned Carmen. I have no quarrel with this poster, for Granada includes these things, but I do have a question. I don't even know if it's connected except I thought of it while cycling in the Alpujarras mountains. Every muleteer I saw talked to his beast from the corner of his mouth, strange guttural squeaks fired off one at a time. The donkey bent back his ear and knew whether to go left or right or to stand still. I was impressed and tried the sound myself. I could just do it. Then one day I listened and knew that it was a frog. So I had my question: Why do mules listen to frogs?

I had no answer.

My frustration at the lack of any answer appeared again when I saw this poster, and now I had plenty of words to say about that. For example, why this emphasis on glamour, these partial views of Granada? But it's true of Andalucia, England, Paris, and any other place which wants to attract visitors. Have you seen a poster of Bath with beggars in it? Or a poster of the Red Indians depicting their culture of warfare? I wanted to see another, truer picture: Granada at the edge of the 21st century, a turbulent, changing, fascinating world under pressure from North Africa and its rhythms and migrants. This one-sidedness is a deliberate attempt to wrap me in cotton wool. What I like about Andalucia is the incredible variety: desert, mountainous gorges, treeless campina, insectless latifundia, sandy beaches, dignified provincial towns, stricken mountainsides, olives and more olives, crackerjack cities, African bag people, cling film coastlines, retired expatriates, people struggling with their integrity...the good, the bad and the very ugly. I could make up my own mind. I wanted to see a poster with all these things and the word at the bottom:

ANDALUCIA

I'd like that. I never did, of course. Why? I had an answer to that.

The muleteers are a hardy lot. I saw them dotted all over Andalucia: in a back-street in Granada, a rubbish yard at El Arahal surrounded by street dogs, trudging along quiet mountain roads to Ronda. They epitomised the tough Spanish peasant lifestyle when perhaps people had to eat broad beans for two weeks because they had nothing else. (And fart for two weeks afterwards.) They appeared a little lost as if the culture which had valued these mules was deeply in the shadows cast by modern Spanish cities. They belonged now to *the hinterland. I identified with this displaced feeling, me on a bicycle in Andalucia just passing through. The locals regarded me as if I were an oddity, exactly the same way I looked at the donkeys. To me they were exotic. There was a donkey in the poster of Granada, a tame-looking creature led by a boy. They were not going anywhere. I have no desire to romanticise this donkey; donkey work is tiring in the sun, boring repetition, going backwards and forwards, thinking the same things, expecting to see what is already known and seeing it. So bit by bit the world becomes smaller; from the Serennias of Ronda, Sevilla is another planet. Yet for this cyclist, some connections are obvious: the insectless campina, that vast downland of wheat and olives, is the other face of Sevilla. They fit together like jigsaw pieces.*

El Valero is at the end of the track from Orgiva, the traveller's capital of Spain. Most of the Spanish (originally settlers from Galicia after the Moors were kicked out) have long abandoned their small mountain farms of intensive fruit and olive terraces, with some pastoral sheep herding. In that one valley now live many Europeans: Germans, Dutch, British, French, Italian. Probably their children's children will consider themselves Spanish or Spanish Europeans. The English girl, Chloë at El Valero, practises her flamenco dance in her pueblo bedroom and dreams of Sevilla, I think — far away from these drought-resistant Aleppo pines. Here the soil is as precious as water. Her father, Christopher Stewart, loves his flock of sheep despite the damage they do to the orange terraces. He wants to be buried farther up the river (still on his own land) by the old farm ruined by erosion, lack of trees and water. Water, that's the thing; where to find it and protect its purity. The alkathene pipe which brings it down the mountain is literally their lifeline. Once he was the original drummer in Genesis ('No future in it son') and now he is a shepherd, a builder, a sheep sheerer, a writer, a seed collector, a lover of Sevilla. Together with Anna Exton, his wife, they struggle with life here — but there are compensations. In a riverside orange terrace there is an emerald lawn, the only tangible link with England. It is a kind of touchstone, a land dream he could never have realised back home.

At night I dream of eagles in this cruel and beautiful land.

While walking in the mountains above El Valero I heard a familiar sound, a succession of sharp, corner-of-the-mouth guttural calls. Straightaway, I understood. They were frogs in a cistern of spring water, a lifeline. And they were the calls of the muleteer. Now I had another question: Why do muleteers listen to frogs? And I had an answer.

What am I doing this for? If I dare to answer I will take another fork in the road. That's the hardest thing. Love is meant to last forever, through fortune and misfortune, in health and sickness, in youth and old age. I made promises I couldn't keep. The truth is I didn't know how to keep them. This crack goes up and down this land. You see it best on the wayside. In the dream I clung to the edge like a dying man and then I let go. A warm rain touched me and little butterflies beat their way back up. My father picked me up and placed me on the ground. It was that same feeling of being carried up the stairs, being held and being taken to a safe place. Some terrible meaning is there. It's here now. Is this what you want to hear Jo? What our fathers did or did not do? To be carried up the stairs is like being carried by a dream. I should say, while I remember, that Jo had a mother, and his mother had Jo, but she had died a long time ago. She was granny's sister, but we knew nothing about her.

I saw him for the first time when the cow parsley was big and breezy, and white clouds were puffing across the sky. An English rural paradise. He was waiting at the entrance and he pulled back the metal gates one at a time. He didn't have a suitcase or thick glasses, nor was he dressed in a suit, at least not a new one. It was old and baggy, double-breasted as if it had belonged to his grandfather. He knocked on the window and stuffed a Bounty Bar into our hands and he ran beside the car, an old black Vauxhall 14, in long bounds, bending low so his face appeared smiling in the window. A big face, long in the jaw with strangely small eyes which managed the trick of staring at us and somehow past us. His teeth were good on top, crooked below. He seemed like a giant, scraping his hair on branches and always waving his long arms. 'I'm so excited.' A warm voice yet high as a bird in places. His hair was cut in a straight line as if someone had put a bowl on his head. The door opened and he beckoned us across the lawn, past the old people sitting in deckchairs and wheelchairs with the day pencilled in before them. The nurses were dressed in blue skirts and white tops, and they carried lunches and pots of tea on trays, and pushed the wheelchairs down to the lake. One old lady raised a bony finger at me, and I stopped, not knowing how to say hello. Jo rubbed her cheek until she giggled. By the bird house at the edge of the shrubbery, he kneeled in front of a white wooden cross. 'It's gone to meet its ancestors. A gift of eternal life...God works in mysterious ways. I'm not sure they'll let me in there. I must have killed a thousand things, ants, woodlice...'
'God will understand,' said Sarah. 'We all make mistakes.'
The parakeet climbed up the wire and took the nut from his fingers. A pink canary hopped down the branches, past hanging mirrors and landed by a pool of water. There were jungly green shrubs growing in there and

nest boxes and water bottles. 'They're nice company and, to be honest, take my mind off horrible things…I'll be really happy the day it says something to me but at the moment it's like talking to a brick wall.' He had seeds for all of them. The parakeets he called Pinky and Perky, the canaries had no names. 'To be honest I did try calling them names but I couldn't tell the difference.' Already he looked older and younger at the same time, as if he were both a child and a man.

He talked non-stop! One minute it was about a woodpecker catching ants with its tongue, then it was his birthday coming up fast or the crash he had heard on the radio. 'But I like surprises.' He stopped when the nurse in blue walked over with our parents. I remember two things; her hand was cold and she called him by his proper name, J.P. Tomas this, J.P. Tomas thinks that. He should know better than to shake hands with dirty fingers. She knew him better than he did himself. 'He loves his birds more than me!' She placed her hand on his shoulder. 'J.P. Tomas. Did you show them the roses? He is a wonderful gardener. He had *Mermaid* in flower last Christmas.'

'I'm doing something with my life.'

'He is.'

'*Whoever does the Will of God is brother and sister and mother to me.*'

'You can't afford to waste your life. Life is precious…it is. Oh! It is.'

'It is.'

LOUISE

For three years Louise lit a candle at Christmas: 25 candles in 25 windows. For three years she lived alone in this mill in the remote Viaur gorge, a long way from home for this French-Canadian woman in her thirties. In a former life in Quebec she had dreamed of being a farmer. So she rebelled against her comfortable home and went to Somerset where she fell in love with an older man; long-bearded, young at heart, very down to earth. He was a farmer with his cows and cereals and sheep and chickens and polytunnels. He was a musician and an engineer. They loved each other and lived together in a caravan next to a mill mentioned in the Domesday Book. Every day of the year she fed the animals, milked the cows, mended the fences, shovelled the shit and, in season, hoed and lambed and harvested. She was good at all this. Ten years went by and she hardly noticed it. In love, out of love, hard time changing. 'I'm a passionate woman,' she says. 'I go through everything. I have no regrets.' She means it. In the end she packed her panniers and cycled to Andalucia sleeping out each night to prove to herself her independence. She dived in at Le Moulin d'Ayres, a place of water, and for two months she hardly ventured out. It was very hard for her discovering who she was left alone with. Her rural neighbours stared in amazement: a young woman by herself, a young woman choosing to live in this rural backwater. 'Where is your husband?' they asked, knowing full well the answer. The elderly women of Tajoi befriended her with vegetables while she in turn earthed-up their potatoes. She studied carpentry and the business of fitting out shops. Slowly the isolation and mournfulness at the mill evaporated. She found another person inside her, a woman in all this tender rain. 'I could not believe so much could happen to me. I had to grow,' she says.   (Le Moulin d'Ayres, September 23, 1996)

VIGELANDSPARKEN

The sun opened the day and the Norwegian hearts. Everyone was in Vigeland Park, in shorts, in bikinis, licking ice-creams, pushing prams, walking dogs; bare-chested skaters in dark glasses glided in and out of the crowds; kids in bulbous helmets and knee-pads trailed behind; girls with all their horizons on view promenaded together; Annie the cheerleader twirled her batons and kicked shapely legs out of a gold lamé skirt. Gusts of Japanese tourists worked their way through the crowds eyeing the bronze figures gazing down from the parapet. Seagulls, perched on the heads and shoulders and buttocks of the naked figures, tilted their eyes for something edible, or imagined they were gods to dump on mortals below.

I walked slowly through this procession intent on seeing the 200 sculptures by Gustav Vigeland. This monumental carver made a deal with the Oslo authorities: If you build me a studio and give me the land I will create a sculpture park for the nation. They agreed. A lifetime's work is miraculously displayed on a long stone axis past Titanic waterfalls and ending in the huge column of basalt which took three carvers 14 years to complete, sometime in 1943 just before Vigeland died.

The great themes of human life are here, from infantas to old age, angry children, ecstatic maidens, conjugal dignity; fathers and mothers standing alone or together or at ease with children, or leaping or leaning against each other or staring gravely at the onlookers. Gustav Vigeland would have loved this festival time – people paying homage to his humanitarian vision by enjoying themselves. I did.

The mood changed subtly by the waterfall where the Titans shouldered a gigantic saucer. It is enclosed by a wall of bronze reliefs of tender infantas and children and first love, youths standing opposite each other, of skeletons between lovers, souls floating who knows where. But what I noticed most was a young man, flesh and blood and in pants only, parading his muscle-bound body before the crowds. He grunted with his karate chops and scissored his legs with each death blow. He shouted at us so we would see him before falling back into the waters. This dis-connected man frightened me but I did not know why – then.

On the top terrace the monolith of figures wanted to touch the sky. Around it on lower terraces were monumental groups of children and infants, men and women in prime and old age, some entwined with each other as if they were trying to go somewhere. Around me visitors chatted or posed for photographs. Suddenly I lost my breath. I felt as if a sack of potatoes had hit my chest. I choked with tears. They flooded my eyes and nose and mouth! I could not control them. My face burned. I had to walk away. I had no idea what was happening. I kept staring at the monolith, the figures climbing onto the backs of others to pull themselves to the top. But where to? Suddenly I understood. By association I had remembered the children and pregnant mothers, the old and the lame, the sick – all victims of the gas chambers at Auschwitz-Birkenau. When they opened the doors the bodies are said to have made little pyramids as they struggled for breath. This monument was completed before the world really knew about Auschwitz and Zyklon B gas.

I was dumbfounded it could scratch this raw place in me.

I walked back past Anne's cheerleader show and the skaters gliding around their fans, people still feeding ducks, girls arm in arm and boys eyeing them up. I sat on a step listening to South American guitar melodies. I gave him three kronors. (Frederikshavn, June 15, 1997)

She sat next to me at Portsmouth Passenger Terminal, French, and a little chic with her blonde hair and matching make-up. I noticed her skinny legs and the stick, and the way she squinted while speaking, sometimes pursing her lips to find a word, to follow her thoughts which appeared now and then to be tangled. She was sick, she told me, and she had come to England to be healed. I admired her courage to talk to a stranger, to open herself. Here at the beginning is my fear of skinny legs, the pale, emaciated eyes. I have to hold onto something to stay upright. Sometimes I appear tied to a thread in this life. I want to walk away from her but I have to listen. I can touch you with my little fingers, she says, anytime I want to. I find it hard to trust. My first thought often is: 'Someone has stolen something from me,' and I am on my guard.

Sometimes the way ahead is hard to see even when you know the right direction. You're here right at the beginning.

'I'm here,' she says. 'Can't you see me?' That's the point. You can't.

'How are you?'

I know. I look into the mirror. I examine my eyes for dark spots, tell-tale holes into which I may disappear. I sense my trembling muscles in my legs, the way they twitch without warning. I will become thinner and thinner. In some lights my face is thinner, the spaces under the eyes paler. I cut my hair short to show less silver. You made them, they say. Each word is an arrow, my concern are the barbs. I am not them. I'm little. I weigh just under ten stone. And I don't tell them that I had all my clothes on. Eat more. They give me more money hoping that this will fatten me. I want to be fatter. I eat twice as much as anyone else. It's a kind of joke: 'He'll eat it.' Sometimes it seems that the more I eat the more I fear that I will lose weight. I cannot fill this empty space with chips. I am sensitive to lactose. Why? It's a mystery. What can't I stomach now? It has taken me two years to track this down. I listen to my belly and its labyrinthine ways. I am not much wiser.

The past taps on our shoulder and we call it a stranger. It's closer to me than you. Out of all those people at Vigelandsparken why did I alone cry? I hid myself in a corner like some wounded animal. I didn't want anyone to see me or to detect my confusion. When this not-knowing is present I can step into the cracks of the day. I can be myself, and I'm scared of that. And another thing: I would like this to be a love story across time and lands, but I may be deluding myself. I can still see the flick of the parakeet gripping the bar to climb back through the cage door. It could have gone anywhere but it loved its little house, keeping the bars on the outside.

LOVE IS STRANGE

*This day belonged to uncertainty. I had to take the train to Granada and was assured the day before that Spanish regional railways carry bicycles. When I bought my ticket I might as well have thrown a wasp's nest at them. The furore subsided and I was told that only on half of my journey could I take the bike, the second part was forbidden. I paid half, hoping to switch trains. At Bobadilla we waited for a train which never arrived; it had been de-railed near Malaga. We waited, everybody doing their best to do nothing. I noticed three Japanese girls, a strange mix of city trendy clothes, suitcases on wheels, yet two had welcoming rural faces, slow and unfettered, with real smiles. The third girl was different. She had fine black hair cut to her shoulders, a broad peach-shaped face with a certain expression, a knowing sensibility not afraid of show-ing itself. She smiled when I looked at her. I felt ridiculously shy and boyish. On the bus which rescued us, she put a handkerchief over her mouth as a pro-test against the Spanish cigarettes. The coach dropped in at every rural station to pick up more stranded passengers. The sunset filled the sky with blues and yellows, and a glorious pink haze covered the snowfields of the Sierra Nevada. I was about to arrive in Granada, an unknown city in the dark. I saw her face reflected on the window, an exquisite gentleness stared back. I wondered where I had seen her before. I kept singing the first part of an old Buddy Holly song, **Love is Strange**. Somehow I imagined my eldest son Ben liking and singing this song too, the unrequited passion of a sixteen-year-old, intensely tender,* *unsure of itself before first love. Then I remembered the face I had seen before in Glen Lyon in Perthshire, the woman sitting with her back to the gorge dressed in white. In her eyes, for a second or two, I saw the same knowing sensitivity. I saw her at dusk, in a place unknown to me, and I still cannot say whether she was mortal or a fairy.*

The bus finally reached Granada. I sorted out my bike and the three Japanese girls had gone. I never said hello, but this unknown Japanese girl is my friend.

(Granada, February 2, 1996)

* * *

The day started with the hoopoe zigzagging before my wheels up the mountain road through the Alpujarras; scrubby brown desert, citrus lush Rio Andarax valley, chasms, snowfields, high mattoral of hedgehog plants and a pink haze of almond blossom. The sky amazed me. Vivid blue skies with island clouds brushed by the wind as if made from whipped cream. I had seen clouds like that in those 'B' Westerns from my childhood of dusty cowboys on the desert trail and under the big sky. Suddenly I was there too, not a cowboy, but a gleeful eight-year-old in a world where the slightest mistake would end badly for me. This edge, this danger I liked, but not too much. I kept singing **Love is Strange** *over and over again, as if these words were the nearest I would get to naming this intimation. I listened for small birds, elusive and fleeting; a white rump, a yellow-barred wing in the giant canna grass. It did not matter.*

These fragile lands are protected by terraces with a bottom lip to contain the ruinous run-off from storms. The Arabs must have placed the big stones to make the terraces, to grow the olives so I could brush oil onto my morning tostada. The olive tree is the saviour of these people: oil for food and money, prunings for firewood, leaves for goats (so cheese, milk and meat); and they keep the sides of the mountain in the same place. All day the sun unpicked my cloud-ships until they were eaten by larger clouds. It did not matter this letting go. Under darkening skies I pushed myself harder. The barrier stopped me at Torvizcon: landslides. I slipped past when no-one was looking. The headwind became a hand in my face sometimes shoving me close to the edge. Around one bend floodwaters had taken three-quarters of the road leaving only a narrow strip of tarmac in the middle with drops on both sides. I could not turn back now. I stood there thinking this is exactly how I feel about this writing idiot, me. I am in too far. 'Love is Strange', he says; almond blossom and biting winds, families beating olive trees with sticks, stones wedged together to break the force of water, an eight-year-old sheltered by this man, delighting at the zigzagging of a bird.   *(Orgiva, February 5, 1996)*

We deluded you Jo, wrapped you in cottonwool. Gave you time but no money, all the time in the world to do nothing. We wanted you to be good, someone had to. And what did they do to Balder? You always smiled. They had taught you well. Was it your first line of defence?

The nurse brushed the grass from his shoulder, swung her watch on the chain. 'Time for tea.' Even then that first meeting was full of bits that didn't fit: the blue sky and the old people, Jo's wide grin, the caged birds, my awkward, silent parents, people talking but saying nothing, green lawns with cut edges and not a daisy in sight. If I stayed there I would become melancholy, a fossil at least. Jo knew the names of all the old people, how long they had been there, what books they were reading, what medicines they took, what they had for breakfast, who was coming to visit them, the names of the flowers and the insects that visited them. He was always giving. They adored him. You could see that from the gratitude in their eyes and the way they offered him their hands. He was sinking under all this wisdom. Is that what it's like when you get old? You just disappear.

THE OLD MAN

No-one will remember him when he's gone. His best friend Jennifer will be in a donkey home, the two heifers he fattens for beef will go to market. The fences of old bed springs, recycled railway sleepers and motley metal posts will be sold for scrap, and so will the drinking troughs of enamel baths and the four rusty tin sheds cobbled together over his lifetime. The narrow strip of land his father bought alongside the Somerset Coal Canal will return to Dunsford Farm, and the traces of his work will be as indecipherable as an Indian coin. He will become anonymous as the land itself.

It would be easy to caricature Don, appearing as regular as the weather, to see only the cloth cap and russet scarf, his day-in and day-out coat tied with bindercord (I never saw him in anything else), to have ears only for his broad vowels and 'Where-be-to's' and 'Get my meanings', his habit of repetition, or smile at the ancient Raleigh bike leaning in storm or sun against the Dunsford oak. That is there along with his kissing side-burns and blue eyes which look at you without blinking. Don is a remarkable man; a little rheumatism in a knee is the only homage to his seventy five years. He is probably the nearest thing to a peasant around these North Somerset coal-fields. He lives between his bits of land near Radstock and Paulton, eating bacon for breakfast every morning before feeding and watering his cattle, baling hay for winter, checking his fences and regularly cutting Jennifer's ingrowing hooves. He knows his knee will put an end to it one day.

He keeps the heifers as company for his donkey. He thinks the world of her. I am touched by their friendship owing no allegiance to the market place. He bought her in 1971 for his grand-children, but they rode her only six times. 'She's my love,' he says, stroking the knob of fat on Jennifer's neck. 'That hump is fat but if I do starve her — and that's what they say — she'll not eat a blade of grass or touch her food.' And again: 'It's I do the work and she looks at I. She's better good looking than I.' I realise what a shy man Don is: his best friend at the farm never answers back. One winter's day with the sun glowing the tan and golds of the oak, I caught him doing absolutely nothing. 'Contemplating the world?' I asked. 'No, no. I'm growing good in the sun.'

I am amazed by his memory; there were 69 apple trees in the upper vegetable field and he names the twelve varieties. He was born a stone's throw away on the Paulton road; as a child he milked cows on this farm before and after school. 'This is home,' he says, 'but it's my aches and pains.' He's tired of pushing his bike up Radford Hill, cutting the hedges down Monger lane. Away from home, there's nobody to talk to except Jennifer. 'I think she understands every word I say. If I say "move over", she moves over.' Jennifer follows Don up and down the railway track. (In the film, 'The Titfield Thunderbolt', he was paid £15 to graze his goats on the embankment.) She waits patiently behind him while he carries a hay bale across his back from one shed to another. Don says the record age for a donkey is 44. 'I could be eighty and she'll still be here.' No, he's made up his mind. Jennifer will go into a donkey home and he'll donate £1,000 to keep her in grass the rest of her days. Suddenly I realise that a chapter of history will go with him. I want to record his memories. 'No,' he says smiling, 'what will I have to say?' It's useless to argue the point. A moment's silence, a smile and a nod: the sum of my wordless affection. I leave him standing beside Jennifer, two still points in this landscape.

(Dunsford Farm, 1996)

TREE MAN

If you want to talk about trees in Oslo you go and see Tore Naess. He is the official spokesman on tree planting in the city, whether a tree should be protected or not, how close a digger can come, choosing varieties, maintenance, public information... His job is to make decisions.

One day he gets a letter from someone saying a tree is dangerous. 'What are the authorities going to do about it?' He visits the tree and recognises the old cupressus which was there long before the homes were built nearby. Some of the branches are dead or dying back, he notices, and that the roots had been damaged during the house construction. The homeowner wants the tree cut down. 'It's dangerous,' he said, 'it might fall on my children or house. We don't want it here.' Tore checks the old reports from the tree specialists — for this tree had a long history. He discovers that no-one knows who the tree belongs to or where the exact boundary lies. He remembers he saw signs of internal rot. They can cut it down, he tells them, but at your own expense and risk. He always says that in writing.

Two weeks later a well-dressed, professional lady about town walks into his office. She stands in front of his desk. 'I hear you are going to cut down that cupressus tree. How can you do that? It's a beautiful tree.'

'It is a beautiful tree,' says Tore.

'You cannot allow this. I have known this tree all my life.'

Tore explains about the damaged roots, the rot at the base, the dying branches.

'But we love this tree. It was there before the houses.'

'True,' says Tore, and he tells her about the tree protection order and how they had tried to minimise root damage when the houses were built. The woman sits down. She is still angry.

'I'm a journalist,' she says. 'I will call in the media. I won't let you get away with this.'

'I tell her she is free to do what she likes. I tell her I like the tree. I would not cut it down just because it obstructed a view or cast too much shade. But it is dangerous. Who will be responsible if the tree falls on the children?'

'But there is growth on the old branches. I have seen it.'

'It is crying out for help,' says Tore. 'That's what happens when a tree is dying.'

'I don't want to see it go,' she says more softly. 'It's like somebody I love.'

'We have to do something before it falls down.'

'I feel so sad,' says the woman. She starts crying.

'I'm sad too,' says Tore. 'It's a problem of old age. We have to do something.'

She leaves his office. He never hears anything more about the tree.

MY WORD

Josephine, the two-year-old daughter of Katerina, will not allow anyone to call her granny old. She's been told that 'old is what you throw away': old garbage, old socks, old newspapers. 'Granny's not old. I'm not going to throw her away.'   (Göteborg, June 5, 1997)

THE POTTERY

May Day – and for the first time I see people in a French village, neighbours talking, young people buying and selling bunches of lily-of-the-valley, the traditional romantic gift. I pushed my bike past the barn with the banner, 'Salon d'Exposition. Entrée Libre'. I hesitated when I saw the old man propped against the barn door, half in and half out. 'Paintings?' I asked. 'Pots,' he answered back. I shook my head and walked on. Halfway out of the village, St Amand-en-Puisaye, I changed my mind. I cycled back.

The pottery occupied a spacious barn, labyrinthine walkways between scaffolding supporting rows of teacups, plates or teapots, all thrown with a distinctive putty-coloured clay and waiting to be glazed: a cavern of industriousness and order. Down into a book, Roger Jacques, the potter, appeared to be growing sideways, all muscled shoulders and chest, yet stooping from a lifetime of throwing pots. His eyes are big behind his pince-nez, clear blue and buoyant in *a sea of wrinkles. It's a medieval face full of expression, solemn, earthy, somehow larger than life, a face I may have seen carved on a misericord.*

The pots for sale are displayed on the tables, domestic and arty ware side by side, while on the floor are the older earthenware jugs, salting pans, and pots with handles to carry them on your shoulder. These he called 'la toule' or 'la bouteille' and were used for storing nut oils, huile-de-noix before the First World War stopped that trade. Little clues – the faded prices, the ubiquitous dust – completed the impression that the pottery had seen better days. Jacques showed me the pictorial tree with the proud slogan, 'Pottier de père en fils depuis 1568'.

'And now it is finished,' he told me without any emotion. He had discouraged his own son from succeeding him. He worked in telecommunications instead. The cheap imports from China ('slave labour') and his government's own taxes had made the business no longer viable. He would keep going until the millennium then call it a day. 'Triste, triste,' I repeated. What can anyone say? There are other potters in the area – the village is famous for its clay – but his is the oldest.

I bought a little cup with a projecting handle, enjoying its simplicity and price. At the door, his face lightened as he remembered the visit by Bernard Leach. He described the English parachutists who had helped liberate their village during the last war. I had scratched a surface. 'We were such friends. Bonne route,' he said.

'And to you.'   *(Avallon, May 2, 1998)*

FINE FETTLING JILLY JOGGER

The barn door opens and out come sounds – the patapat clap clap patapat pat clap; wheels pepper-mill grinding, slow talk, a little laughter, terminal grundlings as the jilly jogger bites into the clay, ladle slooping into the bucket of glaze, laughter-making gaps, the heart-beat of slow motion, fingers drawing up clay, teasing out foot-wells, small-talk, ring ting aling let sing – and this is Tilly and James and Claudia and Caroline. Welcome to the RS Pottery at More on the Welsh Borders.

James Waters is Mr Cross-Cutting Tie, a graduate of The Slade, a musician, a farmer and now a potter. He's integratively challenged, a long time to weld these talents. His hands have to work with his fettling mind and earth-seeking ways. Something he does in the world. 'I want people to see me, to know me by what I do.' There's a picture of him in his home of feeding the piglets, leading the boar into some gritty and low-lying place. 'I'm at home everywhere, but not everyone is at home with me.' Sometimes when the isolation is an expanding hole, he returns to the wedging table or his wheel in the barn patapat clap clap patapat pat. The ball of clay goes down to the embrace of two

hands. Its waywardness and wanderings are tamed until it turns in a still
centre of its own. He leans over his shoulders, first fingertips, then knuckles
pull up the clay until it wobbles and out comes a beaker! At other times the
talk is alchemical, how quartz can cure crazy glazes, the liquid slips of feldspar
and hawthorn ash, silicon quartz or oxides of potassium, the secret of 'chun'
glaze and celadon, the sea greens not from pigment but from refraction of the
light. The chemistry is suddenly cut short and out comes the saxophone with
strident, bassy booms and reedy chortles bring out the underside that he needs,
the full spread of his hands.

I like this productive place driven by quality, where problems are resolved on a
daily basis, where it takes 20 years' of continuous effort and setbacks to build
up a name. I'm glad you can't do it in a day. I envy the tangibility of their
work. A book is five years of dreaming, of fragments, of obscurity. Nothing is
certain, and most of the time I like that. (More/Bath, January 1999)

Tea was served in a large white room where the lino smelled of antiseptic
and boiled cabbages, and you could see the idiot look in your face because
it was polished so much. There were photos on the walls, black and white
school shots, people in uniform from the war standing in front of fighter
planes, nurses outside canvas tents with men on crutches. Jo was in a staff
picture with his arms around older people, and there was another one of
him as a child sitting in a wooden bucket. He pointed to it, saying 'I was
there.' We gave him the train book and he opened it slowly, page by page,
as if he wanted the surprise to last. 'For me,' he said, without smiling this
time, and he said it again, 'For me.' Then he added in his much older
voice, 'My father says don't let opportunities pass you by. For once they're
gone, they're gone.'

'Out of the mouths of babes..,' said the nurse.

'*These people honour me with their lips but their heart is far from me,*' I could
have added.

At three o'clock two nurses came in and unlocked the cupboard, each
taking it in turns to insert a key. They counted out pills into dozens of
small trays. This they did in silence and with a ballet of flicking fingers.
That place upset me but I was meant to like it; in every window an old
person, and in one, Jo. He showed us his room, just a bed and a cupboard,
a cage with two more canaries, and tennis rackets and balls; there were
photos on the wall of trains in blues and golds, red and blacks. How could
he live in such a mansion and in such a tiny room? Sarah said she wanted to
see his eyes, to see what he thought secretly, but he never stayed still long
enough for that. His feet were always moving, just like the canaries in the

cage. My father, all solemnity when he is shy, had the grace to be awkward in public, not to retreat into good manners. He didn't know what to do. I liked him for that. I felt the same. My parents had done their duty but they had no idea of the door that had opened in our hearts. J.P. Tomas had become our friend. The best thing about him was that he was always telling stories, leaving nothing out and that made us laugh. He showed us a cow-parsley flower and a long-legged fly buried in it. 'They're best friends. They come in spring together and the flies die when the flowers go. You can see them holding the dead flowers.' And then later, 'I wouldn't mind being a fly except I wouldn't be able to see what I was doing.' He closed the gate behind us. 'What's the time?' Then he laughed: 'This means you like dolphins and I like ships.'

A week later came another letter with our names printed in ink and nothing crossed out. It was a train coming out of a tunnel with tall trees growing along the edge, and there was a signal box, dinky and lush, like granny's cottage. Above it was a moon with a face inside drawn smiling. It was such a happy face. Sarah cried.

The Good Ship Britannia

"... So the land became a sea and the crests became narrow ships. But where were they going?"

Alas there are no royal commands. This business of wanting and hoping is never-ending. It's the old yearning for transformation and I am infected by it. Someone once said that there are three kinds of people in this world, those who are happy as they are; those who are not and don't know why, and they are always searching for a way out; the third kind belong to their own and are incomparable. To the first the second appear rootless, their life a cat's walk without any destination on this earth; to the second the first appear static, accepting fate as some gardens are designed by the shape of the walls. I'm somewhere between the first two, not-knowing in plenty, and I live with that. One of my earliest recollections was seeing a Rolls Royce on the side of the road. I stopped and looked at it, the ivy contouring the wheels and chassis. Where was it going? How did it get there? This wayside is a royal road. There's a dream here. It's in the world now, but don't ask where it goes.

HOMELESS CHURCH

No-one in Sahagún (that I could find) had the key to the monumental San Lorenzo, the 13th century Mudéjar church built by Arabic craftsman for their Christian overlords. It was locked and that was that. I couldn't get in, and, if I did, I would find it empty or filled with heavenly jingles. All through France and Spain tiny bands of elderly priests rattled in enormous monasteries, seminaries and presbyteries; they kept the candles burning in these magnificent pilgrim churches with ambulatories made for thousands. But for how much longer? At Sahagún I walked around those colossal walls and was childishly happy identifying horseshoe arches made from wafer-thin bricks. The people are like the bricks, I thought. If this church is abandoned, then the people must be homeless. San Trinity, another Mudéjar church, is a stone's throw away. It is no longer a church. One end has been converted into a concert hall for the town, the other is a refuge for travellers. Inside, a winding staircase leads to the wooden floor and a lowered roof; the arches have been ritually broken and painted white. Somehow it all works. If the homeless need a home, then a homeless church needs the homeless people.   *(Sahagún, October 8, 1996)*

EUNATE.

The octagonal church of Nuestra Senora de Eunate means 'The good door' in Basque. It stands beside the long, straight road scissoring the campina horizon of stubble and vines and maize. The tiny chapel is a remarkable fusion of Islamic and Christian themes from the 12th century; a single ribbed dome is supported on eight sides and guarded by gargoylesque faces. A ring of stone arches surround it. Some believe it is of Knight Templar origin or it is a funerary home for pilgrims to Santiago de Compostela. On this day, alone and wet, with a jack-knifed lorry ahead of me and flashing police lights, its charms passed me by. I was impressed but unmoved.

Two nights later in the eyrie of a block of flats in Logroño, my friends Carmen and Sebastian showed me their wedding photographs and dispelled any lingering Spanish stereotypes. They had chosen Eunate not just because it was midway between their two families but for its simplicity. The sixty guests could sit on the stone benches around the altar and gaze wonderingly at the bride and bridegroom's own original designs – the purple bow tie, the customised waistcoat, the white gown. They could hold hands during the blessing. They showered rose petals as the couple left in a recumbent bicycle for two and with its own wind-powered generator. It was then that I remembered the angry words of the old Dutchman, William van de Geer: 'Some people look at all the old buildings but it is the people that matter.'

(Belorado, Spain, October 4, 1996)

Jo had a dream. It was in the little birds which he loved, the way they could fly, but he kept them locked in cages, except his parakeet. He had learned to do that. He never believed that the sky would give back its birds. I don't know why, but it always came back to a bird, this base-line of something small you could hold in your hand and crush without realising it. Something that liked crumbs. That's the hardest thing opening the door. I never expected to find you when I stepped outside. You were there on every back road in Europe, especially when I was tired or alone or I had lost my way. The same silly face or tears, the same not-knowing. There's no escape. There are all these pieces, the little bits which make no sense. Life's like that. But if I put them together will I see your face? And will it start again, that road? I thought it had ended a long time ago. I had forgotten it was even there. But I've got to use my brainbox. You see, things are never what they seem to be.

56

TAPESTRY

Aubusson is world-famous for its tapestries. At the Musée de la Tapisserie rooms as big as aircraft hangars are hung with panoramas of lions and unicorns picked out in greeny blues or antique creams. There is Diana out hunting with the moon, Dido and Aeneas in love, Alaric-sur-la-Chaloupe, and numerous coats of arms from the Kings of France, as well as old favourites from the Bible. For five centuries anybody with a chateau or Bishop's palace and subjects to impress had a tapestry from Aubusson. Very chic. I have to say I was underwhelmed by this pageant. I just couldn't get excited. For me they were behind plate glass: tantalisingly close, yet remote and untouchable. Then I stumbled onto the corridor gallery and I stepped into the poetry of black and white photographs from the 1940's; the world of the créateurs and fabricateurs of Aubusson and Felletin, of smoking chimneys and dying tanks by the misty Creuse river, of rows of sturdy men and women in scarves, intent with nimble fingers and a thousand knots to tie. I saw the old woman in clogs spinning as she walked; two old men in grey jackets and folded scarves hanging out the wool to dry; glimpses into half-lit ateliers where a husband and wife, comfortable on cushions, counted the lines together, their faces touched by the serenity of gentle repetition. I walked up and down at least four times paying homage to Jean Lurçat who renewed the tradition of tapestries in Aubusson with his modern creations. They love this man. I will remember the fulfilled gentleness of his face. I returned to the main gallery and this time the people came with me. The tapestries were no longer huge and impersonal but embodied the weft and warp of private lives. I had stepped behind creation, and they had come to life. (Lac de Neuvic, September 14, 1996)

THE MELANCILLO: A cautionary tale.

Hidden in the remote Serra Vermelha in Portugal is a small farm which the Arabs once called, The Place of the Oaks. They are still there, the cork oaks, the evergreen holm oaks, the deciduous oaks rubbing shoulders with a few sweet chestnuts. Manuel and his wife, Olga, are the latest flowers on this ancient peasant tree, and with care, thrift and hard work from first light scrape a living off the mountainside. This hard, beautiful world they share with the short-toed eagles. They are content with their hardships for they have known nothing else. Every scrap they save: the orange peel for their chickens, the pips they boil to make pectin, the grey water for their peaches, their own faeces to fertilise the fruit trees; they even soak stale bread from the village to feed their geese. A trickle of eggs supplement apricots, plums, bottled preserves and help to make their one delicacy, fruit cake.

One day is like another, up shortly after cock crow, blowing up embers and heaping on the twigs they dried the day before. Though they have a sack of flour and a fine adobe oven they prefer to toast the stale bread and brush one side with oil or eat it with their own marmalade of windfall bitter sevilles. 'My mandarins are worth their weight in gold' or 'Who needs meat?' Manuel is fond to repeat. Nine cats share their house. Two had originally come to control the rats, and they had fattened on those and bred and prospered and were now part of the family. There is another cat but he is a sneak thief and has a number instead, No 10. One day, one week, one year are much the same – until The Storm.

Olga has her own theory about the rain. The dry years which had cracked the mud walls of their home, made water worth its weight in silver, had brought the desert to the edge of their farm. Everyone wanted rain, prayed for it, attended masses for it until their Maker heard their prayers, pitied the honest squalor of their lives and gave Her answer. The rains came early that winter and, though they had never seen so many windfalls, the deep relief was celebrated with home-made plum brandy and slices of mulberry cake. The cats didn't like it. They stayed close to the fire deserting the top room where the water filled a dozen tin traps. All this indoor life had its price. They could not afford to spade the cats; once they had experimented tying leather aprons to the females' private parts but it never worked. As soon as a female came on heat rolling shamelessly on the floor, the young toms would show off spraying every corner of the room. 'You dirty little bastards,' shouted Manuel. His wife dangled them off the ground while he squirted them with ferocious mulberry vinegar to show who is top cat. Then she flung the tom outside.

The rain got worse. The old man who lived in the valley stitching grasses into orange baskets had no memory for such weather. It got so bad that they built a sturdy hen house with walkways of branches, dry egg-laying boxes and generous rations of mashed bread soaked with bonemeal and barley grains. The marbled and rufous-eyed bantams liked their new home and so did the great black-faced cockerel; everywhere he went the bantams followed. But not all were so obliging; three chickens refused this home and every enticement to enter; each night they chose the highest perch, frustratingly out of reach. How Manuel and Olga cursed them. 'The melancillo will get you,' they shouted, but it made no difference. In disgust he called them, The Renegades.

> Ha ha ha!
> We don't care.
> We're the Renegades.

Their leader was a strange cockerel without neck feathers but with gaudy wings and a red coxcomb. He walked in slow motion. 'That's Garibaldi, the drunken opera singer. He's here drying out.' And so he would need to, for it rained every day letting up only at night to spite them. One by one the terraces flooded, trees hit the dirt trail; the bridge connecting them to the village was washed away. Never did they make so much apricot jam; there was nothing else to do: no radio or newspapers or television, and only once in a month did they see their neighbour. He always asked the same question: 'Where can I find a wife?' Then one day, awesome pea-green clouds shadowed their valley. Hailstones as big as pigeon eggs ruined the mandarin crop. They heard the dying sigh of a pine crash to the ground. The air crackled. Then it came – The Thunderbolt. What a thunderbolt! The single incandescent explosion rocked the house, rocketed the cats into the back room and, in truth, though they never told anyone, they held each other as if it were their final moment.

The heavy rains stopped but not their troubles. The melancillo arrived. They knew that because a head was missing from one of the chickens. 'The dirty little bastard,' said Manuel pulling off the skin with his fingers. No longer than a rolling pin, this cousin of the wild civet cat can wriggle through the tiniest crack and is a trained killer of domesticated hens. In a week of dirty dogs, they ate chicken every night. Soon the hen house was transformed into a castle barricaded behind wire. No eggs were laid that week or the next. Each dusk the bantams hid behind the black-faced cockerel. The Renegades looked on from their inaccessible perches:

> Ha ha ha!
> We don't care.
> We're the Renegades.

One day Lucky the cat (Lucky because he didn't float down the river with his brothers and sisters) sprayed Manuel's shoe and he was halfway to seizing him by the neck when **The Idea** brained him. If this stinking stuff nauseated him, surely it would strike terror into a melancillo's heart. All they had to do, he reasoned with Olga, was to daub the spray around the hen house. First he had to collect it.

'Do it here, my darling Tonto.'

'Adorable No. Ten sprayed me on the leg.'

The poor toms were totally confused, but when the heat was on what else could they do? They obliged, and Olga and Manuel collected the odours with oiled brushes. They painted the foul stuff around the hen-house. No melancillo would come near that. That night they heard two melancillos screeching eerily and padding swiftly across the roofs. The geese and chickens went frantic and so did the ducks on the little reservoir. The next night **three** melancillos repeated their open-air performance bringing a terrifying excitement to the chicken-yard. Manuel thought he had not used enough spray, but it was Olga who reasoned: perhaps we told the melancillo that the cats were busy mating? And everyone knew randy cats only had one thing on their minds.

No-one could prove it, but The Renegades had had enough. The next evening Garibaldi, with grave dignity, led the two others to the hen house and, as far as is known, they never left it again.

Jo's picture started it really, the old man sitting in the fork of the tree. Not that we went back. I never wanted to. After that Jo and Christmas came together like a cap and tippet. I don't know why. He was like a beggar boy sitting outside Bethlehem and waiting for someone to arrive. As if he too thought there was someone BIG coming down the road. All he had to do was to wait long enough. We can wait all our lives, remain at crossroads. My father said that it would mean trouble but he never said why. He disliked change and hedged his life against it. He had his routines, brushing his teeth straight after breakfast, ten times up and ten times down, gargling three times, having his weekly bath on Saturday whether he needed it or not, and always giving the pocket money in pennies and counting every one. He rarely made a mistake. I did once, telling him about the sweets I bought. He cut my pocket money in half for six weeks and gave me the lecture about the times before. Perhaps it had been hard, and he wanted only to protect me. I should work harder, choose a direction, be more like him. He had had to pull himself out of poverty, and education was the only way out. Often he ended up by saying, 'We were poor then. On special occasions we had newspapers for tablecloths...' Sometimes they were so hungry they would spend the rent on food and would flit away at moonlight when the owls started to sing – but I think that was just a story. 'You had to survive. It was hard. There's nothing glamorous about poverty when you've got mouths to feed. It's just like being a sparrow.'

LONE'S PERFECT DAY

The most perfect day of her life, she says, was watching the mating dance of cranes on Lake Hornborgasoen in Sweden. Back in the city she dreamed about that place and the wild birds, so one day she returned with a friend and stepped into the endless reed beds by the shore. They were wearing shorts and backpacks; a camera and binoculars dangled around their necks. The reeds swayed above their heads. They pushed them out of their faces; the reeds closed behind them like curtains. Not too far, they thought. Already their arms and backs were sticky from the humidity. Perhaps they should turn back, but the wavering silence and blue skies drew them farther in. They had come all the way from Copenhagen, so they were sure to see something really wild. They swam through the reeds for an hour. Suddenly the land wobbled. A foot went through. Panic buttons. It's a bog! Which way? They hadn't bought a compass. They stamped their feet. The ground vibrated in every direction.

They were frightened now. Oozing mud climbed their legs and arms; they brushed it onto their faces. The sun climbed down bringing slanting shadows; mosquitoes appeared. They found a narrow canal cut through the reeds and followed it to a single alder tree. Her friend climbed up and saw a wooden roof in the distance. They walked towards that until they reached the flooded area. For an hour they cut reeds and laid small branches to make a trackway across the water. They slipped in and pulled themselves out half-a-dozen times. They stepped out of the reeds and onto a neatly cut lawn. It was in front of a red wooden house with pots of Busy Lizzies on the verandah. They flopped onto the grass. An old man in a white summer's suit appeared and was shocked to see the state they were in. 'You must be thirsty,' he said, and brought them iced drinks. Then he looked at his watch and apologised. He had to do something. He returned from the house and stood a few metres away. He spread out his arms and opened his hands. He whistled a few times until small reed birds landed on his shoulders and hat and hopped down his arms to feed. Lone and her friend were speechless. (Struer, Jutland, June 17, 1997)

KARIN'S STRANGE DAY

Karin lives by the Kromme river near Mijdrecht, and she likes birds. One day she cycles to work and sees a white bird with spindly legs and a beak shaped like a spoon — in fact, her first spoonbill. She takes a back road to Woerden and spots a giant black-and-white bird sailing over a dyke. 'That's a very big heron …' But it's her first stork in that part of Holland. In the evening she notices a bright light in the northern sky. 'That's impossible!' It's the comet, Hale-Bopp. Strange day, she thinks, and takes an early night.

(Lelystad-Haven, May 14, 1997)

HORTUS BOTANICUS

In the cafe at Amsterdam botanical gardens, the English couple put crumbs on the table for the sparrows. The Dutch couple shooed theirs away.

(Amsterdam, May 12, 1997)

After my father died, suddenly from a heart attack, I met him in a dream sitting by the side of the road. I sat opposite him and we looked into each others' eyes, saying nothing but everything in that silence. I cried on waking, having to leave him behind. I would have liked to have said: I appreciated your struggle coming up from the ground. I would have liked to have heard: You're carrying on where I left off, going down the small roads, the green roads I loved. As a child I thought that my father had another house and that was far away in the land of elephants and giraffes, that it was a land I must have seen in one of my picture books of the world, of long-waving grasslands, scrub-like trees with leopards on branches, golden-black beetles as big as my fist (and with silver wings), and a land towered over by a volcano higher than the clouds. And at the top of this mountain was a ring of ice and steam and fire hissing from the earth's inner depths. It was a land I sometimes saw when I lay awake in bed. I remembered a fantasy – or perhaps it wasn't – of waking up in a darkened room and seeing the sunlight stream through the window like an arrow. I watched the dust clouds sparkle in that light until the door opened and in came my father with a breakfast tray of porridge and hot chocolate. My father showed me the rooms, the wooden floors, the white stone walls, I remembered best the owls in this land, the ticking of clocks, the little sculptures of birds and animals on the mantlepiece. Out of the window I could see the golden, bent grass rising to meet a blue sky.

TELLISFORD

In rural Bohemia I kept thinking of Tellisford again. Perhaps the low-ranging hills called me, the way they were stacked on top of each other with pine forests for crests, or were broken into islands so the land became a sea and the crests became narrow ships. At other times the road dipped down secluding the views with pine woods and glimpses of fields, some larger with mustard or wheat, but always the road returned bringing something new into the distance. And this is what I remembered: It's a sunny day at the edge of a wood beside a clearing, and an open field lies on one side. I am with my male friends. We are sitting by a fire in the daytime and a copper kettle is boiling. Here at the edge of the forest we are making things with our hands, with wood, green hazel or unseasoned ash, so it is easy to peel and split. Perhaps I am making a long stave from hazel, peeling off the bark in simple geometric spirals which I find pleasing. Flies are humming in the sunlight beneath the trees, perhaps a jay, flashing its white rump, is screeching nearby. Here there is time in plenty; the city world is far away, not easy to find along this network of back roads. This is hinterland country. Here I sit on the earth and hum and drum. I laugh a lot. I content myself weaving hazel benders and cover them with tarpaulin, and we would light fires to heat metamorphic rocks and put these inside a pit inside the hazel house, to sweat and sing, and the darkness would glow with faces and the smell of sage or lemon-grass. This earth medicine held me, supported me, gave me legs to stand on, male friends who I thought of as my family. They fathered me in little ways, and I thank them for that, the male honesty, humour and sensitivity which I needed.

It seems like a fairy tale sitting in that glade with the day before me, though it was my midday. Here at Jílové u Prahy, I am sitting under a tree with a field miraculous with buttercups; red-bellied insects winging it alone over my head. A solitary wasp is nose deep in the embrace of a buttercup. A breeze comes up and it holds tight to the anthers. Every buttercup glistens with the sun. This little sun of earth is what I am after too. (Jílové u Prahy, May 20, 1998)

DIALOGUE

I stepped through the fog of my prejudices at Beijum, a moon of municipal housing to nearby Groningen. Here is multi-cultural Holland; Surinamese, Africans, Poles, former Yugoslavians all finding a foothold in Dutch society; East and West, rural and city; dyke walls with experimental eco homes; swans and redshanks grazing nearby polders. Here lives Tonko Ufkes and Maria Ufkes-Kayatz; he is from Friesland and she from East Germany. They met at an international youth camp back in the 1980's, before The Wall. Her father is a Lutheran minister, his a headmaster and a Calvinist. When they married, their parents, for the first time, met their former enemies. They wondered what had divided them.

Maria's father had been a strict Lutheran and had not co-operated with the Communists. For this, his children were denied a university education and friends were elusive at school. Maria likes it in Holland even though it is crowded and the houses are not as old and spacious. In their home and lives they keep a space to sort out disagreements. Her two children – Maaike and Paul – speak both Dutch and German. Maria's parents find it hard to understand Tonko. He doesn't have a proper job. He is a history teacher and a writer, and looks after the children while Maria works as an occupational therapist. 'In East Germany you either have a job or you are unemployed. Work means everything.' Tonko enjoys caring for his children, getting them up, cleaning them, taking them to school. When one is upset they usually run to him first. It is hard to explain to his parents-in-law that he is not a failure. Conversely, when he goes to the former East Germany, he sees so many grim faces. 'I am the only one enjoying my life.' Fanaticism is the enemy. 'Some people have a strict diet and if you eat the forbidden thing they think you are The Devil.' He spends hours playing cars with his son, making garages, but he doesn't own a car or want to. 'If I had a car I would have to spend more time earning money and less time with my children. There is a choice.'

Tonko has written stories about adults and children. 'They live in different worlds and that's why there is so much misunderstanding.' One of his stories is about a father teaching his daughter skating and he wants her to be good. He brings a chocolate to reward her efforts. She tries and tries and becomes frustrated. 'Her father realises it is his own wishes he is wishing for. He gives her the chocolate anyway.'   *(Papenburg, May 19, 1997)*

Invite him for Christmas? When they had a special Christmas party with balloons and a stuffed turkey and a clown who breathed out fire. I thought of his long arms and legs, his head bowed down inside his small room. There was never room for Jo. I said I would sleep downstairs on the sofa, but all they could say was 'NO'. They had closed their minds. We slammed

63

the door and ran outside without our coats even though it was raining. How our hearts burned! I remember the freedom of getting wet and not caring. Nothing mattered except our question. It was there going to bed and there in the morning. Sarah stuck his picture of the smiling moon and our grandmother's signal box above her bed. I wanted Jo's monster to pinch someone, to make them see sense. Sarah and I made a vow. We cut our little fingers and mixed a drop of blood smearing it on our hearts. We would starve ourselves rather than give up our question. We announced at breakfast that we would not eat anything unless Jo came. 'That's blackmail,' said my mother, 'you should be ashamed of yourselves.' Sarah and I had agreed that we would say nothing, that we would not argue. 'He couldn't cope. It would spoil it for everybody.' I expected them to argue. 'None of us made him how he is. He is different. That place is his home, the only one he's got.'

I remembered the Christmas story. 'We'd give up our room.'

'Granny likes Jo,' said Sarah. 'She likes the way he says "Thank you" for her presents. The way he makes her laugh.'

'We can't just invite ourselves for Christmas.'

'She said so on the telephone, she said it would be heaven.' Sometimes you can't argue with my sister. She glows in the mouth and you have to listen. I expected the world to fall on our heads, and then silence and a voice BIG, as if you had to listen. They stared out of the window, saying nothing and watching a silver leaf float down. Her hand stroked the back of his head, slowly as if time didn't matter. I was affected by her tenderness and the way he received it, wanted it. He sighed, such a big sigh, turning slowly to face us.

'I only want you to be happy.'

I hugged my father. That was why that morning we ran to school singing at the top of our voices and waving our hands at everyone we met in the street.

Change comes with laughter and sighs. Sometimes it comes with tears and howls like banging your fist through a door; or the face of a one-year-old struggling to stand, until one day she rages at her legs and they stay standing; or a two-year-old fighting with a door handle, pulling it blindly until in anger it turns. But I don't want to romanticise this. The 'yes' of my parents had a price. From that day they never quite saw us as children. If they acknowledged our mind, they expected us to use it, especially in homework, household chores, helping to earth-up potatoes, things before they had been happy to do for themselves. I was expected to think before I did anything, and that was unfair. Sometimes it seemed like a punishment. The times for sitting still or running along a grassy path going nowhere had ended. They wanted my trails through the day to have signposts. Now I felt that there was less time in the world. I lost something but I could not find it as I did not know its name. It was about then that I wanted a dog. Tugger was another reason for going to granny's.

COPI

The football-size scruff of matted wool dozed on the marble step of the hotel, all glinting metal counters and chairs, glassy table tops and expensive brocaded curtains. He outclassed the dreadlocked travellers of Orgiva; obviously he had never seen a bath in his life. Immediately he bounded over, spinning on his legs to find a tail he didn't have, and got what he wanted – an orange rolled under the vine pergola for him to chase. I say him but actually I couldn't see. He had to be a male, he was so cocky! He walked on hind legs not to please us but to see the scraps on the table. He dashed onto the streets of Orgiva out-distancing death by inches. How could he see through his veil of matted hair? This scruffy little dog made my daughter Aelfrieda laugh. At dinner he watched us eating, his head following the fork to the plate and back to my mouth, and, when the fork stopped, he stopped too. Madam, the patron, apologised and walked him on two legs to his basket behind the door, Copi peering back folornly.

Copi – a name she gave him – is Spanish for tassel of wool. Once she had had an Alsatian to guard her hotel. Copi had been a street dog and its friend. Every so often Copi appeared when a big bone was lying about. Their friendship was such that he was allowed to chew the bone. Eventually the Alsatian died or was knocked down, but still Copi returned. The patron fed him, and little by little Copi relinquished his street habits and was happy to doze on the doorstep with an eye open for visitors. But he would never accept having a bath. Once she had tried and he ran away for a week. She was forced to accept him as he was.

I was strangely touched by Copi, this dirty little ragamuffin, his intelligence and fun, this rags-to-riches story. For the first time in my life I considered buying a dog and, of course, I would call him Copi. (Orgiva, February, 1996)

* * *

Four years later I visited Tim and Maddy Harland, the life force behind Permaculture Magazine, that flagship for the sustainability movement in Britain. Their business home is part of a former naval communication's centre in Hampshire, a 50 acre site run by the local authority and Earthwork's Trust to create a sustainability showcase. It is a jigsaw of former sentry boxes, abandoned barriers, old rifle ranges, coppiced woodlands, empty matchbox buildings. I find them happy and collapsed after delivering a magazine to press. On the office floor is little 'Pip', their Border Terrier. Within minutes of his chin being scratched, Pip becomes a singing dog, lying on her side and crooning to us. They're smart these Border Terriers. Maddy said that a friend shut hers into the car while she walked across to an orchard. She heard the horn tooting and rushed back. The dog bounded out, peed against a tree, then jumped back in again. 'We're wondering whether to let her have a litter.'

'Save one for me,' I said. *(Bath, November 26, 1998)*

STRAY DOGS

The fear sharpens my eyes, stretches out my ears. The slightest movement at the farm gate I notice. It's a chicken poking its beak into my day or a walnut leaf clattering onto the ground. Steady old boy. I check the fences and chains; all in order. The brute's locked up. And so on... I'm exaggerating of course. At Abbas I cross the Aveyron river and see the hill climbing out and three dogs kicking dust in the road. They see me but providence throws the chain from a motorbike and they trail that back to a garage. I walk cautiously past. Three more dogs come out fighting from another corner – and I am their excitement spot of the day. I keep the bike between me and them. 'Hi gang.' They bark louder. The three other dogs exit the garage. Six dogs circle me barking loudly. A man comes out shouting. They back off. I walk quickly away. I'm a dog coward. I hear the thudding boot and the dogs yelp.

They were only doing their job. It takes courage to test out a stranger.

* * *

A big dream. I see my rightful domain, an ancient place held in trust. I try to get in, but there's no front door. I walk round the back and find a string. I follow it through a small door into a dark shithouse. A huge bearded man is standing there with an equally huge shaggy dog. I'm scared and I know they are on my side. We shake hands. The only way into my kingdom is through this back door. They are the ruthless eliminators guarding this entrance. It's what's left behind that matters. I chew on this: Do I have any stray dogs? Instincts which I disown? *(Cabrerets, September 25, 1996)*

We arrived four days before Christmas. The deal was this: we would spend two days with granny and Jo, and then my parents would come. It wasn't perfect but it was still two whole days together. Two days that had never happened before. First thing Tugger jumped me with his soft wet nose then chased the white hairs in his tail. He raced around the sofa yelping, folding back his silver-tipped ears and wouldn't let us catch him.

He dodged between our legs almost knocking Sarah down. Granny squeezed my face in her hands. She smelt of coal-tar soap, like the coal-fire smells of the house and the wood polish and the brassy bits shining up and down the staircase. Usually we had the signal room overlooking the fields but as that would be Jo's, Sarah and I shared the attic room above that, the room I didn't like because of the picture hanging there. I took it down and turned the portrait of the woman in the long blue dress against the wall. She gave me the creeps the way her eyes followed me. I helped Sarah tie coloured streamers to the curtains and balloons around his bed. She wanted to put a teddy bear between the covers but I said that was babyish. She says that boys didn't understand. I said rubbish. She always thinks she knows everything but we didn't argue as granny was there. Then she surprised us with a finger-sized knitted badger. She put it on her little finger. The badger nodded at us.

'*Rum tum, rum tum.*'

'*Rum tum tum,*' we chorused.

'You remember!'

How could we forget? Since the beginning we had painted faces onto our fingers: *Miss Sad, Mr Happy, Mr Angry, Miss Nosey.* Granny walked two fingers across the pillow, her eyes following ours.

'Once upon a time there lived *Miss Two Legs.* One sunny day she went for a walk.' She walked her fingers up Sarah's arm. 'Up a long mountain. My, she was tired and thirsty. She came to a cave. She dug for water.' Sarah pulled granny's hand from her armpit. 'She carried on walking until she came to a forest. She sat down and a crackalump jumped her and they started fighting.' Sarah pulled granny's fingers off her hair.

'And what about the two dancing beetles? Or the mittens we painted green and gold and put legs and whiskers on? They danced together swinging their legs and pretending they were by the seaside.' She slipped the badger under the pillow with his nose sticking out.

> '*Here he comer.*'
> '*rum tum tummer.*'
> '*HERE COME.*'
> '*rummer tummer.*'
> '*HERE HE COMER.*'
> '*Rum tum tummer.*'
> '*HERE COME.*'
> '*TUGGER!*'

I can still see Tugger's black nose pressed against the french window, his dark eyes quick to follow a bird or a drip from the gutter. He arched his back at a fly and cocked his black-tipped ears when I rustled my fingers. He's a Border Terrier with long bristly hair silver on top and brown underneath, and he had a look in his eyes as if he knew what you were thinking. He wasn't very well and had been to the vet lots of times. They didn't know what was wrong with him. Sometimes he stopped breathing and had to lie down and then he trembled. He got better with rest but no-one knew why. He was an amazing dog. Once I put a piece of bread on a rose bush and Tugger walked on his back legs sniffing it out even though he couldn't see it. Granny made us promise that we would never let him out of the garden, that we would always hold the lead and keep the gate locked. There's a metal fence around the garden to stop him getting out. It would stop a horse or a pack of hunting dogs. 'If a fox can get in, then Tugger can get out,' she said, and said it again ten minutes later. Tugger had his own water bottle at night and lots of doggy chews and treats with bits of chocolate in them and he had coloured balls and rings of bells to play with. That's how he got his name: he never let go once he got hold of them. Granny was daft about Tugger. Sarah said she loved him to bits. Brave Tugger. He was there at the beginning. It's a good job he couldn't talk as I'm sure he knew everything.

Sometimes I think that it wasn't me that went through all this, that it happened to someone else. Perhaps I was somebody else. They say you start as a child then grow up to be an adult, then middle-aged. That's not true. I was old at eighteen. I'm the wrong-way round man. I never understood the signposts. Now there is one pointing at me.

MIXED UP

When I was born I wanted to be held.
When I was two I wanted to find my feet.
       I used my hands to pull myself up.
When I was eight I had my feet and my two hands. I was wise.
When I was 12 my head got bigger. I lost my hands. I scowled a lot.
When I was 16 I had forgotten I had lost my hands.
When I was 18 I was wondering where my cock was.
When I was 22 I was an old man looking over my shoulder.
When I was 25 I discovered my hands. I found my cock.
When I was 34 I discovered an eight-year-old child. I played a lot.

When I was 38 I got through my adolescence. I raged a lot,
I laughed a lot.
When I was 44 I found that young man again. I cried a lot.
I'm 47. I'm old enough to be a man. I want to be held.

(Göteborg, June 5, 1997)

SIGNS

It's late in the day, almost closing at the Tate Gallery and the ushers are looking at their watches. Verona is following the sign to the Jackson Pollock exhibition. By the central foyer she sees the sign 'Work In Progress', and so she peers out of a window. She is immediately caught by the massed volumes, the shadows cast by scaffolding, the patterns of protective plastic. It's the construction site for the new gallery of contemporary art. She laughs to herself. 'Installations are works of art nowadays.' (Bath, March 1999)

* * *

The signs are there: 'Official Loch Ness Monster Exhibition' ; 'It has yet to be proved there is no monster, so beware when swimming'; 'Nessie Alert'. You see the cascading hoops on cards, peering from shop fascias and car stickers. But I didn't see Nessie even by Urquhart castle where the water gets really deep. I guess I should have been looking in my rear mirror. But I did the see the tip of the tail of a monster which strangles the local flora in the Great Glen – but there were no signs for that one, the rhododendron. (Mucomir, April 29, 1999)

EMPANADA

At Torrelavega in Cantabrian Spain I buy a slice of empanada, spicy cockles between layers of pastry. I unwrap it while pushing my bike through the crowded street and notice, for the first time, that I am the object of some attention. (I should say that my baggy trousers are tucked into red socks and a paramedic day-glo jacket singles me out.) Some motorcyclists stand beside their gleaming Kawasakis. They stand doing nothing but saying everything in their all-body leathers, proof of the prosperity in their pockets. Women, luxuriously attired in tribal leathers and silky scarves, laze at the tables. They watch me with a polite yet crackling curiosity. I keep walking, conscious, that I as an older man – old enough to be their father – is the spectre of their worst future scenario. You know: baby zimmer frame, tricycle, pedal scooter, stabilisers, ATB's and 50cc's, Kawasakis, Porsche, the world etc... Despite the morning traffic, a dazzling silence plays along this faultline smoothing all their faces. I am happy with myself, I am happy with them, I am happy with the world – and I show it. I hear the giggles and walk on, stuffing my face with empanada.

(Santander, October 19, 1996)

TEMPTATION

'I'm a serious cyclist,' I say. I had just landed from Santander where the evening before I had watched starlings shape-shifting over the blocks of flats. I was spellbound.

'I can see you're not a plonker. You're articulate too,' the film-maker says. 'I'll make you famous.' I had met him by chance at The Globe in Chagford. Nice pub.

'I don't think I want to be famous.'

He senses my hesitation. 'You'll have the means to realise your dreams.' Bullseye!

'I'll chew on it.' This amiable man flatters me with the prospect of film-chase crews and sound bites on the never-ending roads of Europe. Almost immediately a crack appears in my world. I breathe pure oxygen. It could work. No more penny pinching. I could give them away. The world balloons into boundless opportunities, my name on every one. I think deliriously. I dance on top of it. Names become numinous, The Globe, the Easton signpost. The numbers of pennies add up to nine. I'll need a retreat from the glare, the noise, somewhere to return. I could make it work. And so on. I chew on it, the suspicion of a magical eight-year-old already intruding. I sleep on it. The night brings the dream of starlings, dark against a pale sky, ominous shiftings, a blob, a hand...a claw reaching into me. I wake up thinking: star-doom.

I have my answer. It's only the boundaries which keep me sane.

(Timsbury, October 29, 1996)

That morning granny and I checked the garden boundaries. She made me check the fence and gates, how to lock and unlock the front door in an emergency, where to find the outdoor water and electricity switches. *The wise man tendeth the hearth.* She could quote *The Bible* chapter and verse if you asked her. It was always within reach, like a friend's hand. I followed her through the long grass by the railway track, rising on the other side of the fence as a clumpy, golden field up the hill to King's Wood. I breathed out balloons of mist. Down by the stream, at the far end of the garden, a tunnel dipped under the railway embankment. *Every stone you throw in goes plop plop plop.* Granny once looked into the blue eyes of a fox there, and she could have asked it the time. She herself had foxy eyes, the way you could see them thinking from the inside looking out. We walked back beside the fence picking our way past the rotting apple skins beneath two Bramleys. The lowest branches touched the grass. One tree had a hole at the base as if an animal lived there. In that golden sunlight the gnats rose and fell as if they were caught by invisible threads. A butterfly as big as a tulip turned slowly round on the leaf. I could see through the reds and whites and the rusty holes on the wings. They stabbed my heart that something so beautiful, perfect had to end. It didn't fly away when I touched it but closed its wings slowly. The dung flies were the first to go. Fat, old and tired they didn't stand a chance. The frost took them all. Not even the wall of ivy could shelter them. Then I saw dog shite by my feet, or at least I thought it was until I knelt down. It was nearly blue and full of little stones or seed shells and the crunchy bits of violet beetles. It was in a hollow. I touched it, granny didn't.

'Where's Tugger?' She cocked her head the way Tugger does it. 'Tugger!' She spun on her feet, looking behind the apple trees, at the back of the house, in the coal cellar, up the lane leading to the hill, everywhere at the same time. 'TUGGER, TUGGER!' There was no answer. She pulled up her coat and stumbled back to the house swaying from side to side; she came back holding him inside her coat, speaking sharply to him and pinching his ear. 'Bad boy giving mama a fright. That fox will get you.' Tugger stared back with his wide black eyes and cocked his clever head. Her eyes became small and vindictive. 'Damn that fox, they'll get him. They'll run him to ground.' Again we walked around the boundaries but we found no holes or bits of fur in the wire. Granny is just like Tugger, she never lets go. Sarah was asked to check the fence a third time. 'He might escape and get lost, and he's no match for the farm dogs.'

'Farm dogs!' said Sarah screwing up her nose and punching up her fist, 'I'd like to meet them.'

CAMINO ANIMAUX

I dive in. Two moments not connected by time but by a road: pulling the chain on the 12th floor of a tower-block in Rennes and in that early morning hour the siphoning and gurgling water sounded like an army of pigs being slaughtered. Straightaway I thought of the abattoirs at Auschwitz-Birkenau, the same blind panic at the gassing of innocents. I wanted it to go away but it's here now at Le Puy-en-Velay, the beginning of the pilgrim's trail, the Route St Jacques to Santiago de Compostela.

In front of me is a little golden pig I was given as a mascot. It lives on a safety pin in my jacket pocket. Under my padded cycle seat is Tiggy the badger. When I am tired I sometimes let my left hand stroke the badger's nose. I ask her how the world's looking from down there. I feel I'm stroking my arse and it's made of gold. I have never thought of this before. The other animals I'm always thinking about are dogs. Out of the undergrowth they will chase my bare legs, pull me down. I'll fight off a monster, and then there's rabies and terrible injections. Pigs, badgers and dogs. I have no idea why they're here. I can change this fear. Sometimes I put the youngest child-man onto the handlebars and for the next few minutes we discover the world together – the perfection of dawn crossing the Dordogne, the tinkling moo-bells at Champagnac, two kites lording the thermals at Langeac, the blue haze and prairie lands with old volcanoes. 'That's the Auvergne,' I say. 'It's big.' And it is. We see through my eyes, and in that moment I find peace. The fears are part of me now and not floating out there.

* * *

My luck's out. The brute's standing guard behind the parked car. It's a narrow lane in the Aubrac. The bastard is hiding. They're savage these mountain dogs. He can see me, he'll pull me down as I pass. The owner will be picking mushrooms. Damn him! No-one will know. I cycle past VERY quietly on the opposite verge. I glance back. The dog peeps out behind the far bumper. I see fear, bewilderment and relief. Exactly how I feel. I burst out laughing.

(St Alban-sur-Limagnole, September 19, 1996)

SOIL-LIFE STONE

The day started with three pigs: the sow had farrowed in the night, she said; the boar was on the farm drive following a scoop of grains in her hand, and Susan Seymour gave me a little golden pig as a good-luck charm. I am dressed in my day-glo orange jacket with three luminous yellow crosses on the back. 'You got to look like an insect for cars,' I told everyone. I had my sights on Santiago de Compostela.

It was a dreary day. I started the morning by unveiling to myself the soil-life stone I had carved. I set it on the bank of the old Somerset Coal Canal which runs through Dunsford farm. I danced beside it. I roared my prayer stick around it. I lit sage blowing the smoke onto the four faces. I saw nobody and nobody saw me. If they had I would have smiled. On and off for three years I had carved that old staddle stone which had kept rats away from the grain store. I had inserted it into one of the mill stones, again from the farm. Only walkers and cyclists will see it on this wayside. Four little owls guard the corners, and out of the West comes a snake travelling around the sides to emerge at the top where joyful human figures dance with animals. (I had carved two stones before: one at a signal box at Pylle on the Somerset and Dorset railway line, the other at a hill overlooking Glastonbury Tor.) This third stone is bigger in every way, but the yearnings are the same: to trust in what I think and feel. This stone is a place of animals in me.

At the Cathedral of St Pierre in Rennes I sat in the cool, gloomy darkness and I longed to see my stone there. Straightaway I remembered the night crossing from Portsmouth, sitting in the same place, seeing people – the same people – going backwards and forwards, round and round as if they were lost or had forgotten something, and couldn't remember what. I remembered my children. I saw again the bright-peopled morning of the Wylye valley, the ghost of the traveller-naturalist Hudson, his birds and stones and shepherds, the quintessential traveller in little things. Then my father appeared, for he had shown me his books. The stone standing in the church was like my father but not my father; it was my father standing up for something. This new-born place in me is about trusting that this place of animals is also a way in the world, that my instincts can be trusted.

(Square de Terra Neuve, Rennes, September 5, 1996)

LE MOULIN D'AYRES

If I close my eyes I hear water everywhere, a wind in the sedge or leaves, or rolling in the chestnut and hazel groves clinging to the gorge. Here all is secret, solitary, hidden. A place of water, low travelling Viaur river with reed beds and islands of grass; still and murky leats feed the old mill with its rough-hewn wooden doors closed long ago. Little stone bridges take me over the sodden grass and yielding earth, over another leat or silent pool. I have never seen so much water in one place in France as here. Every so often a walnut cracks onto the stone patio or an apple plunges into the big mill stream. I'm glad to rest, but where am I? I have listened to tales of sorrow, tales of inspiration along this way of St Jacques. The first day here I stood in the new barn and I cried hot burning tears; the dead end of change and I have to go through it and the others must do it too: the one who is losing his sight, the one with a long grief of caring for a dying mother; the woman leaving her lover after ten years as they had stopped growing. I wanted these waters to wash the feet and faces of these people. They touched me with their trust and friendship.

Moona, the young Border Collie, is chewing a walnut and she always has half an eye on this moving pen in case it might need rounding up. She's clever. She spits out the skinny bits, the bitter bits of the walnuts. The leaves clatter to earth, trapped raindrops are released, the drooping sedge hangs its beard: Autumn is here cutting back things and all I can see are the seeds and wreckage. I do not want this mood to cling to me. I want the running water to wash it away... I dream I am above ground now and looking out through the cracks of a rickety wooden shed; a bright day dawns outside and a man is working in a garden. It will be so hard leaving this rickety shed. I can see out but no-one can see me. Here I'm a half person. I made this place from bits and pieces, a sort of refuge from the world, for most of my life really. I do not need to smash it down. I will take it apart how I made it, bit by bit. This new world is here already. First I must say goodbye... How do you say goodbye? With tears and silence, resolution and respect. I have no choice but to be a man to myself, not taking other people's loo paper when I should have my own. Understanding is forgiveness too. I came into this world with blood, tears, rage and joy. I came

73

because my parents loved each other, because my mother overcame her fears. I
will need to overcome this fear of being alone, this fear of dissolution.
I listen to the sorrow of others and it is the same sorrow. I moan as I write and
Moona comforts me with her funny face on my lap, not in submission, but
with a gesture of complicity. There's a water breeze in the trees. Where it comes
from, where it goes, who knows? The leaves come down. I find my earth too
with this writing.   *(Le Moulin d'Ayres, September 23, 1996)*

The sleeting rain came after lunch. I laid by the French window watching
the plops and craters in the puddle outside. I loved watching the raindrops
slide on the window, the way one got bigger and bigger until suddenly it
became so big that it snaked down the glass gobbling up the other drops.
The first ones are dragons and find the wiggliest, quickest way down. The
other raindrops followed them. For a moment the day was a long straight
road with nothing happening on it. Boredom stuck me with its knife. I
didn't want to do anything, especially housework. Then I farted from all the
baked beans at lunch, and before Sarah could say anything I put my knife
and string and three chocolate biscuits into my coat pocket and ran outside.
I climbed over the wire fence and stopped by the stream where the steps go
down. I walked slowly across the field of golden bent grasses. I stopped by
the hedge dividing the field from the railway to King's Wood. It rained
gently. No-one else was there. I liked being on my own.

OUT HUNTING
They were skinning the rabbit when the three city kids poked their heads in by
the door. They watched without speaking as the knife unstitched the skin
while the hand pulled it off like a glove. They had never seen that before or
the shotgun leaning against the bed. They asked for the skin and ran off.
Early the following morning there was a knock at the door. The city kids were
back with charcoal faces, a stick in each hand and a cardigan wrapped around
their heads as a balaclava. 'We're out hunting,' they chorused.
(North Somerset, April 5, 1996)

DANDELIONS
The happiest sight in Calvados, once past the busten barns and relic orchards
with grandparent trees kneeling to earth, are the dandelion fields. They are
here beneath the small domes of apples besoomed with mistletoe, and the tall
heads of cherry gean flowering in the woods on the higher slopes. Big white
charolais cattle graze them down, but what tongue can devour a skyline of
dandelions? That's what I saw — and immediately the nostalgic, pre-spray
memories of my childhood assailed me. I hesitated before I braked.

I heard melodic flints, the elastic vowels of frogs. I noticed the goldcrests, up-beat and yellow and bounding over the waysides of cowslips, toughing it out in the longer grass. I listened to the high-octane larks, all song and standing in the sky. I saw the early-spotted orchids, more dodo memories from English waysides along with the quiet and sober lights of stitchwort, and colonies of Solomon's Seal drooping to attention as if they are obeying the last trumpet call. Perhaps they remembered a woodland here. Perhaps.

I am squatting in the lane behind the field's wire fence. I dig into my jar of petit-pois with my back to the dandelion horizon. What can I say? I have no words to paint this picture. I notice the dandelions by my foot, the fleshy knob of the unopened flower astride each green scaffold. The solar heads, yellow rays cut long and narrow so they do not shade each other, are overlaid from the centre where the anthers, hundreds, ply their trade. The bronzed cylinders snake in all directions, not one in a straight line. Unfathomable black-legged, narrow-waisted flies sleep nose down among them. I stare a lot. The petals are soft to touch, not like paper left out in the sun. Their stems head out to Jones's, the protective mane of green sepals clasp them by their throats so only the rusty pappus tips show. I had seen this before but never quite like this.

I listen. The trails of bird-song reach my ears. They are here all the time! The simplest things, leaves, songs, colours, are beyond my words. I look up. The dandelions go from my feet to the horizon, a narrowing space between two shoulders of woodland. The moving bits I see are insects. Everywhere! If I could plot their pathways I would see lines connecting every flower, a web between the sky and the earth. And me. The tallest dandelions, pappus mop-heads, are the seeding ones. Miraculously they have risen from the dead, the green scaffolding now almost straight. They have broken free from the bandage of sepals, outgrown the fist which held them. I'm amazed by this and the shaved heads of the solitary elders, the protective manes neatly folded back. They are almost invisible. Their work is done and my words are finished. Except – I have never seen a dandelion field with these eyes before.

(St Gauburge, April 27, 1998)

I listened to voles squeaking under the grass. I wasn't in any hurry. I noticed raindrops on twigs and saw upside-down winter branches. Some raindrops had pot bellies, the greedy ones. I dawdled along the side of the hedge, peering for a thrush's nest, until I heard the rumbling of the new road. It hadn't been there before. Now a giant ditch sliced the top part of the wood into two. It's a new road full of new cars. I crouched hidden by the trees watching them and wondering where people went in such a hurry. Where did they come from? Where were they going? Some birds did the same thing sitting on branches. Then I looked left and right and I saw it lying by the side of the road. I thought it was a shopping bag someone had dropped or a lot of leaves pressed together. I knew what I was thinking: it was dangerous to cross this road. I investigated. The shopping bag was made of fur and had stumpy legs. Blood came out of its mouth. It was an old badger with yellow teeth. Its head was tucked into its belly as if it were trying to hide or curl over and go to sleep. It was the biggest badger I had ever seen. I didn't like seeing it dead there, this beautiful animal in the gutter. The cars missed it by inches. It wasn't the badger's fault he didn't look left or right. I couldn't walk away. I stroked the rough, oily fur. I found an old plastic fertiliser bag in the hedgerow and I cut and tied the string on two edges to make a handle for the sledge. I turned the badger onto it. It had a willy. The badger was covered in mud and still soft. Animals go stiff and hard when they have been dead for awhile. I pulled the bag into the ditch and up through the trees, out of the sight of magpies and crows. In the wood, I dug a wide and shallow hole with a stick. I tipped the badger into this and covered him with leaves and earth. I put my hands on it. I felt silly, but I said goodnight.

REAL VIKINGS

The little girls were standing in an alley selling glasses of apple juice from a tray. I walked by, came back and bought one. At least it's local, I thought, in contrast to the global trading in Arvika. I had seen that before. Where is the real Arvika? Perhaps this is it. Then I found Sågudden, a near perfect museum celebrating on several floors the arts and crafts of western Wermland: rural interiors of painted furniture, baroque-swelling flowers inspired by the Bible, peasant wall hangings — a hand-made world made from wood, a rural tradition with all its virtues and vices. The Empire style and luxury was on the top floor, medieval Christianity on the first, and the Stone Age in the basement. This was my picture-book idea of Sweden. I liked it.

Not far away, the farm touches the shores of two lakes, Glafsfjorden and Algsjon, one hundred hectares of wheat and barley lands and forest skirting the small mountain of Vileberget. It is an attractive land, the open fields and stately ash trees tempering the never-ending coniferous horizons; iron-red wooden houses (one with 1812 carved on the door) are set in grasslands among breezy birches; well-worn tracks lead to haybarns and sturdy workshops; to grandparents' homes. In the fields, polished stone axes and flint arrow heads have been found; on the shore of Glafsfjorden are sombre mounds of boulders where Vikings put them a thousand years ago. Nothing has changed, except the water level has dropped by several metres.

Arvika is across the lake, a necklace of lights by night. The Vikings used it as an inland safe port, and from here they could sail or row to Göteborg, and they did. They were converted to Christianity and no-one ever heard of them again. Where did they go? At this farm live the grandmother, her daughter Karin, husband Roland, sons Wiking and Erling, proud Northern names. The milk cows from the old days have gone along with the horse-drawn sledges and pony traps. Today they run two cars, a Saab and a Volvo. 'I know it's crazy but we need them,' says Karin. Their priority now is their children, to pay the mortgage, to give them holidays, take them skiing.

Roland comes back exhausted from his work repping for an agricultural company. He sits on the wooden steps hunched over his big arms and legs. His steely, marksman's eye is dimmed by the heat. He would like to farm full-time in ten years. He dons his blue overalls to fix new sheep fencing. He blames the flies on the sheep. At dinner he methodically swats them; his sons dispose of them. Karin is partly German, straight blue eyes in a broad face, golden pigtails, full lips which smile only when she is amused. She is by nature productive, a rural survivor. Several mornings she is up before 5am to go relief milking; in the winter she works at the plastic recycling factory. Her spare moments always count: she is potting up sweetcorn and squashes for the garden, preserving vegetables, working as a football trainer for the younger schoolchildren. She thinks the Swedes work too hard. Stress-related illness is on the increase.

One week in October, Roland joins his neighbours and they shoot eight moose on Vileberget and each get 55 kilos of elk meat for the freezer. His little dachshund, Alice – an unlikely hunter – picks up the scent and barks and leads the marksmen to the elk. There are strict rules: no mother and calves or males below a certain size. They butcher the elk in a special cabin. Some people go shooting in season every weekend but Roland prefers to be with his children or paint traditional scalloped flowers on the wooden furniture. Back from work we go to their lodge on Algsjon which Karin's grandfather built from logs and planks; it has a burner inside. It is the only one marked on the ordnance map. Erling goes snorkelling at the edge of this wilderness, the Glaskogen nature reserve. Roland recalls diving into a shoal of tiny fish. 'They were so tame I could tickle them. It was amazing.'

They leave me to sit alone by the quiet water where the beaver has chewed the bark and dragged the matchstick branches to make his dams and pummel them with mud. The lodge is a mound of branches two metres high with a long underwater entrance. I sit here for an hour, fencing with mosquitoes, watching wagtails somersault for flies; a loon diver calls eerily; little fishes forever splash back into the water. The sky is made of glass and it floats on the water. Nearby is the other mound made of rocks. It is easy to picture the figures each placing a rock in some simple and moving ceremony. Where did the Vikings go? Is the beaver really here? I have no answers, and this evening that's all right. (Kongsvinger, Norway, June 10, 1997)

FARMYARD – PLACE OF ANIMALS

The sparrows step gaily into the sunlight in the gap between the top of the wall and the rafters of the cow byre. Here comes one, chocolate-hearted, white-cheeked male, dipping to dodge gusts of sharp autumnal air. They come and go from this perch all day long, rubbing shoulders, soothing chattering before launching themselves into the big world. Below them are broken breeze blocks, squashed paper feed bags, coiling lengths of black alkathene pipe tacked to the wall. Hawthorns and hazels shade the cart track branching on one side of the barn; a concrete path, wide enough for a tractor, follows the other to the small dairy at the far end. You pass by this farmyard.

The black plastic covers the cow and pig dung shovelled neatly against the wall; nettles invade the long disused sheep-dip where the half-wild black cats live. No matter how often they breed among themselves, there are always only five or six. The rusty angle-iron gates leading nowhere, the wildling elders drooping berries, the carcasses of vans where the breeding sow lives (Shakuntla, an Indian princess) mark the boundaries of the farmyard. Red-haired Inken, holding the corners of her jumper as a bag, appears and vanishes into the dairy. Twice a day, the five Jersey cows creak and scrape and blow in from Paradise or Tepee fields; the first sign is a feline face, undeterred, by the derelict peanut grinder. Another emerges and they step one paw at a time into the milking parlour. They wait for the morning splash. The dogs, Queen and Megan, know from the word go, and deftly stalk the heels of the cattle, lunging at the tails of Honey and Wispy.

This is midday and the farmyard is empty. I like the absence of a central focus, the derelict impression the bits all make. The smallest activity, a piglet scrabbling and chased by another becomes centre stage. The piglets rock and scratch, the magpies saunter boldly, step sideways flicking their long tails; the lone hedgesparrow stares closely at the ground; the collared dove shuffles and plods like a tortoise. I look up. Beyond the berrying thorns and batch, the spoil heaps of the former coal mines, the rains fall out of grey skies. The first rain and the sparrows drop onto the ledge, beaks behind them facing the gloom and the sleeping calf; they peer this way, that way – a split second – then drop to the straw and cowshit, stretching their necks to examine the sky. It's all too much. They fly back to think again.

A solitary robin is on parade standing to attention. It's sly, too, and knows the tastiest crawlies are in the byre – a fact second-nature to the cave-dwelling wren. It always appears sneaking through the smallest crack, a full stop on the run. The rain comes. The dry stones gasp. The seeding docks and sticky brown heads of burdock are rusty holes in the grass; mould grows on the elderberries.

The black cats are excellent thieves. They know every crevice and mouse den in this longstone barn. The dream of fat mice must get passed from generation to generation, for they never desert this place. The stinking slurry makes green pools by the entrance. The straw is pressed down by the calves and pigs, and rises up the walls until it is cleaned out. Two calves with benign eyes and long eyelashes step back trying to fathom me. The black cat is bolder, changing course and placing every paw in my way. Friend or foe? She hesitates. I stroke her. She pummels my knee.

I am part of the bits and pieces waiting for something to happen or a bird to come along — a spider would do — to give a sense of time passing. Inken strides past meeting my smile with hers. Megan, the black Labrador, investigates but prefers to stare frenziedly at the sleeping piglets. The calf stretches her head through the bars. Megan meets her nose and snaps at it. The calf knows it is a game and repeats it. I stare vacantly into the yard, the cat next to my feet, the dog behind me, calves on my left, pigs farting on the other. Megan, bless her, inches closer and closer to the cat pretending she is not interested. The piglets wake grunting, wheezing, tossing straw, shrieking to wake their mother. I am allowed to be here because I am doing nothing. I am not trying to change anything. This accepting feeling is enough. 'Hello! Fancy seeing you here,' says Susan Seymour filling her pail with water. Queen arrives staring at the piglets, flapping their ears, rubbing their bums. This barnyard is pure sensation and movement, a place of animals. I smile as the piglets bury themselves in the straw and dung, yet they are always sleek and pink with bright human eyes. Down into my belly come up singing hymns. (Dunsford Farm)

CAMINO ANIMAUX

I had no plans to visit La Grotte de Pech-Merle at Cabrerets. I didn't know it existed. My enchantment with the Cele valley — white cliffs out of rusty stunted woodland of oak and box — was hounded away by the approaching storm. The cliffs which had evoked an age-old continuity now tyrannised at every twist of the river, leaning over me and darkening an already dark sky. I wanted to reach Cahors, but the lightning changed my mind. I arrived at Cabrerets at one with the streaming roofs and puddles and water squelching in private places. No choice but to stay...

La Grotte de Pech-Merle, as Abbé Breuil described it, is the Sistine Chapel of cave art. I was unprepared for this underground journey. I tried to picture these hunters — from 30,000 years ago — crawling on their bellies through the fissures, their smoky lights flickering this world into existence, as if light and shadows were independent forms moving as they moved, imagination itself coming towards them to vanish and reappear in another shape; an inner world with its own power. The absolute stillness, coolness, the smooth ceilings and tunnel sides of a million-year-old abandoned river system must have appeared as the hidden source of creation, the home of their Maker. I could walk on my feet through this chain of underground caverns, see by discreet lighting and still

I couldn't speak. The manganese blacks, iron-oxide reds and calcite whites made real this wonderland of stone, still growing, still bubbling, still dripping. Not a straight line anywhere. Here on the inside I saw the twisting guts and crystalline gravity of earth. I saw a footprint made by a girl 13,000 years ago. And what did they bring to this most inaccessible and secret place? Not trees or butterflies or flowers; not their anger or sorrows or unresolved squabbles; neither did they depict themselves directly. They sanctified this place by painting animals: the bison, the mammoth, the bear, the auroch – the BIG animals they hunted in the upper world. They painted the spirits of the animals. They painted Woman, too, the Maker of life. I would have liked to have sat by the two spotted horses – big bellied beasts with tiny legs – and the silhouetted hands painted 24,000 years ago sixty metres below the grass roots. The guide said the hands could be a signature. (They occur in many Magdalenian caves.) I wanted them to be a visible sign of the hunter's wish to touch this horse. The sacred exchange of food for living does not defile it. Here I felt I belonged to the deepest knowledge of ourselves: not just the hunter, but the lover too.

(Moissac, September 26, 1996)

O CEBREIRO

I stoop through the narrow doorway and into a quiet place, a refuge from the elements. The light flickers in through the tiny round windows – white eyes set deeply into this stone wall. They glow with branches buffeted by the wind. I sit alone on the trestle bench in the back room. The tourists have gone. I am curious. This palloza built in the Spanish Celtic tradition sweeps almost to the ground offering the wind little resistance; its thatched roof is supported by projecting wooden beams. It could be from the 21st century; elegant, functional, minimalist. I had not intended to stay, but the flickering lights, the clinging dampness and sudden coolness touched a memory.

I am surrounded by rock, a shell of perfect drystone built on slumbering quoin stones. I like this dark place, this half-light, and I don't know why. It is easy to imagine the brooding figures, an eye on the candle in the backroom or an ear for a child in the cradle. A world of sound, peering looks and shadows and slow movements. I sense I am inside a cave, these eyes my only window on the world. Here I can retreat into this smaller world. On the walls are no paintings of wild animals: the mammoth and the bison have long gone. But the aurochs, the deer and sheep are in the fields outside. This place is a cave but out in the open, in a field. The attendant comes with his keys. I retreat to the church, a cavernous place of pillars, solitary candles and lack of windows. The smell is the same, a luxuriating dampness. The two confessional boxes are in the darkest and most secret places. A couple wander around nervously inspecting the altar,

*touching a sculpture then fidgeting. There is something here, but what? They
are unsure. They have lost the connection, and so have I.*

(O Cebreiro, October 12, 1996)

I didn't cross that road or return by the track. I wandered back through
the wood sometimes running from tree to tree to stop skidding over. I like
being out of control and the shock of pulling myself up. I found a squirrel
trap the gamekeeper had balanced on a log. I smashed that with the stick
and I kept smashing it until it would never work. From the edge of the
wood I saw smoke coming out of the cottage chimney. I wanted to be on
the outside. I felt bigger on the other side of the light in the kitchen window. Granny and my sister were probably baking cakes. They could not see
me, and I liked that. I wanted to be alone. In the corner of the field on the
way back were thistles, bigger than me, tilting over and full of prickles.
They were straight-lined thistles and I pointed my stick at them pretending it were a spear. They were an army attacking me. I charged them
and they fell down. They couldn't fight back, and halfway through I put
my stick down. Their spiny branches, the way they snapped, had no
strength. They were like old people. They were standing at the bottom of
the field and someone had sprayed them with dull golden paint. They
looked sad. The wind and the frost would blow them away. I could not
put the broken branches back. Instead I collected seeds and planted them
on the railway embankment.

There's a band of thistles there now. They've nearly reached the bottom
on their way back to the field.

DESCENT IN THE LOIRE VALLEY

*The little road to Isle St Martin clings to the long-haired edge of the Loire.
Even in daylight the owls prowl this glassy wilderness of tall poplars and eyelet
islands; no telegraph poles or ditches or fences, only a speechless tranquillity. I
understood why this place is special. Perhaps it was the clatter of poplar leaves
to earth, but something made me pull up and listen. The wind blew but it was
not the wind, it was the land breathing hoarsely as if its throat were dry. On
the other side of the road was a field of sunflowers bowed down by drought and
prematurely ripened. The elfin-cut fringes blown back by the wind, faces
unshaved and brown from staring too long at the sun, nodded towards me –
thousands and thousands regimented into lines and staring the same way as if
listening to the same speaker. The more I stared at them, noticed the way they
leaned at slightly different angles, some taller than others or with fewer yellow
petals in place, the stranger the thought that I was gazing at a multitude of old
people from a combat zone. They were like tired birds trying to fly but they*

could not leave the ground. They would be looking the wrong way when the harvester chopped their feet from under their knees. Suddenly I was not free to go. A great poignancy seized me. These sunflowers were all the people that had lived before on this land. A sharp line divided them from a newly ploughed and drilled field. I saw the many many people who would belong to this land in the future. Only I, now, could see this. I fancied I could hear their voices: 'Remember remember, we live here too. Protect us, you the few, who live here now.' What kind of world would we bequeath them? I had no answers. Only tears covered my face for being alone on a Sunday afternoon and far from my loved ones.

Several kilometres down this wetland paradise, I turned a corner and came face to face with a nuclear power station as if it were a supermarket by the side of the road. 'Lighting Up Chinon' the sign said, and behind that was the monolithic concrete block without windows or adornment and set within a compound of tarmac and electrified barbed wire. I had to cycle past the gigantic concrete dish cooled by tumbling water and billowing steam across the road. I hated their secrets. I hated this siege mentality. I hated this anonymity. I hated aluminium, the lighting up of more roads, the refining of agrochemicals. I hated this centralisation of power. I covered my head and roared with anger at this invasion.

In Loches I felt silly. I had seen Le Donjon before but where? It looked like a castle of square straw bales in the Lochois, but it wasn't that. This dominated the rocky peak of the medieval town as if someone had placed a giant brick there, except it was creamy-coloured and made of massive blocks of volcanic stone without any windows. This fortified tower of the Counts of Anjou was built nearly a millennium ago, literally as a stronghold of the warring court. In the 15th century it became a state prison, and from the routine brutalities permitted in its cellars we coined our word, dungeon (I think). Down I went to see. I wish I hadn't. I joined the well-fed tourists entering by small doors into a dozen airless caverns, the homes of terminal malaise. In one cave a cardinal had endured twelve years. **'Trop ennui a qui attend'**, he had scrawled. Then I found the exhibition of graffiti from the walls of Le Donjon. The scratches depicted ships, angels, runaway deer, a suffering Christ, windmills – the only links to their makers, their private hopes and despairs. This tenuous humanity confronted the anonymity of Le Donjon, and then I remembered.

I had seen it before from the outside, in the Loire valley where a beautiful sky had fallen to earth. I had seen another tower, a modern symbol of power without windows or adornment.   (Loches, October 9, 1996)

Life feels like bloody hard work sometimes. We make it so complicated for ourselves. Where's the point in that? Letting go seems about stepping out of your skin, if you see what I mean. Sometimes the world flies by and I am going much too fast. This uncertainty breaks my heart. I cry for no reason. Is love to be measured by time? A good relationship lasts forever? I am just like everybody else picking up the pieces.

CAUTIONARY LOVE TALES FOR PILGRIMS

In the perfumed air of La Maragateira, there is a dangerous beauty. The little birds click their warnings from the upright broom and tree heathers; in the mattoral of Hermes oaks, the circle of sheep expands through the golden grass; guard dogs turn to bark their warnings; the echoes travel as far as the indented horizon of the Montes de Leon, a monumental jawline for the unwary. Snow-poles dog the tiny road stringing together the great cairns and hermitages for pilgrims, the mainly urban wanderers who brave this wilderness each month of the year. They shelter from the heat under pools of poplars in dried-up river beds or listen to the speed-windings of crickets or dodge the whippet shadows of lizards. But on this glorious day silence submerges the half-abandoned villages, the works of ages tumbled by a succession of hot summers and the bright lights of Astorga and Ponferrada. Nothing stirs this hot afternoon; perhaps a Bot fly drones for a victim or a raven grundles to itself. The very few locals gossip and peel potatoes in the shade of their timber balconies. Stray dogs lounge on the collapsing walls in the village. All is quiet, except for someone singing.

'Oh! I do like to be beside the seaside. Oh! I do like to be beside the sea...'
He stops mopping the tables and stands to mock attention. 'All shipshape and Bristol fashion, Captain.' He doesn't salute, that's going too far.

The Captain enjoys his private farce. It brings some companionship into the daylight hours, tames a little this strange land and the language barrier. He likes the challenge of running the pilgrim's refuge on a shoe-string. He likes the pilgrims. They fill the gaps in his life with affection; in return, he gives them a clean bed, free breakfast and his good nature. 'That's me, a practical fellah. I'm the softest touch on the Camino,' he likes to boast. His kind, watery eyes glisten. He knows when he's happy. He puts away the mop when he recognises a strange whistling sound. He runs past the piles of firewood to stand by the road where a metal rail separates the unwary from a precipitous finale. It whistles and ricochets as if someone is tapping it. The Captain runs back to put on the kettle. He's expecting visitors.

Ramon, the Canadian, looks like a washing line with socks and pants dangling from his rucksack. Beneath the cream cap and a grave Calvinist dignity, recent tear trails have smudged his dusty complexion. Next to him stands José, the thinly-disguised migrant worker with a plastic bag looped at the end of a stick; all hands and sinews, shrewd, pointed face and oily hair in rings to his shoulder. He is a good listener. The woman is in her forties, well fed and normally cheerful, but perhaps the sun has sealed her lips today.

Ramon is shamelessly unselfconscious and speaks aloud: 'This day is the happiest day in my life. No-one can take that away from me.' This display of tenderness and quiet intensity touches them all, and they happily seek each other's company by the fire as the heat surrenders to another cold night.

Ramon is the first to speak. 'Everyone says "love love love", but all my life I have been angry. First my marriage ended. I was so angry with my wife, myself, with everyone. I was too young to know how to save it. I forgive myself for that. I lived alone for twenty five years. The first years are the hardest. You have to face yourself, and then you get strong. Then at fifty they dumped me on the garbage heap. The boss said he had no more work but he lied. That was six months ago. I sat in my house. I was more angry that ever. Then, d'you know, I remembered a childhood dream of walking to Santiago. I couldn't get it out of my mind, a road in the mountains, peace and heat, perfume in the air.' A smile melted his tight lips. 'I forgive that man. Yesterday was that perfect day of my childhood. I thought I had lost it, and he gave it back to me.'

* * *

The Captain plays nervously with his fingers. The others stare into the fire. Emotion always embarrasses him. The hard lines in his face reflect his thoughts, the knocks of a hundred journeys in Khartoum, Bolivia, the Australian outback, of a hundred different bars. 'I will tell you a love story,' he says, winking at the others. The woman stifles a groan. 'I had just come back from Mecca flying in goats and sheep from Turkey. I had bought a pad on the Old Sol. The locals were still weighing me up. So I goes into this bar and I see 18 bottles of San Miguel on the counter, my favourite.

'Who's the lucky man?' I say.

'You,' says the barman. 'For your birthday. One bottle for every two years.'

'How the devil they knew, I don't know, but luck's luck. I opened two and said "Put the rest in the fridge." I worked my way through that lot, and by this time there was a merry crowd of locals watching me. The crafty devils. I knew their game. They wanted to see me flatten my honker. I got to the end and said, "You've made a mistake."'

'A mistake?'

'I'm 40. There should be two more Miguels.' I drink them and walk slowly down the street. I know they're watching. So when I get to my door I turn round, tip my hat and kick out a leg. They've loved me ever since.'

'You must have a dream,' says the woman. She had been listening with her head resting in her hands. She stares into the fire. 'Without a dream what is there to live for?' The others listen.

'I am a respectable woman, married with two grown-up children. I loved my husband – well once I did – but what with this and that we grew apart, and still lived together. We had our routine and it worked, sort of. To tell you the truth, I was terrified to change it. But I missed love. Is that a crime?'

'Go on then,' says the Captain, thinking of the barmaid he had known in Old Sarum.

'I am in my forties. Time is running out. I needed to be at peace with God with this yearning, and what better place than the holy shrines. I went to Fatima, to Lourdes. I even walked to Canterbury. I met him on this pilgrimage. From the first moment I felt attracted to him. But he is married, and so am I, and we are Christians... responsible adults. God knows I didn't know what to do. We wrote to each other, discreetly, and decided to go on a pilgrimage together to find the answer. What harm could there be in that?'

The Captain strokes his rather large nose and says nothing.

'You might think me a wicked woman but I had no choice. So we walked and talked, and held hands in all innocence. Then halfway across the Meseta I saw a figure crouched by the side of the road. Strange, I thought. There are no buses on this road. She lets us get closer and closer then jumps out in front of us. It's his wife. The husband goes running one way, chased by her, I go running the other. I never saw them again. That night I cried myself to sleep. The next day and the next day I walked across the Meseta. I don't know what burned in me, the injustice, the futility, the consciousness that a chance of love had slipped through my fingers. In truth, I was devastated. I felt so small. I could look twenty miles ahead and see the jagged mountains. Dragon's teeth. I would have to cross that. On this gravel path were countless footsteps of pilgrims all going somewhere. But where? To Santiago? To God? To a loved one? Or running away? From what? I knelt on the path and wrote in big letters:

AMOUR

'I had a dream and now it is broken. I felt so foolish to be like this a thousand miles from home. Then I remembered, of all things, the story of the pedlar of Swaffham, a silly story about dreams. A man leaves his starving family because he keeps dreaming about a fortune he can find on London Bridge. In the end he has to go. He walks up and down the bridge for three days and finds nothing. I know how he felt. Then a shopkeeper laughs at him and tells him how stupid he is to believe in dreams. Why, he had dreamed only that night of a beggar from Swaffham who had treasure hidden under his tree at home. The silly fool didn't know it. When I had finished crying, I saw that the mountains I thought I had to cross were only clouds on the horizon. I had got it all wrong.

'I'm a fool,' I said. Then I shouted it out to the sky, 'I'M A BEAUTIFUL FOOL!' And I felt much better.

Ramon laughs longest until more tears smudged his cheeks. 'I know what you mean,' he exclaims. 'I am so serious.' He jumps up stretching out his arms. God! You are so big. We are so small.' He winked at the others. 'But your mercy is great. You have only to fart and you will blow us away. If only they would listen, let love into their lives. Their miserable lives. Why Lord? Why me? Why are some greater than others? I know I am a sinner. But you have given this light so I can see the rottenness of their hearts.'
He grins through his teeth.
'Do they listen? Do maggots understand? Pin brains! You cannot hide from me. I see you fornicators. You can't even do that properly. But God is merciful, just one of His blessed tears will water your crops for a hundred years. Do not incur the wrath of God's shit! If only you would listen. I know what's in your hearts. What evil lurks there. You premature ejaculators! Put away your neighbours' wives. Give me their names so I can admonish them personally. Love is not enough. Is it the sword Lord? Is that the only thing they understand? I will wield it for you. To open their hearts...with such tender mercy. It will hurt me more than it hurts them.' Ramon dropped his arms and a rare smile transformed his face. 'I'm a fool too,' he says. The woman embraces him. 'I like you better like that,' she says.

José is the last to speak. His pilgrimage is life-long and they know it. With the slightest twist of his wrist he signals for their attention. His stubby fingers which have picked grapes and peas and apricots, washed a million plates in Spain and Portugal, motion to the window. 'They're singing tonight,' he says in his sandy voice. The silence settles among them, but the crickets sing ten times louder. 'No-one knows where they are. If you look here, they're over there. If you look over there, you are lost already. Love is like this. You can never look for it. Some say only the Lord gives it, but they are wrong. The land gives us love.' He flicks the butt of his cigarette into the fire. He stares into it. The lines around his eyes cease to worry.
'There is a garden outside León, only a hectare, but the land is the best. The only trees you see are in this garden. Outside are factories and wire fences or parking lots or maize. But inside it is beautiful. A deep yellow soil, and not one stone! You should see what it grows. Potatoes as big as footballs, carrots you can't pull out. It takes two to pull one carrot out. The sheep can't get in. A red brick wall surrounds it. It is a work of art. The gate at the front lets in the truck every morning. It collects for market pimentoes and peppers, baskets of hot chillies, plum tomatoes, aubergines...apples and pears and plums. You pick them just by standing. The chickens get the rotten ones. The best eggs

please! The foxes don't like it. They can't get them! The bees are behind the house. Honey for breakfast is normal. The house is white, not big not small, a practical house with a cellar for potatoes, a shed for the pig. The wood is cut and stacked against the walls. You cannot put your finger between the chumps. Carmen plays here or on the swings with her friends. On hot evenings we sit under the vines. We drink our own wine. The best grapes! The water in the well is clean and sweet. On Mondays we bake and eat fresh bread. In winter we never go hungry. Enough potatoes, onions and bacon, enough of everything. In winter I pick oranges, bitter ones to mix with juicers. I twist them off the tree. I eat as many as I like and more. No-one tells me what to do...'

'But,' says Ramon with his ruthless honesty, 'there are no oranges in León.'

José says nothing. The woman glowers at Ramon. 'That,' says José raising his shoulders slightly, 'is why it is only a dream.' His infinite patience, acceptance of his lot, shames their silence. They have no answer. They think of the homes they will return to and the long road ahead. José goes to bed before the others. He is gone by dawn. It is on the mountain, perhaps by one of the cairns, that he searches for his cigarettes. The envelope has his name on it, and someone has written: **'El dinero para la tierra para construir la casa blanca, con nuestro amor.'**

THE SHADOW IN THE FLAMES

"My heart will always fly to you like a bird, from any place on earth, and it will surely find you."

Etty Hillesum, *A Diary 1941-44*

Love, love, love, say it often enough and I feel unclean. All my life I have got this message: love everybody but not yourself. That's selfish! The devil will get you for that. He takes care of his own. He'll truss you up, chisel out your eyes and force-feed you as sausages into a gaping mouth. I am not all good. Everybody needs a few vices. We start off with our good intentions and end up in deep water. I never knew what door I had opened by going to Central Europe; there's a long shadow there, but it's not love. I had a warning back in England, when, by one of those coincidences we call strange, Thomas had come into my life. He had been a tramp for 26 years, 'a lonesome hero' in his own words, of the roads in Britain, Europe and America. His haunting eyes, hair touching his shoulders, his genuflecting hands somehow suggested that he was an angel from an apostolic brotherhood. He told me stories of Hudson Bay, the lonesome travellers with their long coats concealing bundles of twigs wrapped inside newspapers – the kindling kept warm by their body heat – of hiding caches in a dozen places along the road to await their next visit. He gave me a Radar key to open invalid toilets anywhere in Britain, a tramp's trick for a dry night. I should have guessed that this key had a symbolic meaning. He said I might need it if I were stung by a wasp. I had to push it into the sting until I felt the pain, and then the metal would take out the poison. I took it, I must say, partly to please him.

I saw him once more, and this time he was serious. With his silent intensity and warm hands, he entrusted to me a small black box containing a rosary and a white, artificial poppy inscribed with the word 'Peace'. He asked me to listen as he recited the Lord's Prayer in Hebrew, and he did it again at my request. I did not need to remember it; it was his blessing on the cross. These were the words his life-long mentor had taught him, from the man who had been sent to Auschwitz as a child. He remembered the wagons, the arc lamps and the barking German orders. He had blue eyes and was selected to go to the right. His brother had brown eyes and was selected to go to the left. Left was a tunnel, and who knows what lies at the end of a tunnel? He never saw his eight-year-old brother again. Thomas asked me to place the poppy and the cross somewhere in the Auschwitz-Birkenau complex, and to do it with a little ceremony. Without words, I accepted the burden of his trust; his mentor had said that after Auschwitz the burden of belonging back in the world had been his greatest trial. I put some seeds into a packet – sea holly (*Eryingium maritimum*); yellow-horned poppy (*Glaucum flavum*). I had the idea of scattering the seeds, a symbolic gesture of making a garden of remembrance at Auschwitz. I told him that I would return his box with a little soil from that place. (I never did. I wanted to leave Auschwitz behind me.) But I had wanted to know what could grow out of such a rejected soil.

TRALEE SPIRIT

He was crouched by the ferry security fence scribbling into his pad. First impression: long black hair, bearded looks and a spring curled up in his legs and eyes. Mid-forties at a guess. He fired off his thoughts, all honed by the necessity he chooses in his life. He is interested in just about everything: old trombones, BSA's, music technology, master classes, building work, instrument technology, flute and saxophones, sailing boats... 'I have a lot of irons in the fire,' he says spurting out laughter with his words. The creases reach his ears then subside. Budapest was a dynamo ('Watch out West'), they stole his bike in Bratislava; he cycled big loops in Poland, Hungary and Austria, over the Alps without pants; he busked in Paris, lived the low-life with Turks and Africans in Munich. He dreams of building an ocean-going yacht, and has the pine already seasoning back home in Ireland. Where was he going? He may go to a London music school, get into his boat building project ('but you need £150 just for two tins of paint'). Maybe he'll go travelling in Africa. He had a sister in South America. He has relations in the Cotswolds but they never replied to his letters. He was very interested in tramps.

'There was this old man in Kerry, mystic with his words and wandering around. He came into my workshop. His coat pockets swung close to the ground. He pulled out a big magnet. He emptied £50 in coins onto the bench. Where did you get that from?'

'You see,' he says, "wherever I am I look for the one-arm bandits. I bide my time then stick on the magnet. But I only ever does one jackpot in each town."

(Saffron Walden, June 22)

Granny had another way of looking at it. What you and I would call rubbish, she collected. She hated throwing things away. She kept a box of useful things that didn't fit anywhere else, 'The last stop before the dustbin'. In it were sherry corks, white sheep bones, paper weights, bits of copper pipes, marbles, empty thread spools, mother-of-pearl buttons, old coins, glass stoppers, postcards, insides of cameras, electric motors, pegs and almost anything else. We loved tipping them out and taking turns balancing them on top of each other to make amazing mobiles you could walk around. They were balanced so carefully that one hair could tip them over. We played on the same side against the box and, if one of us lost, then we both did. Another game was to choose ten different things and see how many you could balance off the ground in a minute. Those were the happiest times I remember with Sarah, making things out of nothing with only our fingers and time. I made patterns out of the buttons and Sarah wove the coloured threads until they became a bird of paradise.

HAT

The girl liked putting on hats, anything she could find: real ones, saucepans, an ice-cream carton. She liked that the best and walked about the supermarket amusing the other customers. 'What a nice hat,' the till lady said.

'Don't be silly,' she replied, 'it's an ice-cream carton.'

(North Somerset, May, 1996)

'It needs to be sitting in a tree and not on a carpet.' The threads we tied onto the fireguard and twisted over our heads to be tucked into the table-cloth. I spun crinkly paper into streamers and along the threads. She pulled the table closer until we were sitting under a web. I saw her eyes. The grandfather clock ticked to itself. The coal fire behind us, when I listened hard, talked too. Granny was upstairs sleeping.

'We could be anywhere,' said Sarah, 'anywhere in the world.'

That was in the room below. A hundred years ago? Yesterday? Who can bring it back? The past is here now. It was impossible to travel in Central Europe without thinking of the fate of the Jewish people. They were there in the cracks of every day; in the wagons in railway sidings; in every big chimney; in children holding hands; a tramp pushing a hand-cart, in names like Zilina, by silver birches and wooden shacks, at the end of railway lines, in glossy books. I was always drawn to the bookshops and glossy images to haunt my eyes. I had seen them before but never so close to the actual war theatres.

I felt tremendously sad before those pictures of mothers and children running away naked, a hand appearing from a gap in a covered goods wagon, people digging their own graves. Not only were the Jewish people betrayed but also the German youth. Goering had told his SS death squad formations that genocide would not harm their souls while 'removing the bacillus of Europe'. I remember watching the 50th anniversary of the liberation of Auschwitz. I saw the youths holding the perimeter fence, and one had such peace on his face as if he had walked through fire and come out the other side. I howled at the time. I wanted him to be part of my family, and in my mind he eventually appeared with a basketball cap and baggy trousers. I wanted to belong to him and him to belong to me. I called him the Birkenau kid. I wanted him to find a way in the world which would bring fulfilment. I did not think this odd; it came naturally to me. And then, in France, the first dream came knocking and I had to listen: *I am in Auschwitz. I am trapped in the corner of a wire cage and trying to dig a way out with my hands. But I know it's impossible. The guards will get me. I fall back resigned to my fate.*

This may have remained a private drama but I remembered Vigelands-parken when life barged into my face. I had never heard my friends expressing these thoughts or emotions. A common response might be, 'I don't like thinking about it. It is too distressing.' But there are connections, an impetus which upsets this reason. What if I were there? It's impossible, I know that. But what if I am connected in a way that I cannot explain? There are ties, but who tied them? And to whom? And when? And why? This doesn't make sense. I am not Jewish. I was born in 1950, about five years after the camp was liberated by the Russians. But I still have my question: Was I in Auschwitz?

Sarah made a nest out of bones and pipe ends, and sat in the middle. Beside her was a plastic flower in a jar; she pretended to smell it. There were postcards on the floor: date palms in North Africa, a steam train by the seaside, another of a horse-drawn bus. 'This is my place,' she said. The fire behind the tablecloth made everything glow, and so did the shadows around us. She twisted two streamers and tied them around her hair. Is this my sister? She amazed me. Sometimes I hardly knew her, the way she changed with her different voices while mine stayed the same, they way she could talk in a silly voice as if she were very small, but when I looked into her eyes she saw right into mine. More like a fairy. I played this game as if it were real.

'Am I pretty?' she said, waving a stick with red and yellow paper tied to the end. This game we played together where magic came out of the end of her stick. On her lap was one of granny's toy lions with the stuffing falling out. 'You are...in Africa. Africa is full of noise.'

'*Curooo curooo.*'

'I'm waving my wand. A little bird says: "Follow me".'

'*Curooo curooo.*'

'I can't see anything. I twitch my fingers by my nose. I listen. I see yellow butterflies as big as dustbin lids. Leaves talk. Butterflies watch – with yellow spots! Ants, zillions, carry twigs over their heads. I step over them. Water drips onto my face. I jump across streams. I swing across branches.'

'*BOO!*'

'I cross swords with sword grasses... '

'And... '

'Monkeys laugh oooOO oooOOO. They scratch their bums.'

'*Curooo curooo.*'

'Parrots flick their tails. Insects hum. Red eyes watch from trees. I push back leaves. I knock down spiders. I run into a field of golden grass. I shut out the sunlight with my fingers. I open them one by one. I'm surrounded by trees.. I'm alone.'

'And did a girl appear waving a wand? Did she say: "Are you lost?" Did she say that?'

'Yes.'

'Did she say "Follow me." And... '

'She has no shoes. She whistles and a ginger cat brushes her leg.'

'"Don't be afraid," she says.'

'The cat gets bigger...'

'And BIGGER.'

'It's a racing lion. She has far to go.'

'We climb onto the cat...fly over streams, over rocks, over paths made of shells, over yellow flowers. She puts one in her hair.'

'Did she say: "Listen?" Did she stroke its whiskers saying: "I'd never leave you." Did she?'

'Yes.'

Sarah squeezed the lion until the straw bulged out of the sides. She pushed that back in and smoothed it flat. 'Is her house pretty like mine?'

'The house is made of twigs and tied with grasses and flowers. I crawl in. The floor is made of blue stones and pearls.'

'Poor boy. He's lost. He wants to go home. Hold tight! Close your eyes. Can you see me?'

'No.'

'*GrrrrrRRRRR!*'

'A lion!'

'Don't be frightened. Climb up.'

'I'm holding its ears.'

'Did the lion say, "We have far to go"?' She flew the lion around her head breaking the threads and streamers. The fireguard fell down. Sarah curled on the floor laughing. Granny stooped to see us.

'Am I interrupting my dears?'

Sarah held up the lion. 'We're playing.'

'I thought the house was falling down.'

I thought the house was falling down the first time I heard my father crying. That he, too, had darkness behind him, and I might never find my way out.

ULM MINSTER

At Ulm Minster I find the shade to write some postcards. Opposite me, sitting on a bench in the shadows, is a man with grey thoughts, with receding hair, grey jacket and trousers, and in an ill-fitting shirt. He smokes a cigarette, sometimes wiping his chin with his shirt-cuff. I avoid his eye. He probably wants money. I ignore him, rehearsing a little speech in bad German against any demands. I see him as homeless, and the long lines on his face, the slightly hollow cheeks, confirm my suspicions. Minutes later a couple go up to him and, in return for money, he gives them two tickets. Only then do I see the door beside him and the steps leading up to the famous steeple. Now I notice his neat, golden glasses, his wrist-watch, his polished boots. I hear his dignified bass voice calling to the server in the little tourist office. A wave of sadness releases me from my closed mind. (Ulm, May 11, 1998)

HORIZON JEUNE

I am ashamed to say I did not want to go inside. The scruffy clothes and young smokers put me off. Perhaps I'll be robbed. Who knows? I tried to find alternative accommodation without success. I pushed my bike up the Clermont-Ferrand road and back to the purpose-built flats. At the entrance I remembered the dream from the night before: 'I am in a room with strong, traveller type men. I am uncomfortable but it's okay. I uncover some dogs and feed them water. They love it and come to life.' I walk in wary, yet curious. The director, Daniel Rapinat, made me tea in the communal kitchen as I was thirsty. He is a tired bear of a man, not typically French, all in black, expressive eyes, and the look of someone who knows how to listen. The jigsaws – my prejudices – fit together. This hostel is for the homeless young, my worst scenario for myself. 'The problem is everywhere,' he tells me, 'in the paysage, in the city. It is forbidden to squat the many empty properties. All of France is sick. There is no solidarity. The farmers sell their land just to stay solvent.'

I tell him about the LETS scheme (Local Exchange Trading Services) where people exchange skills; time is the only currency. 'Everyone has time,' I say. He smiles now and says he likes that. 'But there is nothing like this in France.' No, he is pessimistic. Les Foyers de Jeune Travailleurs is a private initiative offering a home and education for the young homeless (Un espace de services: Logement − Restauration − Formation − Emploi − Santé − Sports − Loisirs − Information). 'They have to sign and keep a contract or they're out,' says Daniel. I liked this man. There was nothing I could do, but I wanted to do something. I felt an enormous sympathy for this struggle for a home and work when many of the conventional role models are past their sell-by-date.

(Aubusson, September 14, 1996)

THE NARROW LINE

Christine and Annémie are girlfriends in a small Flemish town, a business-like landscape with go-to-work fields, saluting poplars, horizons of potatoes without any signs of elves or goblins. They are proud of their vegetable garden, the carrot seedlings, shallots, spinach tops and onions. 'Why are you growing potatoes,' says a neighbour, 'when you can buy them clean at the super-markets?' Christine smiles. Once they walked from their house to Santiago de Compostela, 110 days on little tracks. They invited friends to say goodbye, lit a fire, exchanged farewell poems and songs. They made a miniature garden with a mirror in the middle to show them their true faces. This simple ceremony touched them all. They ritually shaved off their hair; they had to give up something. They carried pilgrim staffs. It was important to them that they start from home. Their pictures were taken in Santiago (and in their local paper on their return) holding hands as they ceremoniously cut a red tape. 'I had a different relationship with time when I got back. I didn't rush so much,' says Christine. 'I realised that we had to change our life here and not in Africa. That's why we made the garden.'

Annémie decided to work part-time. 'I had worked before with young offend-ers. We lived in a house together. There I realised that there was very little difference between them and myself. At crucial times I had been helped across difficulties. They had not. Sometimes the line is very narrow. A little push and you're over. It could easily have been me.' Annémie would like to walk to Santiago with the young offenders. 'One positive experience can change your life.' I believe her.

(Watervliet, Belgium, May 9, 1997)

LA PETITE CHOUETTE

Something sad touched me in Moissac. It was there in the rain and in my tiredness, in the full hotel and the tacky place I landed. It was there in the face of the teenage beggar outside La Poste, trying hard to be civil with his out-stretched hand; there too in the grey flagstones and the loaded sky. This sense *of things not meeting is what I'm after. I sheltered in the cavernous entrance of the former abbey church of St Pierre: Christ-in-his-Majesty and the Four Evangelists guarded this portal. A Gregorian choir sang from within – but I knew it was on a time-switch and that the church was empty. I had seen the famous cloisters, a millennium of Christian contemplation, once the glory of the Benedictines of Cluny; many of the saints had lost their noses and some had initials carved into their cheeks, perhaps during the Revolution. This settling of old scores had created nothing new. I could not warm up this morning.*

Then I saw the youth crouched inside the church entrance keeping dry and chipping away at wood; a smile in a tanned face. I sat beside his row of sculptures: a madonna, a little owl, a horse's face carved as an ash tray. Straightaway I liked their simplicity, their naïve tenderness. I liked the little owl best with its heart-shaped eyes. It was easy to see the trouble in his eyes, the grime on his collar. He was in his late thirties, homeless and struggling. 'African wood,' he said, 'it brings good luck.' His name is Patrick, of Spanish origin, and his three children live in Northern France. A familiar story of domestic faultlines; they were married for ten years. He likes carving. The owl took three days to make – at 150 francs it's the equivalent of £6 a day. His Madonna is a pious Catholic virgin and he expected to complete her that evening. He liked the atmosphere of churches. He had carved at Avignon and Lourdes where the pilgrims can be generous. I tell him that I love carving, that I have three children and I know the pain of separation. The pain of broken hearts converged for a moment. 'Where's the sense in all this?' I asked. The moment passed. I kept picking up 'la petite chouette'. I showed him the owl feather I had taken from a bird on the wayside, a beautiful, embroidered feather. 'They always bring the dream. What's yours?'

He thinks for a moment. 'A home, a garden, some trees...perhaps a child. Yes, a child.'

'Everybody wants these. Nothing else?'

He smiled, raising his shoulders. I gave him the feather and some practical francs. I walked out of Moissac and the sadness came with me.

(Condom, September 28, 1996)

LUCK

Gerard Coupechoux counts his fingers to number the teenagers living in his street, the Rue St Jacques, the old road out of Loches. Two hundred years ago his troglodyte house – cut out of soft tufa stone – is rumoured to have been extended by the executioner at Le Donjon; business, after all, was booming during the Revolution. There were two weathervanes on his house to acknowledge his status. Anyway, perhaps he gets to eight then shrugs his shoulders. 'The others have gone to Angers and Poitiers and Tours. It's a shame, only old people and children are left. What is there here for them to do?' (The houses get sold as holiday homes, the land for maize and more maize.) Gerard is an exception. He studied at Tours but came back to teach mathematics and chemistry at the secondary school. With his moustache and chiselled features he looks a little like Hercule Poirot, and is a good listener, a touch inscrutable. He is unmarried but likes his own company. 'I have visited 55 countries and hope the world is not too big so I can visit every one.'

Even with education, he says, luck is important. His grandson has luck. After university he takes a menial job with a motor company in England to improve his English. They like his friendliness and willingness to do shite work. A job comes up in West Africa but no-one volunteers. Then someone remembers he speaks French, the main qualification. Africa swallows him up until a post comes up in South America. You have to speak French and Spanish – and he can – so he gets it. Two years later he's flying back to London and talks to an old man sitting next to him about his experiences. The old man listens intently and hardly speaks. Back in London his grandson discovers that he has been offered a prestigious post in North America – the old man's job in fact. He had been flying to London to interview applicants at the motor company. 'That boy's the one,' he told them.

He is still only 26.   *(Loches, October 9, 1996)*

I put my hands over my eyes. I don't want to see this. That's what granny did when she prayed. She closed her eyes. She always did the same thing, locking Tugger in the kitchen, put beans and onions and potatoes in the slow cooker for a soup at lunchtime, then went into her room and whispered to herself. Sarah said she was praying, praying for us, for Jesus, for everybody who needed it. That's why she prayed so long and why we had to tiptoe to the toilet and not pull the chain. We prayed at school assembly every morning but granny did it by herself. She never talked about it or said we had to pray. At school we prayed that the world will be saved, that people will love each other, that they will have enough food to eat, somewhere to sleep or someone to help them across the road. Then we closed the door, and it was always a full-stop, never a gap or a possibility.

LOOKING FOR FATHER

I am in Sorø, a small town in Zealand, Denmark. I wanted a quiet place to write but I'm right in the throb of a teenage café, young love on the walls, tentative kisses, lounging girls chattering in Danish, eyeing up the blokes on the street and collapsing in laughter when eyed back. The blow-up photographs are in faded colours, athletic youths with bulges in the right places, their faces ironed cool, slightly sad as if something is weighing on their minds. Something is weighing on mine. Something is choking me. I hide my face so the girls cannot see me.

99

I will have to get into this. The juke box songs are full of eternal love: **'I never want to be in love with anyone else but you.'** *I am standing on my dis-eased ground and it hurts. I call him Exima, a blessing or a curse. Here I might waste away, sealed up in some interior far away from the athletic young loves. Whenever I inadvertently enter this place I want to lock the door with rules and principles, to shut it tight with purity. I do not want to be contaminated by it. I know the voice. I have listened by the door.* 'Can anyone hear me? I'm disappearing. I'm wasting away.'

'Lucky lips are always kissing.' *No-one kisses this thin man, this skinny youth. Once I entered that curtained room and saw him lying on the bed; he had long curved nails that no-one had cut and hands that had not been held. He was like a sloth clinging to a desert tree, surviving in the hardest terrain. I cannot believe he lives alone in this room without parents.*

* * *

On the island of Fyn is a statue of the cow Audumla; with the milk of human kindness she suckles Ymir, first of the giants; from a salt lick she fashions Buri, the ancestor of the gods. Nearby lives an older woman who welcomed me into the attic she shared with the largest cat I have ever seen. The cat only leaves when her mistress visits her parents in Jutland. On her walls is a lifetime's collection of jewellery, hats, feline faces, clothes and books on every subject under the sun, especially on pathways into the inner world. By day she is a counsellor leading people into their working lives; at home she is on the other side, with cosmos. She eats and smokes and laughs in her temple: part Christian Madonnas and glowing hearts, golden cherubs and infantas everywhere, an old Danish print of people walking to heaven, to the other side; a map of the solar system and stars twinkling out of wrapping paper. Mother Meera and Sai Baba are here too. **'All the love in the world won't take me away from you.'** *She is a generous woman, always giving. Sometimes she is lonely and badly in need of love.* 'There is no God wagging his finger at you,' *she says.* **'I won't let you down again.'** *I have to be true to myself. I'm sad. I've scratched this place again.*

The cat reminded me of Anne Frank. She, too, under the German occupation, had lived her life within a few walls. She could only see a patch of blue sky and dream of the day she would be a writer and find a way in the world. 'I wander from room to room, downstairs and up again, feeling like a songbird whose wings have been brutally clipped and who is beating itself in utter darkness against the bars of the cage,' *she wrote in her diary. I had wanted to visit the transit camp in Drenthe where she was locked into one of the 100 trains going to Auschwitz-Birkenau. This was not the destination she had dreamed of. I went to the wrong Westerbork and never saw the railway track broken and pulled back over itself as a monument, or the 100,000 stones for* the men, women and children who wished they could 'swim away in their tears'. Chronicling her first kiss, sending letters to each other in the hideout, watching raindrops glisten like silver, she wrote accusingly: 'We all want this war.'

The journals of Etty Hillesum let us see the hospital barracks, a mother rebuking children, 'If you don't eat then mummy won't be with you on the transport'; dressing and calming babies for destruction, people swallowing poison at breakfast; the trains leaving at 11.00, the platform staked out by the green uniformed guards, the faces crammed at the barrack windows, the unpainted wagons, the Camp Appeals Officer with briefcase under his arm struggling to pull people out; then the Commandant appearing like a star, walking with military precision, immaculately brushed hair under his green cap; the head of the Camp Service Corps, black cap, black boots and black coat and yellow star; the hands in small openings in the wagons. The dream of poisonous green gas is already in Etty's mind. 'If there is only one decent German then it is wrong to pour hatred over an entire people.' She believed there were two parts to this drama, the victim and the aggressor. She refused to be a victim. She chose to go to Auschwitz.

I once dreamed of a game called 'Nazis and Jews'; a victim boy stays silent, he has no rights, it's safer not to grumble, to be brave and strong, not to have feelings. And inside are the dreams. '...A little piece of blue heaven surrounded by heavy black rain clouds,' wrote Anne. If Exima is my Jew, then who is my Nazi? The gaol-keeper? I have always been scared, ashamed of this wasted part of me. When I ignore him, he knocks at my body. I want to collapse into purity. Or become bullet-proof hard. When I'm too big, I lose myself. My jaws seize up. I'm a hard man with a hard cock, and he's frightened of women. They are death to this place, but it's too late now. I'm a complex man. ('We Europeans,' says my friend Olga Gomez, 'are dangerous people. We need to understand ourselves.') This dis-eased land is home ground, my back-yard.

I'm carving a sculpture of an older man, like a priest, and he is blessing an animal. I know that he lives in my solar plexus, some kind of king, someone who knows what is sacred, what needs to be eliminated. I have covered myself up with fear to protect myself. When I am in this place, holding Exima, I whistle in his ear. I promised I would show him the world. Here I stop looking for father. I am father.   (Sorø, May 27, 1997)

We waited for granny in the kitchen, time standing still, Sarah making pony tails in Tugger's hair by threading in silver and red cotton. I watched the colours creep out of the sky and up the lane, along the tops of hedges and the funny hump-backed hills in the distance. They were islands in the sea or the backs of creatures buried in the earth. There was no sign of snow but the ground mist came out of the shadows as if it were there all the time. The sun takes everything with it, close and far, and I always think I'm going with it too. Along that lane will come Jo, and I will open the front door and my father will be smiling and put his arm around both of us.

Whenever I felt lost I imagined his arms holding me, rocking me and there were no words, only his eyes and the warmth of his hands. If I told Sarah that she would smile, the way she did when she thought that I was losing it again.

THE LIGHT OF YAHWEH

The abundance of regional breads and biscuits, the two smiling people in home-spun clothes, the painted sign – Pan Biologique – worked their magic and pulled me out of the market day traffic at St-Jean-Pied-de-Port. Almost at once I was sitting in the chair drinking weak, black tea with a chocolate biscuit. They were both in their late twenties and married, both German and with an extraordinary tenderness for this stranger on a bicycle. This acceptance bewildered me, but I did not argue. The food came fresh from their community ovens where, they said, it was baked with love. I believed that. 'How did you come to be here?' I asked the man. His gravitas and simplicity befitted his long beard and radiant brow. His wife listened to every word, her lips trembling with sympathy. After university, he said, he went to the Taizé community and became intoxicated by the love he found there. He found a faith in God. It lasted six weeks. He returned again and again but each time his new-found faith surrendered in a shorter time to the world's pleasures and obligations. Passion animated his voice and raised his hands, 'I wanted to do something with a pure love, and all I had left was my music.' But his teacher tells him that you can only play music if you are unselfish. So he goes to Taizé for the seventh time and joins the silence group, but in his heart, he says, he is still selfish, secretly enjoying the showers and talking into the night. The last day he cries out in the silence for his Maker to show him a way to love. Outside some musicians are playing, so he gets out his fiddle and plays a bit. They smile, so he comes a bit closer and they play for an hour. They invite him back to the community. He has lived there now for ten years.

'Peter,' he says gripping my arm, 'we have found a way to live. Come and live with us forever.' He is serious. He tells me of the rottenness of modern life, the greed in people's hearts, the never-ending contamination of sex, drugs and money. This evil has to be rooted out if love is to flourish. Suddenly his face becomes home to an exquisite tenderness, the eyes lose their intensity and his face relaxes. 'Everyone likes the journey but they don't want to find anything.' His solemnity speaks of oneness with his tribe of brothers and sisters, and the root of faith before Christianity – the Light of Yahweh, the One and True God.

I stood in the long shadow cast by his sincere piety and exhortations to love. I wanted to tell him that only darkness can make light glow; that peace-making is finding peace with ourselves and who we are left alone with. Instead I said there are many ways in the world and we must respect differences. He chewed on that. I tell him that I am a writer. He shakes his head.

'You will make a joke of me.'

'No. I will talk about this moment, you and me.' We shake hands and I loose myself into the market mayhem wondering where the religious zealot in myself is hiding. (St-Jean-Pied-de-Port, September 30, 1996)

The next morning the sadness overtook me on the long ascent over the Pyrenees to Roncesvalles, a mournful sadness with the dripping beeches and cracking chestnuts. I saw clearly the humorous Dutch and Flemish faces from the refuge, listened again to their small talk and intimacy, and admired their buoyant sanity. One had received 23 letters at the last poste restante. They left together, I left alone. My tears eased this isolation. I choose it. I say the spaces make me tender. Then the young German's face appeared, the smooth brow, the exaggerated tenderness on his straight path to God. Suddenly I had seen him before, in every pilgrim's church in France, in Moissac, and especially at Conques: Christ-in-his-Majesty at the centre dividing the wicked from the virtuous; the exaggerated virtues etched on the faces of the Saved, the companions of saints and angels, their divine inactivity to compensate for their toils on earth; while Satan, with his serpentine snares, fed the doomed to the monster's mouth or burnt them, hung them upside-down or set squat demons with deeply-drilled eyes to chew out their hearts. The Medieval message is clear: eternal tenderness or unpardonable damnation. There is no middle ground. God is perfect, His creation is perfect. All that is not perfect cannot be from God. It is the work of the devil. How I longed to put a human heart into that middle ground – and no fairy lights in the great shell at Roncesvalles could dispel this. (Roncesvalles, October 1, 1996)

The cottage at night is an island, and the nearest farmhouse is a light at the top of the lane. I think it's a star as it never moves. Once, as a child, I found a star that had gone out. I found it on Streatham Common, a green rubbery thing like part of a tyre, but I thought it was a star. I tried to throw it back but it kept landing on the grass. In the end I threw it up and walked away without looking back. It's still up there.

'I'm not scared of a lion,' said Sarah, threading strips of tin foil into Tugger's hair. 'Only a ghost would frighten me.' Sarah didn't believe in ghosts, and lions might as well be ghosts because we were never going to see one. I said that ghosts belonged to places just as granny belonged to the cottage. They were see-through until they wanted to say something. Sarah smiled as if she knew everything. She really was impossible.

'Perhaps ghosts are there all the time,' I said. 'They can show themselves if they want to. They are just waiting for someone to come along.'

'But why do they hide?'

'Because people don't want to see them. They're afraid the ghosts might hunt them.'

Sarah said she hated hunting and didn't even like cats chasing mice. 'They're so little they don't stand a chance.'

'Being small doesn't mean a thing,' said granny. 'The cleverest creature I know was a mouse, but it was caught by a cat.'

'Did you rescue it?'

'Nature's cruel, and there are too many mice. But something made me stop. Another cat came up and the first one licked its face. For just a moment it took its paw off the mouse's tail. What would you have done?'

'Run!'

'The mouse could see the edge of the path and the long grass, but it was exhausted. It would never make it, yet this was its only chance. What did it do? It ran behind the first cat and *stopped* by its tail. When the cats searched in front of them the mouse stayed still. It waited and waited and then tiptoed to the edge. It escaped, because it didn't lose its head.'

THUG

Aurora Erlander is a northern girl from Oregon and the great grand-daughter of Swedish pioneers. She is a serious girl, on the lean side, with straight blond hair to her shoulder, straight face and unblinking eyes. She is a dancer and says she wants to find the bigger connections in her life. She is unselfconscious. At porridge time she leaps from her chair and trolls around the table pushing the tender air around her and giving way to songs in Swedish. Then she returns and calmly spoons it in. 'I have so much energy,' she says. 'I can feel my legs and arms tingling.' Well, one day at the farm in Limousin, she sees the resident topcat, Thug, with a lizard under his paw. The tail is missing and the poor thing is scrabbling to escape. This is nature, she tells herself, and does not interfere. Thug eventually gets bored with murdering lizards and strolls away. Erlander picks up the lizard with the bruised mouth and the missing tail. She hums to it, sings to it, dances slowly in the garden with the lizard in her hand. She places it on the outside windowsill below her bedroom, beside a saucer with milk and bread sops, and goes away. An hour later she notices the lizard is gone. That night she goes upstairs and sits on her bed. She leans back and switches on the bedside lamp. Beside her on the pillow is a lizard without a tail and a bruised mouth. It is curled up sleeping.

Another time, another victim. Thug observes that during construction work on the barn a colony of pipistrelle bats exit each twilight from a crack in the cob wall, a metre off the ground. So he sits there in the happy hour leaping up to claw the flying leaves – but they are used to dodging twigs at high speed. There is simply no contest. It's as if he's being paid back with frustration. This goes on for a week until, on the seventh day, Thug is observed to lose his marbles. In fact he is stir crazy, not the full shilling. He still waits by the crack but no longer leaps up as the bats glide over his head. He sits there motionless until fatigue, frustration and loathing opens his mouth into a gaping hole. At that precise moment, a bat flies in – and you can be sure it never came out again.

(La Cellete, September 12, 1996)

DESPERATE COMPANY

The door opened and light filled the cavernous room; neatly-rowed tables and chairs jumped out, a fireplace without wood, the stone floor, the high ceiling, bare walls. An unforgiving coldness gripped my throat as I stepped inside. The adjoining kitchen was the same, made for cattle with rows of sinks and a grid-plan of electric cookers. Only one worked. I found a pot and nothing else. Add onto that I was streaming wet and steaming with a cold. I sat in the dining room feeling utterly deflated. I tackled a bottle of Galician red and that helped. Then I noticed a movement by the wall. Rats, too. I could see you. A shadow catapulted in my direction, keeping to the side of the wall, then rushed the fireplace two paces away on my left. A minute later it stepped out of the darkness. A mouse! And frightened of its own shadow. It retreated, then emerged again. Suddenly I knew it was alone and hungry. It was trapped here like me. I dropped a piece of chestnut. Inch by inch it braved the open space. I whispered encouragement. 'Come on then.' Hunger is stronger than fear. It bolted back with the chestnut. I dropped another piece. 'Everything's all right. I'm your friend, remember?' Whiskers grabbed it on the rebound and dived back into its den. A minute later it crept out and stopped halfway, peering up at me. 'Good mouse,' I said. 'We're friends.' For one moment I swear we stared into each other's eyes. I rolled a chestnut halfway to its den. It rolled it back the other half, paw over paw, and I never saw that mouse again.

(Santiago de Compostela, October 10, 1996)

LONE'S MOUSE

When a mouse appears, she stands on a chair. 'I'm that kind of person,' she says. Another time she is in Sweden for a teacher's conference. In her hotel room, straightaway she notices the dead flower heads on the floor, a speck of dirt in the sink. That night she wakes up, ears red alert; it's a scratching noise in the bedroom. 'We have a visitor,' she tells her fellow teacher. She hits the light. Nothing there. Somehow she goes back to sleep. An hour later another scratcher, and this time close. The light! The mouse is behind the headboard and on the shelf. It leaps onto the floor. She dives under the sheet. Now it's impossible to sleep. She sits up in bed with the sidelight. The minutes plod by. This is madness. She dims the light, but her ears are scanning the room like radar. It comes from behind the cupboard and creeps down by the wall. She steals out of bed, pushes aside the cupboard and plugs the hole triumphantly. Lights off. And something is still in the room. She listens. She tiptoes to her bag on the floor. Lights on. She picks up her hat and out jumps a mouse. Who is more scared? It's been eating a sweet. So she puts the sweet just outside the open door. She pretends to sleep. The mouse creeps out from under the bed. She stifles the noise swelling in her belly. It approaches the door. She silently pulls back the cover. It stands on the threshold. Lone hardly breathes. It steps into the hallway. Lone dives out of bed and slams the door. It's 4am and peace, at last, attends her sleep. (Varde, June 9, 1997)

After dinner granny shut the folding curtains, tucked in the velvet sausage at the bottom of the door to stop the draught and I knew the night-time had come. I'd make a den from the cushions on the sofa to sit inside and granny would let me eat dinner on a special board I put across the cushions. Tugger dozed at the foot of the sofa but he always kept one eye open. Granny sat knitting in the armchair with her elbows on the wings and behind her was the grandfather clock with a picture of a boy and a girl at a well, from the Jack and Jill story. That's the only noise in the room for an hour, the knitting needles, the clock talking to itself, a coal slipping, and a warm feeling would grow in me that I was safe, that the night was around me and I was deep down like an animal in its hole. And as soon as I thought that I remembered the dead badger.

I asked granny about the new road. When granny's knitting she's always thinking, slowly as her knitting needles, bit by bit, watching the points cross, and she won't speak until she is ready. 'It's always the clothes which don't fit which get passed on.' Her words made no sense and yet I remembered them. She made me think. By her feet sat Sarah sticking together chains of coloured paper for Christmas decorations. No-one wanted it, said granny, except the council and the people who made it. Most of the land had belonged to the Colonel, but she wouldn't hear a word against him. A good man, she said, and he had put up the security fencing to keep in Tugger and keep out the hunt. 'They go wild when they're on the scent.' She heated up the poker and plunged it into her glass of porter until it sizzled and bubbled, and then she laughed, showing the

106

gap in her teeth. I think she revelled in her oddness. Her own mother, our great grandmother, had drunk a glass of porter each night in the winter, for the blood. Sometimes at night if the wind was blowing from the North, she could hear the traffic in the walls, a droning noise like a huge wasp coming up the stairs. If she woke up she couldn't go back to sleep. 'It was meant to take the heavy traffic out of town but now there's as much on both roads. The worst thing is that it cuts through the woods. How long can you keep darning a sock before you throw it away? The badger died because it always follows the same way. They can't change. Fifty-five thousand badgers are killed on the roads each year, that's one out of every sett. Imagine that one person in every family was killed on the roads. It's worse than The War.' She paused: 'Imagine if one person in every family, instead of being killed, could live for peace. It would repay the lives of all those people, make some sense of it all. '*Is it not true that five sparrows are sold for tuppence and not one of them is forgotten in the thoughts of God?*' I didn't know anyone who had been killed in the war. It happened to other people.'

'You never talk about it.'

'Is that true? I am always thinking about it. The waste, the absolute waste. And you can't bring back one hair of their body. Losing brothers or sisters, whole families gone overnight. How could anyone understand, adjust to that? You cried but you never forgot the senselessness. The sun went out of our lives. The young men went to war singing. Later it was heaven to get away from The Front, even if only for a day.' Her memories she kept as black-and-white photos on the mantlepiece; her brother was there in khaki and smiling with his goggles across his forehead. 'It's long, long ago now, and who can remember that? When I go his memory will go too. That's the way of this world. "*For there is no power but of God.*"'

'I'll remember him,' said Sarah, 'and the kind things you said about him.'

'There's somewhere, I'm sure, where we'll all meet again.'

SEPP

I thought him a typical Kraut, a name I remembered from my childhood comic books: cropped blond hair, a nose and jawline chiselled from hard white cabbage, all edges and each one unsmiling; a robust build from peasant stock but no face to remember. I recognised at once this prejudice, this underhand, comic way of distancing myself from him. I wanted to imagine he was made from clock parts. He hardly spoke to me or anyone and this confirmed the impression of a hard, ungiving German with absolutely nothing personal about him. Almost at once there was a flaw in this picture. All evening at dinner he hadn't spoken but his face softened when the little girl came into the room.

Without words, he played a game with her by wiggling a spoon on his plate so it became a dancing figure. She liked it and he did, too, smiling for the first time. Using a pocket dictionary, he said that he had a daughter at home, except he didn't see her very often as he was separated from the mother.

He came from Berlin, from The East. 'One city, but two people,' he said in faltering English. For nine years at school they had taught him Russian. He could still hardly speak it. 'Useless,' he says, and says it again, reinforcing the gravity lines in his face. I had thought them hard lines but now they appeared prematurely aged. He sighs a lot. Perhaps he just can't find the right English words. 'The West Berliners carry on as normal,' he says, 'but in the East everyone is dealing with change.' The industry is kaputt, much of the land polluted by chemical industries operating without environmental control. He had cut his long hair in spring. 'It's good to change.' He had finished his horticultural diploma, but only the farmers' sons had jobs. Now he is studying for his Master's in agricultural development in the Third World.

Then I asked about the Berlin Wall. I was unprepared for the tightness growing in my throat, some inner drama untethered by his words as if I had participated, been there too. His faltering speech held everyone's attention at the table, all English people. 'It was a typical German revolution, after work only. Nobody strikes.' The demonstrations had started in Leipzig in the summer of 1989 – The Monday demonstrations. First there were 2,000 then 5,000 and so on until by October over 300,000 East Berliners demonstrated for change. Sepp remembers rallying with other students at a checkpoint on November 9, 1989. They asked the guards when they were taking it down. They laughed at the students. Sepp went home to bed and just before midnight 3,000 demonstrators went to the checkpoint. The East German captain had to choose between shooting them or letting them through. That fateful decision decided history. A balloon of excitement and tears rose in me as I recognised that this struggle unites us; that Sepp's freedom is mine too.

Sepp's dream is to travel. Before The Wall, he had visited all the Eastern block countries: been to Prague six times, knocked on the main door at Dracula's castle in Romania, been robbed twice in Albania. After The Wall, he had cycled in Sweden, worked on a cattle ranch in Argentina and was learning English at Dunsford Farm. Travel had been his father's dream, but politics and hard times had put the brakes on that. 'Education is the only way forward. Once I believed in a half-God, Karl Marx, but now I think of him as an intelligent but fallible human being.' No-one in his family believed in God. 'I would like to but...' He was reading the Old Testament, the first six books, about Aaron and Joshua, but he did not care for the wrath of that God. Unsure of himself, gloomy about the industrial world, Sepp had no firm beliefs. Then he quoted these lines from Swinburne, words which he loved:

'From too much love of living, from hope and fear set free
We thank with brief thanksgiving whatever Gods maybe.
That no-one lives forever, that dead men rise up never;
That even the weariest river winds somewhere safe to sea.'
(Dunsford Farm, Somerset, December 12, 1996)

EAST-WEST

Jacob and Conrad are nine-year-old and seven-year-old boys from East Berlin and the former GDR. Their mothers brought them to a farm in Limousin. Conrad's mother hitched, Jacob's came by coach. While they worked on their spiritual sensibilities, the children played. Jacob wore all his clothes despite the heat; Conrad ran around naked within ten minutes of arriving. When asked to play in a water fight Jacob said, 'I'll have to dress properly.' He returned in his swimming trunks. Conrad jumped in — literally. Jacob lived by the book; Conrad didn't know one existed. Jacob was born before The Wall came down, Conrad two years after.   *(Aubusson, September 13, 1996)*

SMART ARSE

There was a lot of shit coming out of me when I crossed into Germany at Bourtange.

Two minutes into Germany, these things happened: a tooth fell out; I dropped my thermos; I lost my hostel card and the runs knocked ominously at a little door. I saw an unmarked van crammed with police. I had seen none in France, Belgium or Holland.

'Schweinhundt! Why don't you use the cycle lane?'

'Don't shoot me. I didn't see it.'

'Shoot you? How can you think that? We hang you from ze lamp-post.'

'Mein Gott. Vat dis dat?'

'That's my silver wand. I use it as a fly swotter. It's very practical.'

'And de frilly knickers?'

'Ventilation. It gets hot on the saddle.'

'Ze vhite sheet on your head?'

'Stops me sweating.'

'Ze pink dress?'

'Illumination. It's important to be seen.'

'Ve can always spot the English, can't ve Hans?'

Garbage, as usual, straight out of childhood comics, the helmeted sadists with their fiendish techno gadgets; the light shrinking in a dark sky, a battle for survival. This writing is full of bits that don't fit. Here's another one:

'Grandma, we got your bicycle back,' says a Dutch banner at a German football match. I laugh at that.

Three minutes into Germany, I see a crippled child steering a motorised buggy; his mother rides behind in a flamboyant, olde-worlde dress. Fragments of conversations stick with me:

'In Germany they mob you, they can't leave you alone. There's always someone above you and they have to put their thumb on you. If the voice says "do this", you jump and salute. You must do this.'

'I am legally allowed to take time off when my wife had a child but they think I'm the crazy one, that I don't like to work. I get stressed about it. You should work, work and work and at 65 you jump into the casket and they close the lid. It's wonderful for me to sit here and not rush to work. I can see my children.'

'I always had to have the best. I would polish and polish my bike and if it had a scratch on it I went crazy. I'm changing my mind. I think I'll buy a small camera next as it weighs less.'

'I think we're frightened to love our country. Everyone is looking at us. They'll think we are nationalistic.'

'I'd like to retire to a tropical island with parrots and seashell beaches. Perhaps there's a village. I'd have a bicycle.'

The Germans go everywhere: Bali, Zanzibar, the Caribbean is their backyard; toilets are plastered with paradise beaches, conch shells are on the carpet, painted parrots in the conservatories, fetish masks in the hall, African gemstones on the mantelpiece, New York skyscrapers in the kitchen... I'm exaggerating, but I rarely heard Germans talk about travelling at home. Here at Hedeby, the once largest town in the Viking era, this silence puzzles me. There's not much to see, it's true: ruffled water by reeds and green-strip fields; some big trees on the monumental semi-circular rampart, cow parsley at the verges. Here, in 980AD, Al Tartushi – an Arab merchant from the Caliphate at Córdoba – saw the dead pig sacrificed on a pole to Sirius; he likened the singing of the natives to the barking of dogs; wandered around the 60 acres of the town, the exotic wooden-stave homes; he saw bronze casting, weaving, coin minting, women wearing make-up. This was metropolis at the far end of the ocean, on the North Way and Europe's oldest northern trading centres. The monk Ansgar preached here between 826-829. In 1050 Hedeby was 'burnt in anger from end to end' by King Harald Hardrada of Norway and the treasure was dumped in the Kattegat to escape vengeance. The survivors left it as a grave. This land, historically in the disputed territories of Schleswig-Holstein, has one of the oldest churches. It has never been found. Hedeby is a lost world from the Viking era, imaginatively re-created in the burial-ship rooms of the museum. German children peer at the intricate Frankish jewellery, the small Christian crosses, the bits of shawls and pins, the antler technology, the satellite views and charred timbers. They stare a lot, chatter in long lines and are then shunted out. *What have they in common? It's the past on the doorstep, the fertile home ground.* (*Hedeby, May 22, 1997*)

TRAVELLING AT HOME

Johannes Zanq was born in a village by Frankfurt, in the shadow of that densely populated region where you can see church spires every three kilometres. He has a goatee beard and listening ears, fleshed-out hands and face, and there is something of a priest's style, his mix of silence and mirth, his rock-steady eyes. He is a marathon running man: Berlin, Denver, New York, next week Vienna. He likes travelling at home in Germany. 'I used to come back from Bolivia, Egypt or Israel or America and realise that I knew nothing of Germany.' So he cycled and walked around the lakes in Mecklenburg, along the Moselle Valley near Luxembourg, over the mountains of Franconia or down the trails in the Bavarian forest. 'I never knew Germany was so unspoilt.'

Before he could remember, he had loved playing music, especially the piano. But at 19 he thought of becoming a priest and studied theology for his vocation. At 21 when his doubts were greater than his convictions, he quit the seminary. 'In one day, on two separate occasions, both my mother and father suggested I go to Israel.' He thought he would go for three weeks but stayed for 18 months learning Hebrew, living in a kibbutz, the West Bank and Gaza. Only once did he encounter a reminder of German history. 'An old kibbutznik told him that he preferred not to speak German as he had learned that in a concentration camp.' After Israel he decided to revive his childhood love and studied music therapy at Vienna, and now he works at a neurological and psychiatric hospital near Deggendorf. He plays music to patients in comas and looks for flickers in the eyes or some sign that the music has found a home.

One stroke victim he remembers well. This man could speak but only in his own language. 'After some hostility he gradually realised he could express his feelings in sound, a language that everyone could understand. His notes became stronger and he experimented with his own compositions. After three weeks his wife said to me: "I never thought this would make a difference. I have bought him a xylophone."'

Johannes announces that he has been offered a job as a music teacher in Bethlehem for three years. 'My first reaction was 'Great!', then I thought 'I will be 38 when I come back. And I would like a family. In Germany it's important to buy land and build a family home. This I do not want. Then I thought, what a challenge. I will have to learn Arabic and Hebrew again. My parents are religious and will probably think of it as a ministry for God.'

'But what if you return as a Hebrew?'

'They will be shocked.'

'You might fall in love with a Palestinian girl,' I say.

Johannes smiles. I think he would like that. (*Deggendorf, May 16, 1998*)

BRIGITTE GABLER

First a puzzle. Two nights I stayed at Ulmer-Tannenplatz, in a quiet suburb with well-tempered bungalows and at the edge of a wood. Two nights I awoke and listened to water bubbling and going somewhere. It wasn't raining and there was no wind or wild weather. I checked the bathroom; the taps were shut and the radiators off. I lay awake puzzled. Brigitte Gabler who lives here was puzzled too. There was no spring, and it could not be the neighbour. Perhaps I had been dreaming. Brigitte is a retired teacher in German and English, and some of the passion she finds playing the viola is in the music of her words too. And in her unclouded blue eyes. She peers out of a compact, firmly hewn face, her hair sober and curled and sometimes she stares who knows where? At these moments she appears wise and childlike, listening to more than the words. I liked her and secretly wished for such joie-de-vivre if I should be seventy.

A young Polish student, Kamila Markow, lives here too. Brigitte had met her as a lost hitchhiker and somehow they became friends. Brigitte could be her grandmother. She helped her to come to Germany and study antique restoration. 'I am living my dream,' says Kamila simply. She has brown, big listening eyes, soulful attention. They glisten when she thinks of home and her younger sister and boyfriend in Glucholazy just over the Polish border. She is homesick. Their friendship, owing everything to chance and nothing to the market place, touches me. Brigitte lives off a teacher's pension and enjoys walking Felix, her dog. 'He is my teacher. He needs so little. He really knows what's happening. He senses it.' At other times she visits viola players in England, Czech, France or Scotland, and for days she will live her passion. Her violas hang on the walls as some hang pictures.

As sometimes happens, when time is known to be fleeting, perhaps an hour left to talk before our ways part, there came an exceptional ease between us. I fried both sides of an egg. 'Such a shame,' she said. 'I'm English,' I replied. Felix watched the food travel from the plate and the fork return. She hummed a tune. 'There were hundreds of songs. We would sing them at home, with my friends. We had no television them. Who sings them now?' In her soft and faraway voice she sang this lullaby by Johannes Brahms: 'Guten Abend, gute Nacht..'

Her father was a typical Prussian and a bookseller in Ulm. They lost their home and shop in the Allied bombings and lived after the war in a room in the country. She worked on the land but it was hard work and there was no time to question her state of mind. She had been fifteen when the war ended and for some years had been part of the Hitler youth movement. She showed me a photograph of herself at 11: picture-book German, flaxen hair in plaits, clean and clear lines looking steadily at the camera. Like a Girl Guide with the kerchief in a ring. 'We had a leader who was 17 and we thought the world of her. We helped the poor, the families who had lost their father. We believed in our Führer. He could trust in us.' She pauses to find the right words. 'We never thought or questioned. We were so young. Hitler told us that we would be a great nation, that we would find our self-respect again. Who could not want this?' After the war she became a teacher of English and German, and slowly she questioned her old beliefs. 'There were no big moments. I came gradually to change these views. After the war I went to see my youth-group leader on her birthday, and told her about my misgivings. "You are a traitor," my friend said, though she still took the present.' Brigitte says that she loves her country but Germany is a word that is too small for her identity.

'Do you think of yourself as a European?'

'I am Brigitte Gabler.'

She liked talking about Felix, how he follows her around everywhere. 'He is the easiest one to live with. People build Towers of Babel but what are they built upon? Felix knows. He needs so little to be content.' These days she prefers individuals to big social groupings, one legacy of the war she thinks. Though she belongs to the Reformed Lutheran Church, she does not go to church. 'I am with myself. Here is my church.' She folds her hands and speaks with a smile. 'What are we dependent upon? That is my question.' I had no ready answer, and so another puzzle ends this page.

(Dillingen, May 12, 1998)

'We won't meet the dead badger,' I said. 'It was stiff by the time I buried it. Now the beetles will get it'. I told them exactly what had happened, where I had scooped out the earth, leaving out the last bit of saying 'Goodnight'. I didn't want them to think I was silly.

'You did right,' said granny. 'How many people must have passed without stopping. Perhaps they never saw it or thought it mattered. But you did, and that's important. You mustn't blame others. We see differently. We've all got something different to do. Sometimes the only thing we have in common is that we might get run over by a bus.' We laughed at that. 'Even with Jo, what he doesn't know he doesn't miss.'

'I've heard that before,' said Sarah.

'It's the truth.'

'He's always talking about his father, as if he's here or he's going to meet him.'

'He died after the war. Jo was only a child... It's so sad. He's buried in North Africa, killed by Rommel's Afrika Korps.' She intoned something from the Bible and touched her forehead. 'It's history best forgotten.'

'Jo doesn't forget.'

'Who can bring back the dead?'

'Jo can't go back or forward. He's been forgotten.' There was no answer. Granny stayed silent until little by little the clicking needles slowed down as if someone had switched off the power and a gentle heaving sound took its place. Her hands lay folded on her dress, one over the other. Sarah tugged the yarn to wake her up, and she tidied away the wool and let granny put her weight onto her shoulders. I helped her up by supporting her other arm. She smiled appreciatively. 'Sometimes I feel hundreds of years old.' They went up stairs together. I watched the sparks creep up the back of the sooty chimney, like tiny torchlights out on a dark night, marching somewhere. Something terrible must have happened to go out searching in the night, to be hunted like that. The lights went out one by one and the last was always the brightest. I wanted it to last but it still went out. I am always worried about fire. I might not being able to get out. I shovelled ashes onto the coals and scraped off the soot, and then I tamped it down with the poker.

The long narrow room upstairs was the old operations room where the men pulled the levers to signal the *UP* or *DOWN* trains. Everything is gone except one lever which granny kept polished and had painted blue and gold. They used it as an attic for years and then made it into a spare bed-room. It was whitewashed and had bunks on one side and tea boxes down the other, and at far end was a small window facing the hill up to King's Wood. Opposite the beds was an oil painting of a woman in a blue dress with high shoulders and ringlets in her hair, and, in the half-light, I thought they were snakes. The varnish was dark with age and all you could see properly were her eyes. I had to take the picture down and turn it against the wall otherwise I couldn't sleep. Outside rose the moon, and the grass sparkled by the stream. It was going to freeze. I wanted Jo to see King's Wood bright under these night lights. He would go to the mud pool with the logs which you can walk across if you are careful, or bounce stones across the ice. There we would be alone; we could say the things we had never said before. Many times Sarah and I had talked about how we would balance across the backs of fallen trees, see the marsh bubbles popping next to our feet every time we jumped, drop a penny wish into the springhead, say hello to the gremlin in the railway tunnel, visit the pond where the black newts lived. It was our secret place. Nobody went there as it was hidden. It was really a bog full of squelchy mud and, in summer, giant dazzling dragonflies came and stared into your eyes. They turned their heads from side to side to see what you're thinking. They were not frightened of us and we were not frightened of them. Around the pond was a stone wall which vanished in August under rushes with big woolly willies, but at Christmas the rushes had gone back into the mud and the leaves floated on the water. Jo would come here. It was the only place we could really be alone.

We would show Jo the two cooker apple trees in the garden, Badger Hole and Wellhead, because if you closed your eyes and touched them you could see a badger's hole with the earth scraped up or hear the sound of water. Here you could ask questions – 'Where does the fox live?' or 'Where does the biggest conker grow?' – and get answers. He would go into the tunnel under the railway and shout his name until it came back to him twice as loud. I wanted him to come up the winding road and go up and over King's Hill. One day he would go down this road and the ginger cat would jump out of the hedge and lick his fingers. And every time he came to mountains Kitty would become a roaring lion and he would fly over them and land safely on the other side. I wanted him to do all these things.

The Solstice night did not say no.

Sarah snored above me in the top bunk, and I liked that. I lay half-awake with my eyes still open. Every time I closed my eyes I was back standing by the window and looking for something I couldn't see. Then I opened my eyes and listened, but the night said nothing. I turned in my bed and turned round again. I was neither asleep nor awake. I remember that. I heard a soft tapping in the room, irregular at first, a few beats and then silence, then a few more, then silence. It became louder as I listened. I thought it was the radiator until I remembered I wasn't at home. I thought it was Sarah teasing but I could hear her snoring. My ears stretched out a little. I heard a soft roaring in the distance but that was the traffic. I listened, more awake and too tired to move. Pins and needles skated down my legs and arms. I moved my eyes. The tapping came from the opposite wall, by the tea boxes. Rats? Surely not. Again I heard the tapping, and I turned my head. It was outside of me. I saw the outline of the picture, the dustlines on the wall. Something was pushing it. Then more silence, more beats. But still only softly. I didn't get up. I couldn't. My heart palpitated. Someone was knocking on the wall, knock, knock, knocking, and no-one answered. I couldn't open my mouth or move my hands. Only my eyes moved. Every beat and the wall bulged, made a little round bump. And another bump becoming bigger. I could not move. The biggest bump popped. A tiny fist poked through. The fingers opened, the hands of a baby. They disappeared. The hands came through with the elbows. They went back into the wall. I sat upright. My hands and face and sheet were cold with sweat. Sarah snored. The night, the white-washed wall, were empty.

Only my heart was drumming.

And who am I left alone with now? I run away from you.

TWO DOVES

We passed like ships in the night except it was Gloucestershire in the daytime, and he was a painter and I was finishing building a garden. Almost the first thing he said to me was about a job in Wotton-under-Edge and how the lady had asked him to clear out and paint the gutter. At one end he saw a white dove nestling among the leaves. 'It has to go,' she said. So he felt like a murderer with his long-handled broom shooing away the bird. He found two dove eggs. 'They have to go,' she said, and so reluctantly he lost them, some-where. He forgets where. Two weeks passed and he returned to do the second coat. 'It's back again,' she said. So once more he shooed away the dove and beneath it he found two more eggs. He shook his head. 'I was amazed.' He put them somewhere dry and out of the way, hoping that the mother might come back.

His philosophy is simple: 'No stress.' His words flowed as easily as the storm-shield paint, his early morning walk with his dogs, his courting days and the neighbours crowding the black-and-white TV where the picture got smaller and smaller as the generator faded; the old lady who told him to put away his fancy cleaning spray. 'She used wet newspaper, then dry and clean and crumpled up. It's the printer's ink which gives it the polish and sparkle.' But he had enough, his family of four had flown, though they came for tea every Sunday.

I asked him where he came from, and his eyes looked away, somewhere. His father was in The Navy during the last war. They were evacuated from London, all five children in one bed. He woke up one morning and his mother had gone. 'She had done a bunk.' They were parcelled out to relations, except he and his sister went into a children's home. After the war his father collected the three other children but left the two in the children's home. The mother never came back. I was touched by his story. I feel the ripples now, and I have no idea why. (Bath, 1998)

THE TENDER ZONE

'Another little job, jobby jobby, little jobbies jobbywobby. Wood wood woody, woody woody woodpecker.' The baby talk is part of it, the play with words out of cold wet mornings, sparking some warmth, some conversation. Full of bits and pieces, long fragments and more in the debris and sentences like: 'I've lost my way. I know nothing.'

116

'That's what happens to wicked boys,' I say. 'They work off dodgy karma.' I elaborate. 'When God comes he will say: "Look what you didn't do…"'

'I know nothing,' says Rob mimicking Manuel from Fawlty Towers. He smiles as he says it. It's a good defence. Often silent and soulful, Rob plays a close hand. He's taller than me, a little thin, he says, but he can't seem to put on weight. His fair and silver hair shows signs of ginger, and he's long in the bone, in his arms, legs and face, very freckled, very Scandinavian. And older too, in his mid-fifties. His still, blank eyes sometimes twinkle at some mischievous thought. Perhaps he was once a Viking, but he doesn't have a beard or drink out of horns.

What's incredible is that he's from Balham, my own stomping ground as a child. I lived the first five years of my life in a prefab on Streatham Common. Rob lived around the corner in Sistona Road, the house his father bought for a few hundred quid after the war: it's worth a quarter of a million now. I met Rob a few years ago still free-falling after his marriage break up. He's looking how to start again. Sometimes he is gloomy and it shows in his long-boned thoughts. The nightmare of relationships which go wrong. His tolerant, humorous face subsides into blank verse. 'I have been honest all my life and I have nothing.' Once he believed in reincarnation but not anymore. 'This is it,' he says. 'Who knows what's round the corner? You're a long time dead.' It's useless to argue or point to the paradise of a fly. Words are no good. It's the action he's looking for. How to start? That's the big question. 'Mama mia. Take me home. I want to go home.'

Rob wants his ashes to be spread on Tooting Bec common in the woods, the big oak trees still there from his childhood, the bright days, skipping the light fantastic, Saturday nights at the Locarno on Streatham High and the last wave of the Teddy boys; his navy-blue mohair suit, hair slicked about, the stiff shirt, the men – with their pints of beer and fags – standing on the outside eyeing up the women dancing beside their handbags. Stumbling back to Sistona Road through Tooting Bec common with a bird in the hand was the dream… Dreams. Once there was a dream. 'I know nothing.' The conversation is in flashbacks: the girls that let you fondle them, the time he went to the laundromat and the girl invited him back for dinner; the next morning his house-mates cheered when he opened the front door. It's a dream now. He would like a relationship, a loving relationship. 'What shall I do?' is a recurring question. He travelled several continents in his youth following the surf; now it challenges him to take the bus into London.

Silences say more; at the end of the day Rob sits, does nothing slowly, just looking round, seeing what's been done, not rushing off, the opposite of a roof gang, in and out; sitting back in the car, the distant lines of the Berkshire Downs, the clumps of Barbury castle, criss-crossing lines of field boundaries, twenty miles to see at a glance, the gravity ebb of conversation, few words, silence before this Cotswold patchwork. A long way from Balham, 'The Gateway to the South'. This is the country life. We are the Balham boys. A favourite game is the whining voice: 'I wasn't doing any harm.'

'On yer bike.'

'But, but, but...'

'On yer bike.'

We floated wooden boats on Streatham pond, climbed the big willows (still there) played down by The Rookery; were old enough to remember the London smogs of the Fifties, the policemen with flares at traffic junctions. I like these associations and the inarticulate sense that we are brothers, perhaps the brother I never really had. I never said that to Rob. He still has his South London accent, slightly nasal with drawn-out vowels. South London is still a picture which is intact: the security of family, the old wooden tea-hut on Streatham Common, the clothes shop on Streatham High where he bought his shirts ('still both there, absolutely amazing'); his first job at the optical business regrinding German war binoculars and re-spraying the frames; little businesses down back streets, long gone.

'A little this, a little that,' he intones characteristically. He is wise with his words to others; do the things that you are interested in now. Slow down. No stress. He has had to learn the hard way .'What shall I do?' he asks himself. He wants to develop a skill for his older age. Not woodwork, though he makes wonderful boxes, containers for others. Perhaps painting, but he doesn't know. Finding the will to change is the hardest, how to act on a financial tightrope. And then there is the subtle drama of his own son seeking independence, the very things he is searching for at 55: initiative, risk, direction. Do the bonds which tie his son, tie them both? His son will leave, and that will leave him on his own. He has to change, he knows that. He cannot face the quiet weekends, the silent slipping away. I tell him I've pictured him in new clothes, in blues, red and something warm, and he is walking confidently somewhere. 'It's coming,' he says. 'It's coming.' Once on Winter Solstice day he twirled a bull-roarer around his head, and that same night he dreamed he was swinging a cleaver into a black cloud of buzzing insects. It's the cutting edge he's looking for, the decision to open the door. He says he's going to buy some new clothes to go out there. Maybe, maybe. This is the tender zone. Join the club.

(Bath, 1998)

I couldn't go back to sleep or stay in bed. I tiptoed down the narrow stairs listening to the grandfather clock in the hallway, always the same, never too fast or too slow, and that calmed me. I stepped over the squeaking boards. I listened for Tugger locked in the kitchen and straightaway the basket creaked and something scratched the door. The clock chimed five o'clock, five hours ringing in my ears. Tugger whined behind the door. I opened it slowly and muzzled his mouth. He understood, his silent eyes growing big in the gloom, and he allowed himself to be led on the lead. I took biscuits from the kitchen, put on my boots and one of granny's overcoats. I pulled a woollen hat over my head so only my eyes and nose stuck out. I was not prepared for the frost or the stars over my head, the air freezing in my mouth. I walked along the railway track brushing the ice from hazels until the brambles blocked the way. My nose started to hurt. I looked back at the house. The frost stuck like snow to the ivy and tiles except where it melted by the chimney. I never wanted to go back to that room. Never! The pine trees of King's Wood marched into the field as long shadows. I felt safer outside, by myself. Lights, glinting, circling, came out of the stars, granny's pinpricks in the floor of heaven. I could reach out, touch one and take it home. '*Star-light, star bright, first star I see tonight...*' I shivered. I stopped by the chainlink fence and the wooden post, where the field turns and the stream runs along the bottom by the apple trees.

Little bits of ice fell onto my face. I felt silly crying like this, not knowing why, not knowing whose hands they belonged to. They belonged to nobody. Like me. I didn't belong to granny, mum or dad or my sister. The post stared back at me. I touched it, half remembering something. I scraped off the frost until I found the arrow carved onto the side, no bigger than my thumb. It came up to my chest. I must have been that tall when I planted the tree. There was an oak leaf, just one. I put my hands around it as if I were saying my prayers.

Back inside the cottage, the frost had iced the little window, bringing grey ashes into the room. I saw the dustline but there was no hand or hole. I tapped the wall. It was solid. Sarah still slept. Only I had seen it, and so only I would know.

THE OAK TREE

Near Belléme is the Forêt Dominiale. Here I stopped to allow nature her exit and afterwards I leaned against the sunny side of a tree to whittle some wood and time. I gazed at the forest floor at my feet, the many flotsam leaves and fallen twigs, a ruin of grey-world shadows, inscrutable and unknowable as Mars. It's home to the fungi world. I saw the hunting spider patrolling this kingdom – and was ever a kingdom so improbable and bizarre as this? I carved, enjoying the warmth in my fingers and the fleeting glimpses of gossamer and the suddenly appearing Solomon's Seal, distinctive with its chequered lights. It was a few feet from my right foot. I noticed the acorn, its brown shell breached by the taproot disappearing at right angles. Then another acorn, the two halves of the nut enclosing a crimson interior. This one had a taproot and a slender upward shoot. See one, see another and within a minute I was sitting among a forest of tiny oak leaves, green slivers becoming bronzed elders under this leafless canopy. They were doomed, of course. What fruit can grow under the shade of its parent tree?

I continued with my carving, and now I saw them everywhere, the dull lights in my eye banished by a single seedling. Perhaps one of them in some future season would grow to replace its parent. How many millions of acorns will have dropped here to fertilise this ground? I would contradict nature's conservatism by planting a seedling on the other side of the road. I would give it a chance, but now I had my problem. Which one? The smallest I dismissed as impractical; many, the size of my fingers, I could have choosen. I hesitated, still undecided. They all deserved a chance. No, in the end caprice had her way. I chose one with three leaves arranged as a wheel, a travelling oak. I planted it with a little rough blessing.

(Les Boistiers, Preaux-du-Perche, April 29, 1998)

THE DEER

First thing in the morning, the deer looks up from the wayside and sees a strange day-glo orange man pedalling out of the Viaur gorge with its steep-angled trees. It leaps over the hedge, all handsome antlers and speckled flanks. 'A fallow deer, how wonderful' I think. I peer over the hedge. The deer stops among the red broadsides of Limousin beef cattle fifty metres away. Immediately it turns and stares at me. So do the cattle. We are spectators to each other and we will go our way, and that will be that. I'm happy. I want to give something. I sing 'Morning has broken...' The cattle nudge each other; the deer glances back at the cattle. They contract one pace, but still stand their ground. I stand mine. We like staring. I finish the song. 'BYE GANG!' I shout and walk fifty yards up the hill. I glance back. They haven't moved. One hundred yards. Just the same, still goggle-eyed. I stop at the top of the hill. I look back one last time: it's a still-life scene, the deer surrounded by the cattle. They are dumb-struck. So am I.   *(Conques, September 24, 1996)*

* * *

Another time I am walking along the old Somerset and Dorset railway line at Pylle. I see a stag and its hind gambolling across a field three hundred metres away. I wave my arms above my head, just for a lark. Immediately the stag does a right turn and kicks up turf as it runs towards me. It's a joke. I keep waving my arms. It keeps running. It eats half the distance, another quarter. I stop waving my arms. The stag pumps out steam as it slams on the brakes, turns about and charges back to its hind.

120

MUSIC AT NIGHT

On one of the green hills above Tiverton is a small stone house facing a sheltered dell and a field cropped by sheep. The lack of signposts, the turnabout lanes, the sudden descents and blind summits, conspire to create a private landscape with odd names such as Black Dog or Cruwys Orchard. My friend likes his privacy. Sometimes when the prevailing winds have stopped combing the treetops, a profound silence climbs out with the shadows and, little by little, the ears stretch to tap the sounds: the creak in the winged-back armchair or the thumb smoothing another page. On this particular night piiiiin piiing piin suddenly leaps over the roar of the burner then disappears. It does it again until our friend stares hard at the ceiling and the attic above that. It sounds like someone dropping a bouncy ball. Impossible! Nevertheless he climbs the stairs and sneaks through the door. The light shows a mouse holding a rubber ball in its paws and trying to bite it; but each time it is just too big and drops pinging onto the floor.

He inherited a cupboard with the cottage, an old cupboard with a door missing. Not much good, he thinks, but too good to throw away so he puts it in the attic and forgets about it. Days, weeks and months unravel without a knot, in fact two years go by and the memory of the cupboard collects dust. Then one day he finds a door. This will fit my cupboard, he thinks, and he screws it on. He swears it happens like this: something between laughter and coughing disturbs his reveries one night; probably the flue grumbling. A few nights later, the same except louder and the distinct impression of a thumping sound. He peers hard at the front door. That cat! Another week goes by, the same thumping noise and muffled cry, this time louder. He sits up, antennae switched on and his composure is challenged. He goes upstairs and flicks on the light. Nothing! He peers everywhere. Still nothing. Now he is rattled and the next night he realises that he is listening. He can't help it. The banging starts on cue, then comes the hoarse coughing. This is too much. He tiptoes up the attic stairs and prises open the door. The same nothing, the same grisly silence. Pins and needles skate down his neck. He searches everywhere, and something makes him open the cupboard door. His hand feels inside. It's empty, of course. He leaves the door open. The following nights are blessed with silence and now the dark side of his brain is working. Something makes him go back up and close the cupboard door. The next night he hears the same thumpings and moans. In the morning he drags the cupboard into his van and flogs it in Tiverton. He never hears a thing after that. (Timsbury, October 28, 1996)

All through breakfast I kept my secret and in the time after while making gingerbread men on the kitchen table, the three of us working together. Granny made the tea expertly, heating the cup first with hot water to keep it snug, pouring that out and then tipping in the milk. She could tell the difference, I couldn't. Sarah said that the women had to work all day to pick the tea and got next to nothing. They had to carry babies on their backs in the sun.

'You children...' said granny.

I rolled out the pastry until it was flat, floppy and bland, just how I felt. We were told that Jo hated breaking off the arms and legs so we made some into teddy bears. I broke off the arms and legs. The hand kept coming to the surface; it would poke through the pastry, prod me in my eyes. Sarah and granny stood side by side, both in aprons, my sister going backwards and forwards greasing the baking trays and warming them in the oven while granny folded the pastry. I belonged outside them. I kept pushing the night away. She talked of her own mother, great granny Beatrice, and she rested in the silences, leaning on her elbows and letting her eyes do the talking. Cold hands, cold water and a metal spoon were the secrets. 'That's why shy people make good pastry and warm people make good bread dough.' Sometimes I think great granny was with us telling us how to pick and roll the pastry without crushing it, how to flick it over using only two fingers. When she glanced up her eyes were always new inside her worn face. Sarah cut out the gingerbread men and brushed them with eggy milk; we used currants for eyes and smiles. That's what I liked about granny's world, it stayed the same and I wanted it to. I wanted silence between me and a door, a lock that would not open. I wanted to escape but I kept returning to that wall. The signal still says WAIT. It's always said that: there's nothing behind the wall, it's there for your own good. Don't go any farther; there's a hand on my shoulder holding me back. There is something here I need, and it's not a ghost. I have remembered another dream from Central Europe: '*I am making a garden around a small country house. It is an intimate garden with quiet corners to sit, simple materials of brick and stone, flowering trees for shelter. In the house I see a man singing an exquisite base-line melody. I am shy of this man. I walk to the front of the house and see a memorial stone. On it is the single word,* 'Israel.'

You can never stop being yourself, however irritating that might be. I am always telling people that there are lots of creatures in the wood and not two of them are alike. It's only because they are different that the wood is there. I mean if we were all woodlice what kind of world would that be? Hi troggie. How's life? We wouldn't need to ask any questions. We'd know already the boring answer. Not that I've got anything against woodlice;

someone's got to be a woodlouse. I'd rather be a badger making detours and crossing my tracks sometimes. I'd make a rendezvous on the wayside. I'd listen to the moon, but I don't believe half of what she says.

LIMPING PAST TRAFALGAR

I had seen the photographs in the pit of November in England – the white scree of Moorish Zahara de los Atunes within sight of Africa; the glassy sea of Cabo de Trafalgar, the umbrella pines against the blue sky. I thought of rhino-ceros beetles, parasol mushrooms too big to clasp with both hands. I thought of spumy whales. I thought of Nelson, the picture of him dying on the deck, and a primordial reflex gripped my throat. I forgot about the rain. My comic-book history filled in the space, Hardy supporting Nelson, English honour and tenderness in this exotic corner. (I didn't see the sand on the deck to stop people skidding on the blood or the bits of 5,000 British seamen killed or maimed in point-blank broadsides.) I dared myself to trust this teasing fantasy; there and then I decided to cycle around Andalucia in January.

At Zahara, a row of lamp-posts ended dramatically in the sea. They looked how I felt, surreally out of place. I had the beach to myself. The locals were sheltering from the storm and probably pipping olives in their dens. The men were in the bars, drinking and talking, their voices clicking an octave higher every hour; two lovers, arm in arm, peeped their noses out-of-doors and ran back to the Hotel de Gran Sol. I had nowhere to go. The storm came out of Africa ladling black clouds one on top of another, spitting rain and sand relent-lessly across the beach. The headlands of Cabo de Trafalgar buffeted a sea pleated with white waves. Even then I knew I wouldn't go there. I hadn't seen any whales. As a souvenir, I pocketed a red heart-shaped stone.

Two days later I escaped to Barbate – and simultaneously the bearings in the bottom bracket and back axle clunked ominously. I could not believe it. My first impressions of Barbate were not encouraging: a squashed rat on the road, flooded marismas outside the town, a gang of stray dogs, lean cattle splattered in mud; a Sunday morning with thunderburst clouds and empty streets. My kindergarten Spanish failed me. I pushed my bike into the town thinking I might never cycle out of it.

I had reckoned without Doctor Valencia.

All I needed was patience and a drink at La Parada, a local bar specialising in atun-a-la-plancha, Barbate owing its existence to the tuna fishing industry. (In the local church are six giant murals of Christ by the water, standing on it, calming it, and always surrounded by Spanish-looking fishermen.) I hesitated outside the bar, the tawdry neon light, a long narrow room crowded with men mesmerised by the television. I walked past, came back and went in. One or two nodded at my friendly face, the others watched resolutely the Spain v

Tunisia match. Straightaway I was struck by their camaraderie, their baggy cords, brown or black leather jackets, flat caps; the rich and old, grandfathers and sons, nearly all with a cigarette tucked into their mouth. A newcomer would put his arm around his friend's neck and they talked just inches apart. Some brought in their ten-year-old sons and they were patted affectionately. My English horror of showing affection to men publicly was soothed by the gentleness I saw in these often hard-worked faces. I was touched by their solidarity regardless of age or class, or so it seemed to me.

Without hesitation I nominate Dr Valencia as the patron saint of distressed cyclists. If ever your bicycle should break down pray that it is outside Barbate. He is nothing much to look at, a skinny youth with a shrew-like face, eyes set too far back and only the ghost of a smile (and a cigarette) parts his lips. His skill is well-known. Throughout the ninety minutes he took to fix the bike, a small, constantly changing audience stood around him. One shook his head, another clicked his tongue in disbelief at those dextrous fingers. Not once did this go to the doctor's head or flaw the flow of swift, decisive twists of his spanners. He lined up the bolts, tapped in the right place, tuttered at what he saw and showed us the worn tracking for the bearings. The parts he placed on a clean cloth, the way they had come out. He cleaned away the dirty grease, washed out the socket with diesel and blew it dry with compressed air. The messy business of inserting new bearings, greasing them, spinning them for me to see, became a sequence of little twists of his fingers. The wheel spun as if it would go a mile without stopping. The bottom bracket was a terminal case, but within half-an-hour I had a new bike; with a few jabs of his screwdriver he reset my chainset adjusters. For the first time everything worked. He had saved my journey, and what's more he charged me peanuts. The generous tip he refused with a beatific smile, but wisely pocketed it the second time.

Dr Valencia, I salute you!

I left Barbate without seeing the sun or hearing the whirring rhinoceros beetle land to earth. I left Hardy supporting Nelson on their deck. I had been helped through a crisis and not collapsed. It's only later I realised that all my worst pictures had silver linings. *(Barbate, January 28, 1996)*

WAYSIDE BLESSING

Dear Exima, my friend and exile, I am in no hurry. I have never written a letter to you, and never from a Zealand wayside on the road to Kalundborg. I could not pass it by, a beautiful Hound's-tongue flower, deep purples fading to Forget-me-not blues, all gently hairy and nodding among pollinating grasses smooth and light to touch. I had to sit down here, take off my socks and shoes, pour myself a cup of tea — and do something I have never done before, write you this letter. First I ask you to forgive me for walking past your door, most of my life. I hadn't even known it was there. When I did find your door I was curious. I see you lying there now, long nails, scraggily hair and all the balloons in the room as if you had been having a party. I have to say that you reminded me of my brother, John, whose life appears to be like yours.

So here I am again on this wayside, this detour in my life. I am enjoying seeing the world, names of places I had only ever dreamed about. I want you to feel at home with me. I know you get scared, I get scared too. I imagine the worst is going to happen, that I will be betrayed by my best friend, catch a wasting disease from a good woman, wake up with terminal pains over which I have no control. You see, I'm frightened of trusting my body. I have no idea where this comes from. Perhaps it was there on my first journey into this world. Who knows? I have tried to know, but wanting to know seems another way of leaving you behind. I want to be your friend. Life is too difficult otherwise.

Do you remember when I wrapped the coloured streamers around my leg? Or when I dressed up as a little man, hunch-backed with a girt big cock, one-armed and kneeling in slippers? How I laughed! I felt that we were together, having a party. I understand you best with this laughter. I lock the door when I explain you, as if you are in a box and I can forget about you. Foolish man. Then I see you everywhere, in others, in the land, especially in my fears. They prod my body in its vulnerable places. You are speaking to me, this little man is beautiful. You want me to remember myself. I am content here; everywhere are insects, fat, winged beetles, St Mark's fly kissing geraniums and buttercups, the breeze silvering the grasses. This wayside is a church, a sacred place, all the native things are here: insects, wild flowers, rubbish, poor soil, the things we pass by. I have only to sit here to be at home on this ground. I want to give you my blessing: May you have ground under your feet so that you can stand. I will stay with you, shelter you from the bright light and feed you a father's love for a beloved son or brother who has come from night into the day. May we live together always until the cows come home.

(Ubby, Zealand, May 28, 1997)

'Tell us about Jo.'

'You are like Tugger. You don't let go. What do you want to hear? My sister – your great aunt – had returned from nursing in North Africa, following the Allied forces in the desert. Jo's father was in the desert air force. He was shot down, early on; he was only just out of school. He had blue eyes and a patch of ginger hair behind his left ear, but that had gone by his teens. My sister nursed him in the canvas hospital behind the lines. There can be a very special bond between nurses and the ones they care for. Quite special, but it was not to last.

125

'That was a gentleman's war. "A war without hatred," the papers called it, against Rommell's Panzerarmee. It gave us hope when things were black in Europe. The Allied landings in North Africa helped to defeat the Axis powers. The Germans were professionals, the English amateurs. But that first week of July 1942, the battle of el-Alamein was the turning of the hinge of fate. That's what they said. It was a drought-stricken land, just sun and stony ground and dunes like waves in the sea. Nothing grew there, except stones and misery.' Her faraway eyes paused. 'He was always a chattering child, telling me the names of everything he saw and heard. I'm his godmother. Did you know that? He's such a good boy.'

'He's not a boy,' said Sarah. 'That's the trouble, everybody treats him like a boy. He's six foot! No-one says anything about him. It's as if he's not there. They don't want to know what he's thinking or doing or what he wants. He's our uncle but we never see him.' Granny held both of Sarah's hands. She pulled hers away.

'We do our best. When we look back it may not have been enough, or the right thing too late...'

'I know it's not anyone's fault and everybody loves him. But he's got a life too. He's got lots of time, but it's time to do nothing.'

'*The Powers that be are ordained by God.*' What would you have him do? If you opened the gate, he would not leave. He is happy. What more can we ask for?' I felt cross with myself for arguing with her. Sarah filled the heated trays with gingerbread men while I put currant faces on each one, and sad smiles on some. Granny placed them onto the middle oven shelf, doing it slowly and carefully, the way she knitted her thoughts together. Off came the oven gloves, and she set the timer and kissed us on the cheeks. She went to her room. It was time to pray.

TRANSFORMATION

My sister Simbana is a brave woman. She is not afraid to turn a page. In the middle of her life she sells her house and most of her belongings, puts the money in the bank and goes and lives in a bedsit on the Welsh Border. She is touched by the hands-on wisdom of the farming folk, their worn and beautiful lived-in faces, and touched also by the unseen company which attend her solitary journey, with whom she is left alone. It is her time of healing, she says, a time out with the four seasons and without a plan. Each day she walks in the woods before the dawn and at dusk, and is quiet enough to surprise the deer or find messages in oak leaves. She is intensely alone with her griefs and her joys. The child walking beside the woman is herself. One day when she thinks she cannot bear her grief anymore she visits Caldey Island and sits in a

cave, a safe, surrounding space lulled by breathing water and answering reson-
ances. The cave befriends her, and she is amazed by the peace she finds there.
A second and a third time she visits, but on the last day she stops short of
entering. Another sound roars out, then silence, then the roaring, wondrous
sound. It is not the water. It is one of the monks chanting. 'I have never heard
so much passion in my life.'
She takes it as a good omen. (Bath, October, 1996)

TRUST

Bué describes herself as an earth woman, and looks it too – sometimes expressionless and flinty; sometimes her long-boned face is as soft as wayside flowers.
She is fifty and full of dignified silver hair, Northern jumper colours and a
tough serenity tested at Greenham Common. Our paths crossed while washing
up at a farm in La Creuse. She says she has lived with the consensus of other
people, and sometimes with their own horrible selves. She laughs at that. She
has just sold her stake in an English community and has no idea where she is
going '...except it's south, perhaps Andalucia. It's harder for the others staying
behind with their questions. "Why are you going? Where are you going?" I
told them all I knew: "I need to change".' She is not sure if she will come
back to England. 'I experience my independence as a relief.' The previous day
she had left Paris and a meeting of the Peace Brigade, an Amnesty type organ-
isation offering practical support for human rights. Once she had sat on a roof
in Guatemala being the doorkeeper and a silent witness, while dozens of
indigenous women demonstrated solidarity for their rights. 'After that, I could
have gone anywhere. I had so much trust in people.'
(Aubusson, September 13, 1996)

I went to the corner window behind the curtains in the living room. I
always went there when I wanted to be alone. I put my head on my knees
and leaned into the wooden corner. I closed the curtains leaving a gap in
the thick strawberry brocade so I could peep out. I pretended that I was a
cat hiding and no-one could see me. I could see everything, even a mouse
tiptoeing by the door. I could hear its little heart go *boom boom boom*.
Sometimes with Sarah we would make shows and take it in turns to be the
audience. This time I rocked myself until I was quiet. I wanted to sleep in
front of a sunny window. The hoary blue sky gave everything a dream-like
quality, as if I were passing through, as if everyone were on their way to
somewhere else. I fell asleep, I remembered nothing.

Then I heard a voice, but I couldn't see anybody. I opened my eyes and it
was dark. I was alone. I heard someone talking softly, a voice muffled by a
handkerchief. I didn't move. Slowly I heard the sobs and sharp intakes of

breath. I recognised granny's voice. I should have come out. I should have said, 'I'm here'. Instead I spied through the gap, the cowardly streak of not wanting to be seen. I saw granny with her back to me and she was talking to a photograph, stroking it as if it were a baby. It was the special one in the silver frame from the sideboard. 'Never mind,' she said, 'for us, for us. I'll remember you.' Then the front door slammed and in came Sarah shouting, 'Coming!' Granny stood as Tugger came barking into the living room, and she quickly placed the photograph back onto the mantelpiece. Her tears were wiped from her cheeks and she followed Tugger back into the kitchen. It was as if nothing had happened. This is how they keep secrets I thought, and so I would keep mine.

VESOUL NIGHTINGALE

I am here on the step of my cabin cloaked in a blanket and woolly hat. A lorry rumbles into the night. It cannot stifle the liquid notes of the nightingale. I had been lying in bed listening to its night song for perhaps an hour, struggling with inertia and a sleepy head. I counted to three and here I am. A bell rings but I am all ears for this song I have never heard in England, only once in Friesland when Bram the bee-keeper silenced us with his finger. It is a love song: why else would he (forgive me she?) sing half this night before dawn? Little plaintive notes are often repeated or chuckled out or held in the back of the throat and warbled about. A shy piper drawing out its notes, drawing from me a tender response; tendresse, as the French say. Other birds emerge with song liberating the dark spaces one by one. The nightingale improvises as a knitter may from different patterns but it is all in one piece, the air tapped out as single notes, then liquid and fluty or as a sudden wheezing, or trilled out solemnly. I close my eyes. The cool inbreath of air, a dog barking, more lorries drowning the song but not my attention. Frogs join in, two base-lines sounding under water.

The best part is the slow descent, the repetition of longing in those simple notes, then cut short so it never descends completely into pathos. I have never listened so intently to a nightingale before. I notice the stars for the first time, The Plough above my head. Is this song also the promise of a blue sky, anticipation of the morning's winged feasts? Is it a love song? There is no reply. I respond to its piece-meal splendour teasing from me a longing. Is it tenderness? It is not important to see this nightingale. It is there in all my childhood picture books, singing songs, infanta songs of love and longing; something belonging to the nature reserves of the mind, not to be held in the hand. I understand the frogs when they listen to the nightingale. They croak their base-lines as I croak these words.

(4.30am, Lac-du-Vaivre, Vesoul, May 5, 1998)

SINGING MY SONG

I am in the back lane beside the Argyll Hotel, a private place hedged with old Fuschia magellenica and thickets of glossy green wands to filter the on-shore winds. Halfway down on my way to the Iona harbour, a song-thrush stopped me, perched at the end of a branch and not more than an arm's stretch away. I could see each dark spot on its fluffed-out breast, and it still didn't move. Out of its beak rose the thrush's song. I could no more do justice to it than walk across the Sound of Iona to Fionnphort. I listened, my belly listened, my toes listened to this escape of jubilation, for what else could convey the inventiveness of its song, something new at every turn, plaintive, whistled, chuckled and strung together out of thin air. I can picture this bird vividly. I listened a decent time and still the notes eluded this pen, but this is a small thing. Nearing fifty I wonder about my own song. More comes in pieces, bits that do not seem connected, and there are pauses where nothing happens, and sometimes the same thing goes round and round and I wonder how they can be connected, if they are at all. I would like to hear my song played from beginning to end, but a song can take a lifetime. I sing it best bit by bit.

('Cruachan', Iona, 7pm, May 5, 1999)

THE SINGING GATE

On a whim I decided to give my headache a tour of The Machair, so I cycled across to the west end of the island. I stopped by Cnoc an Sithein, The Hill of the Angels, the green mound where cattle are said to have been blessed until recent times. It's a small wedge of turf and it always catches my attention, its distinctive whale-bake contours and base-line gravity. Just past it is the metal gate barring the way to the daisy turf (and some of it is a golf course) by the sea, the Bay-at-the-Back-of-the-Ocean. It's an old five-bar gate, entwined in places with rusty barbed wire. I was about to open it when I heard a low humming sound coming from the gate, the wind behind me playing on the wire. I touched the bars, the wire but it made no difference – except now I distinguished a base-line coming and going, and a higher ascending note. How strange, I thought, such delicate sounds from such an ugly gate. After five minutes, quite entranced by this chance music, I meandered across The Machair. Here the wind had more space to roam so I pulled my hood over my head. Slowly and imperceptibly I heard the singing gate again, but I was hundreds of yards away. I heard the same mellifluous weaving of sound, no longer the lone notes but now in a choral arrangement. I felt a curious sensation at my temples as if I were being touched, and pleasantly so. Suddenly I started to cry, the gates on the tears unlocked and something rocking in my chest. I stopped crying. I listened to this wind harp. Where did it come from? I

stopped by the gate again. I heard the same sounds I had heard at the begin-
ning. My headache had gone. I looked at The Hill of the Angels. It said
nothing enigmatically. Minutes later the sound disappeared, and I could not
recall a note, then or now.

(Iona, May 5, 1999)

The Dome

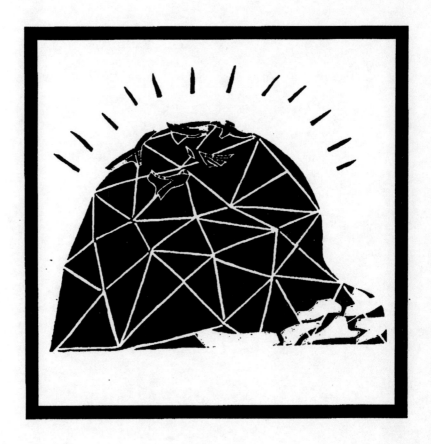

" 'Dreams,' said the cautious Penelope, 'are awkward and confusing things.' "

Odyssey, Homer

Jo arrived last thing out of the morning, the clock striking midday. I didn't know whether to shake his hand, just say hello or hug him. I stood limply before him, and so did Sarah. He dropped his brown suit-case and stretched out his hand, all plump fingers and each one warm. 'I like you.' He held onto my hand for at least a minute. 'I like you, I do.' He was huge in his black coat covering him up except for his face, pear-shaped with high cheek-bones and ears sticking out of short grey hair. A happy face, always on the move. 'Pinky's crossed over,' he said straightaway in that high, bird-like voice, and raising his suitcase as if it weighed nothing. 'One minute he was flapping around. His eyes went funny. He must have had a stroke.'

'They don't want to hear about Pinky,' said the woman standing behind granny and smiling at us as if it were a joke we shared. Her blue and white uniform peeped out like soft feathers beneath her coat, and I knew she was Jo's minder.

'I do,' said Sarah.

'He'll go on and on.'

'Closed his eyes...he'd just gone to sleep, peaceful. He's gone to a good place with all his other dead mates. Heaven's like that, isn't it? Nothing lives forever.'

'*See how the deaf can hear, and the dumb can talk.*'

'We'll meet again somewhere. What vicars say is true. It will come to us all one day. I think that will be in the next world. It makes my mind boggle.'

'There's always a reason, a reason for everything.' Tugger leaped up licking Jo's hands and face and wriggling his body against his legs.

'I like you, I do. When I'm walking my legs start running too.'

The nurse thanked us formally for inviting Jo, as if we were doing it to make her happy. Every word she said had prickled me. 'He's so excited to visit and they will miss him back home. He is his own man now and he must decide. Don't touch that.' Jo pulled back his finger from the face of the grandfather clock.

'If you're good God will look after you. If you're bad you go to the Devil. There are always two sides to every coin.'

'And two gingerbread men,' shouted Sarah from the kitchen. I helped him off with his overcoat, then granny fitted his long legs under the table while the nurse brought in a cup of tea and a plate, put a napkin on his knees. We were always doing things for Jo. The teddy bear went in head first and he used his sticky finger to pick up the crumbs. The spilt tea he poured from his saucer back into his cup.

'Manners!'

He poured the tea back onto the saucer. This time everyone laughed, except Jo. He stared at us seriously. 'There's a right way and a wrong way.'

'It's what fills the heart which comes out at the lips.'

'I did the right thing. Perhaps it had had enough. There's no way of knowing, is there?'

'Pinky's at peace. Let's leave him there.'

LAST RITES, LAST LAUGH

Characteristically he stood in the empty space between the door and the steps, going nowhere but strangely available, dramatically on the spot. Everyone entering the youth hostel had to pass him and he peered cherubically into each face. What did we see? An old man in shuffling slippers and pink and green trainers beneath his white overcoat. He idled on his stage; English fruitcake thought the Continentals, and so did I, and with affection. I liked his pixie, peaked cap and absolute disregard for formality. He told us he was 80.

I have had a life of perfect freedom,' he said melodiously to no-one in particular. 'I have no regrets. My father's dying words to me were: "I admire the way you live my boy." My three sisters never so much gave him a roast Sunday lunch after he was widowed. After he died I went off on style: pale suit and coloured baggage on Victoria Station. I went to Australia for the first time. I was on a luxury liner with my seven cases full of beautiful outfits. He waved his arm. "The name is Allington. The Presidential Suite..." People connect a nice speaking voice with money. When I wear the bracelets they'll be from Cartier so run like mad! I went to Australia five times...South Africa five times. All the working class went to Bournemouth.

'People...Half are shits, half are good. I have had 70 jobs. You can't bully me I told my bosses. I don't have two children. You can kiss my knees. My only brother was married with a lady at 21. He was in the spare room for the last 30 years. She would only give it when a £10 note was presented.

For heaven's sake, what kind of life is that?...I'm living in Southend. I went up the Social and the clerk said it would be three days before my money comes. How pathetic. By the time I got to 60 I always saved half my wages in the Post Office to go travelling in the summer. I have had several executive jobs where I have engaged people. I pity the people working in offices. Wasted lives. There are people who are unemployable. In those days they wore ties and shirts and navy suits. They didn't look too awful. There are so many shabby people now. You can go to Oxfam and buy things. This peaked hat I bought in Morocco. Poor little man, out in all weathers.

'I only ever borrowed twice in 50 years. I had the indignity of having to ask. I have had serious operations with cancer. I don't think I'm going to live very long. I have had my chips. I'm quite prepared to go to sleep in a hostel bed, in a room somewhere. I'm not tragic about it. I certainly don't want to go on until I'm 90. I have had a divine life. I have had many lovers. I have known several leading ladies. "You never been kissed?" I said to one. "Never fell in love? You must be half dead." Now with my experience, I say: How lucky never to get into that trouble.

I'm reading Lili Palmer's story. I never met Noel myself but I wrote to him in Switzerland and he wrote me a nice letter back. My sister said you must keep it, but moving about you can't keep things. "The pleasure you gave me..." He was so brilliant. I had always seen his things from the gallery.

'Life is so interesting. It is. I used to work in my parent's public house, in the saloon bar. Nothing in the upper storey there, I'm afraid. They have no conversation, just bigger TV, new wallpaper. Their lives are empty. Intelligent people educate themselves. My parents always gave me a reference: "We would have him back."

'How old are you? You must have learned a thing or two about life now. I cleaned seven days a week, picked plums and strawberries if I had to...I worked in hostels. I put the music on in the morning and brought them a cup of tea in bed. "The sun has got his hat on hip hip hip hooray..." We all laughed.'   (Saffron Walden, June 23, 1997)

MIDDLE GROUND AT AQUÆ SULIS

At midday precisely, while the Abbey church bells were ringing, I threw a golden coin into the circular pool. I wondered whether to throw just a penny, one with the Queen's head; but no, this was a golden wish for myself, for my middle age. I am 47. It's always the same wish, fulfilment, wholeness in this life. I always say it at the same place while gazing down at the firmament of little stars; in fact they are countless coins lying at the bottom of the pool, and each one is a wish. If I could hear each coin splash surely I would hear the longings of this world. Afterwards I come and lean against one of the look-

alike Roman pillars, attracted by the playful steam swirling on the waters of the Great Bath. The water is green and sombre. It's a good time to visit, few people, and each one is alone with their electronic guide. I come here alone yet I always imagine that I am part of some enormous crowd coming to whisper their wishes. We are equal before these waters as we will be in death. This tenderness for our mortality abounds here. It teases my thoughts and I can never quite express or know this sense that I am passing through, and this is a good place to acknowledge it. Perhaps that's why I keep coming back.

The steam expresses this better than any words. It's here one moment, gone the next. And it's always coming up. Where does it come from? Where does it go? I don't know. I am full of head cold and I am distant. Everything outside me appears solid: the solitary siren of a seagull, the clip of shoes, echoing children's voices. I am at the bottom of the well, emptying me, and I wish I could enamel this place and wear it as an emblem for this bottom-line January day. This backyard face, this unexpressed part brings me here, when the distance from the inside to the outside is at its greatest. I wish for some middle ground to connect up the parts, middle ground in the middle time of my life.

A soft rain falls; every raindrop is nailed to the water. The mist still rises. A pigeon croons; people stay inside. I come here not to find anything, not to ask any questions or drop curses into the sacred springs. I come here to do nothing. Absurdly I see my friend's face, Marko Michel, Bath's own folklorist. His face appears smiling out of the water, The Gap, as he would say, into the Other World, the place where people come to die. I do not need to make a spell upon this place for its magic to work. It's a common feeling as the offered coins testify, this longing for continuity in life and in death. Several times I have dreamt of the circular pool and seen the colossal Madonna's statue carved in stone, and staring equally at all-comers, or is it Minerva or Athene or one of Cerridwen's faces? It doesn't matter. This deep underground spring – said to be rain which fell 10,000 years ago on the nearby Mendip Hills – is rusty red at heart, heated and bubbles miraculously. The waters pass on to the Avon river then to the Bristol Channel and so to the sea. I will pass on, but the wish will stay for the middle ground in this life, more acceptance of the changes.

(The Great Bath, Bath, January 19, 1998)

'A quick walk.'

'Promise,' said Sarah sticking me with her eyes. I crossed my heart and showed her my open hand. We understood each other; everything had to be traded. Tugger understood by running between our legs and thinking aloud with his tail.

'Bad boy,' said granny, easily catching his back leg as if she knew which way he would turn. She didn't want him to go. 'You'll run away, won't you?' Jo looped his arm around Tugger and granny released him.

'He has a way with dogs.' Tugger lay on the lino with his leg cocked up, showing you know what. 'Enough of that.' She made me promise to keep him on the lead, to wrap it around my hand three times and never to let go. 'You must be the master.' For Jo she found a red bobbly hat and pulled it over his head; she squeezed his face between her hands and tapped his nose. 'Whatever you do, stay on the paths.' She always wanted to know where we were going.

WALKER

The delicious moment arrives. I appear from nowhere and pull up beside him on the back road from Aberfeldy to Dunkeld. His two walking sticks pace his feet along the tarmac. I walk beside this older man, still lithe and with his hair and clearly pleased to have company. He is two-and-a-half weeks into the walk from John o'Groats to Land's End. 'It's my way of preparing myself for retirement. I didn't want to just fall off the edge.' We discover we are both Peters, and shake hands on that. At 61 he looks too young to be retired, a friendly, enquiring face spectacled and now stubbled.

'We must look a fruity pair. You with your placard and me with the day-glo jacket.'

'My grand-daughter says that granny won't kiss me if I have a beard. She's only four.'

The walk down from Wick had been hard, with blisters already appearing on both feet. He had jettisoned the tent and several pairs of socks. On the mobile – it's his lifeline, he says – his wife told him: 'I'll only tell you once. I told you so.'

'She'll tell it to me again.'

And then there was the pressure of sponsorship (he was walking for MS). His business associates from the banking world – where he had controlled a £120 million budget – had sponsored him honourably, one even giving 50p a mile, and that's £500. But his poor feet! The dark thoughts of failure already cast their shadows. 'I cannot face failure, letting all those people down and especially my wife. She has complete confidence in me.'

'The first half of any journey is always a descent,' I tell him. He says he wants to believe that. In three weeks he hasn't once thought about his working life, only the people he left behind. 'I miss the crack though.'

I can see that it is not easy walking on the tarmac. 'It ain't the 'unting and the 'edges that 'urts the 'orses' 'ooves, but the 'ammer 'ammer 'ammer on the 'ard high road.' He laughs at that. He says he is building up confidence to walk on the mountain routes, a little show of vulnerability. It's the same with me, I tell him. The long silences of walking make him garrulous. 'I can't stop talking...After five days it was so hard that if someone had pulled up and said

"Jump in", I would have jumped in.' The meagre company in bars, the same dreary lasagne, the glut of chocolate bars had taken their toll. And still seven weeks to go.

'I can't believe about the Highland Clearances. In one town half the streets were in Gaelic, the other in English. They had been brought to the coast and left there.'

'Just like the ethnic cleansing.'

'My mind keeps returning to a patch of land near Cardiff. I keep thinking I could make a garden there.'

'Why not? It's a good way to go out.'

I identify Sweet Cicely (Myhrris odorata), the fragrant umbellifer, then Bird Cherry (Prunus avium). 'It's a Notherner's tree. See those stretch marks, typical of Prunus.'

'You've opened my eyes.' He keeps a journal. 'I'll have to give a talk you see. I saw a lamb just taking its first steps. It was amazing.' The rusty flanks of a hare meandered across the road. 'This is what it is all about. Do you embellish your stories?' he asks.

'The truth is so much more interesting, the gaps, the silences, the ambiguities. I'm always interested in what I remember.'

'I wonder what I shall tell the Rotary Club.'

'Don't try to make it interesting. Knock that on the head.'

'What do you mean?'

'Start with your fear of failure. That's a good place.'

(Strathmiglo, May 8, 1999)

FREEDOM WALK

Jorgen, the architect, showed me the walk behind his home in Jutland: a woodland trail leading to the open heaths and the six hectares of grass for his daughters' horses. He made me see the boundary mounds criss-crossing this land, all that remains of the Iron Age field systems of Skonager. He loves the things which belong to places: fossilised sea urchins and the old stone axes his grandfather found on the farm; the sand-shaped vindsten stone, the Oslo conglomerate rock dropped in the Ice Ages; the bowl of amber pieces collected by moonlight on the Jutland coast. All the fruits of walks, but he remembers another story best.

In the Cold War days, when he was 23, he visited Prague on a student architectural tour. The first evening a young Czech touched his denim jacket and asked to try it on. He did this and then asked to buy it. Jorgen said no. Away he ran with it, and Jorgen's passport in the inside pocket. They fought on the station platform and the Czech youth fell onto the track. It was electrified. A rail-guard saw this and called the police. They took Jorgen to the station. No-one understood a word. They took him by van to a prison and he was marched down and down and locked into a cell. He was there by himself for 11 days. Then he was locked into another cell with five others, including two captured trying to escape to the West, one for illegal private manufacturing. 'They were not bad people they just had the bad luck to be caught.' In the adjoining cells were prostitutes, robbers and rapists. He had no possessions. The little he had – soap and tobacco – he shared. After two months he was brought before the magistrates. He faced a five-year sentence if the Czech had been seriously hurt. Fortunately they accepted his version of events and he was ordered out of the country.

'When I got back I understood what freedom is – to open a door and go for a walk.'   (Esbjerg, June 20, 1997)

JOHANNES DEPRAETRE

All through South-East France I heard about the Belgian who had been walking for three years.

'Are you him?'

'No mate.'

'He's walking to Jerusalem next year...'

'He's going to take Holy Orders...'

'I met him on a hill. He gave me a beer.'

I had seen his face beaming out of newspaper cuttings at St Come d'Olt and at Condom: a tall lithe figure, trimmed beard, purposeful. At Portomarin in Galicia I knew who he was the moment he sat opposite me; a light heart out of the Galician storm. He shared chocolate biscuits from his bag, confounding an earlier story of meanness. His scrapbook was full of testimonials from Bishops, signed Compostelas, the European routes of the medieval pilgrimages to Santiago de Compostela. He planned to walk them all. 'I am not showing you this for myself,' he said seriously, 'but you asked about me.' He had left Belgium on September 20, 1993, to walk non-stop for four years. His great plan was to work with the homeless young in Latin America with the Salesians. 'What you see on the streets is the tip of the iceberg.' He was walking to test his vocation. After Santiago he would walk to Fatima and then to Rome. 'If others laugh at me it is in one ear and out the other. You see, I had been helped as a child. You can never forget that.'

                                                            (Santiago de Compostela, October 15, 1996)

LES DEUX ANGLAIS

He stepped out of the hedge onto the road to Aire-sur-l'Adour: a husky, bearded man in his sixties with a face tanned by walking too long in the sun. He toiled under a large rucksack.

'Are you Serge?'

'Non,' he replied.

"You're English!"

Mark Flynn had walked from Le Puy-en-Velay, but would not wear his St Jacque's shell until he reached Roncesvalles.

'How did you know I was English?'

'The accent,' I said, 'and the worn spectacle case clinched it.' I had yet to see a Frenchman with a hole in his shirt or mud on his boots.

The town is a fine, airy place, bustling and at peace with itself in the wide streets. The gîte is shut so we shared a room at the Hotel de Les Deux to keep costs down. He is a retired headmaster of preparatory schools in Wiltshire and Derby, and now lives with his wife in a house of their dreams near Brest. At sixty they had planted an acre of garden with sapling trees.

'Winters are quiet,' he says, 'but once a year we do the grand tour of all our friends.' He misses rugby the most and the school's social world. I am glad of company and the easy, courteous talk. We know we will never see each other again.

Ritually he empties the contents of his rucksack onto his bed and takes the weight off his feet. One by one he examines his blisters, pricking and covering them with a non-slip plaster; creams and oils calm the aches. He hobbles backwards and forwards across the room. 'It's therapy.' He is very English with his drawn, determined features, gentle eyes, strong in an understated way. But now he is tired. He listens carefully to my questions and considers his replies. They had made friends in Brittany, enjoyed the conviviality of twinning with a Cornish village. 'But there's always a line. We have no illusions about that. I will always be an Englishman.' I realise that he is old enough to be my father, but on this road age is irrelevant; it's the person that matters. I'm empowered by this equality. We swap gossip: 'William from Rotterdam is four days behind you; the Spaniards, Sol and Paco (she is a nurse to the old man) are walking for the handicapped. 'Did you meet Johannes? He has walked 16,000 miles. They say he will take vows.'

Over dinner, he says that he never gets lonely — there are so many letters to write — but admits that life is short on revelations. 'It's disappointingly parochial.' Perhaps it will be different in Spain when he meets his son. We don't talk about religion. I tell him that I am up to my neck with writing. 'It's now or never to realise my projects. I'm determined.' He believes me. I'm evangelical about cycling and slyly mention the 70-year-olds I've seen touring Britain. Then he talks about television clichés. 'Someone goes into a building and they always fall off the roof. I think, I've seen this before, and after thirty minutes I'm certain.'

Now it's morning. He teases his beard and laughs. 'I might leave it on. See what the wife thinks.' He pauses, 'I didn't catch your name in all our talk.'

'Peter Alfred Please.'
'Mark Flynn.' We shake hands.
'Bon voyage.'
'I'll be catching the boat back on October 21st.'
'Trafalgar Day! That's nice.'   *(Navarrenx, September 29, 1996)*

I whistled the way Tugger understands, two short ones and a longer one, and I did it again. He barked high-screechy and chesty like a fox, pointing his ears at me and then at the door. Jo snapped the chain onto his collar and wound it around his wrist. 'Three times. See!'

'Be back by lunchtime.'

'I promise.'

The day had brought its own magic: a sky made of white tissue paper, the air frozen and from the North. The grass crunched like oatcakes as we walked out; cabbages bowed to the ground, the raindrops were frozen into beads of glass. A silent world without horns or murmuring cars or answering voices; everyone was away in their own worlds. I kept thinking: We're doing this, really. Jo went into slow motion at the style, lifting up one leg until he got stuck, and I had to hold one leg (and the lead) as he lifted up the other. He shifted his weight onto the other side. 'I did it!' I was amazed. Tugger led us up the field of bent grass, now hummocky and glassy. The wind had blown them the same way, the rain squashed them, the frost brushed them white. I zipped my jacket to the neck. Tugger cocked his ears at the ivy but I didn't let him dig for the vole. Jo broke off the top of a hogweed and spun it ahead of him like a satellite. Everywhere were silver cobwebs; so many spiders yet not one to be seen. Tugger pulled us up the hill towards King's Wood while Jo swung the lead expertly from one hand to another, never becoming flustered or cross when Tugger changed directions. The stream had iced over and the water moved under it like tadpoles, sometimes quickly as if waiting for something. You could not tell whether they were coming or going. Tugger, of course, jumped onto the ice trying to bite them and we had to pull him away.

Behind us our footprints were a string of shadows. Jo waved his arms and legs, their shadows trailing down the hill behind us. I did the same, and we swung our arms and legs together. Two crows sat on the single big ash tree ahead of us, lumps of coal with their heads buried in their feathers so only their beaks stuck out; the ash keys were matted stars. Farther up, the new road cut through the lowest point of the hill, and here, while the world moved, we stood still. We went to the wood where I had buried the badger.

I would surprise him, say: "Here's the badger." But the badger had gone! The leaves were scattered and lay frozen where they had fallen. Tugger buried his head into the hole and followed his nose in small circles.

I told Jo about the badger, and he made me tell it to him again. Dead badgers cannot walk. A fox must have dug it out, but there were no padded trails or other clues that we could see. Tugger strained at the lead and pulled us into the wood, and such is the way decisions are made and a small dog sets unseen wheels in motion.

The trees of King's Wood kept the world at bay. All around us pine needles shed solid bits of ice sparkling in the air, becoming piles under the drip-lines of branches, a fairyland before our eyes. Tugger snapped at them, Jo caught them on his tongue. 'OOOO!' I stamped my feet to keep them warm. Then Tugger found a scent and buried his head up a trackway where they dragged timber out of King's Wood, now frozen mud, sharp and awkward to walk over. We stopped at a footbridge, uncertain which way to go. 'Perhaps the lion knows.' He covered his face with his hands.

'Lion!'

'I'm hiding.'

'Here!'

'He can't see me.'

'He's coming.'

'He'll steal me away.'

'It's a joke,' I laughed cruelly. 'The lion doesn't exist.'

'Let's play dead lions then.'

LION ON THE MOUNTAIN

Once a lion lived on a mountain. Everyone in the village knew it was there. They could hear it roaring.

'Stay on the paths,' they told their children.

'Don't go in those woods whatever you do.'

'Come back before dark.'

That lion made their hair tingle, circulate their blood a little faster, stretch out their ears, sharpen their eyesight. They knew the lion's ways. Most of those who went up came back down again and, if there were exceptions, there was usually a lesson to it.

'Remember Jones.'

'That's moonshine for you.'

'They only found his belt buckle, two gold teeth, a pile of tin buttons.'

'In a neat pile where the brute spat them out.'

'It's God's judgement. They never learn.'
Then someone said the lion had to go. 'What about the children?'
'We're not safe in our beds.'
'Someone should get rid of it.'
So they shot the lion, trapped the bear and the wolves, shot the eagles just to
be on the safe side. Now everyone could go up the mountain. But nobody ever
did (except the sheep and the goats). One mountain looked pretty much like
another.

* * *

Watch out for the wolves,' he says. 'There's a pack lying up in the woods near
Kongsvinger.' He sips a glass of water and swallows several different coloured
tablets. 'I'm 71 and I have angina. I have to take things easy.' His wife sits
across the breakfast table, two solid Swedish types; frank, level-headed faces,
humorous eyes. They had climbed the Pyramids, walked along the Great Wall
in China, explored nearly all South and North America. But there was
nothing like Åmal. 'My wife was born here. We have been coming from
Stockholm for the past 40 years. The richest man in Europe lived near here.
He returned from the Alaskan gold mines with suitcases of gold nuggets.'
I tell him about my cycle journey, and he shakes his head. 'The gnats are
terrible up North, and the midges...they get up your nose.' He laughs
carefully. 'Watch out for the horse flies. If the bites go yellow you must go to
the doctor at once.' He closes his newspaper. 'The Swedish police are too soft.
They are either amateurs or they are tired of police work. Less and less
policemen but crime is getting more and more, muggers and rapists and killers.
And now the Hell's Angels and the Banditos (whatever they're called) are
fighting each other in Stockholm and Copenhagen and Oslo. They throw
bombs at each other. It's not safe. A passer-by was killed. I'm not just scared
for myself. We need tough action to get rid of them.'

(Kil, Sweden, June 9, 1997)

Tugger changed his mind by dipping off the track and up a deer trail into
a pine plantation. Laurels brushed our faces with icy leaves and snappy
twigs. Out on the other side we stepped onto a ridge bordered by ancient
pines. I had never been here before, an old wood boundary hundreds of
years old; another one ran parallel to it and we had to step over the
overgrown roots criss-crossing between them. No-one had been down here
for a long time, and we didn't know where it went to. Tugger kept his nose
down padding between the woodland grasses until suddenly six metres of
nothing stopped us above a stream where steep banks were overhung with
laurel cover for the pheasants. On the far side towered straight beech trees
with numbers painted onto the trunks; they were going somewhere, but out

143

of the picture. We should have turned back but Tugger's straining lead tripped up Jo, and with a single leap he disappeared from our sight. Granny's face came rushing up to meet mine. 'TUGGER! TUGGER!'

There was no answer. I scrambled backwards sliding under the laurels, dipping under branches, pushing others away, until I reached the headland where a grey ribbon of water passed beneath a fallen tree linking both banks. Without thinking I ran across. 'Come on!' I shouted. Jo sat astride the log pulling himself across; a snail would have outdistanced him.

'I can't move.'

'You can.'

'I can't. My feet are dizzy.'

He was stuck, ridiculously so. I talked to him like I did to Tugger, telling him to obey, to stay calm, not to panic. I gave him my hand and he gripped it as if he were drowning. I pulled. 'Hold my hand.'

'I'm going down.'

'Hold my hand!'

'I'll fall off!'

'Hold my hand!'

'It's coming!'

'It isn't.'

'It is. He'll steal me.'

Never give up, said granny into my ears. I gripped his hands. You're coming to me. I pulled myself back, Jo moved forwards and so we see-sawed to the far bank. 'I did it!' he exclaimed.

'TUGGER!' The freezing air bit the back of my throat. I fell forwards into tall grasses, icy wands as thick as fingers. The ice cracked under our feet. A robin ticked me with angry notes. I stepped over ferns, scrambled over boulders to cross the stream again. 'TUGGER!' The wood did not answer. I ducked under branches, skidded over icy stones, waved my hands into frozen cobwebs. Then a marshy place jumped up in front of us and there were shadows of dog prints running across it. Willows slapped us, the ground rocked under our feet. 'oooOOOOO!' moaned Jo, but I pulled him across. Up we climbed again from tree to tree to reach the ridge and the black iron railings, the section before us crushed by a tree. The wood ended here. Below us, unexpectedly, faint sunlight streamed into a small valley shaped like a horseshoe, the sides covered with hazel twisting into the sky. I had never been here before or seen this valley floor invaded by brambles, beach-head landings in a sea of bent grass. I pulled Jo down. The smoke drifted out of a chimney as if it were a tin kettle on the boil, a strange dome with ropes tied across the canvas and secured by stakes in the ground. Weak sunlight glinted on the canvas; the ice tinkled harder. I had never seen a tinker's bender before. The tree hid us well and Jo melted the cobwebs on the bark with his breath. In his hand was a hazelnut where a squirrel had chewed it in half, and another one had a pea-sized hole.

'That's a short-tailed vole, not a squirrel.'

'Shut up,' I whispered. A man crawled out of the teapot pulling down flaps of a furry hat and kneeling to tie up his boots. He walked along the edge of the hazels away towards the lane. The door opened and shut, an engine spluttered into life along with the rattle of metal parts and smoke signalling above the hazel. The engine faded and the back of a red van disappeared past a tree. A pigeon waited on a branch, a bulldozer fluffed up and twice as big to stay warm. I whistled the way Tugger understands, two short ones then one longer. I did it again. A dog barked high and screechy. It had to be Tugger tied up somewhere, but his face pushed open the flap and then went back in.

TELLISFORD

I thought I was finished with Tellisford, but it was not finished with me. Several times through France and Germany, usually among folds of trees and bare hills, I kept thinking of that little wood off a back lane in Somerset. I smiled at these associations and revelled for a while in those woodland glades with the ferns signalling in the shade; the rutted tracks with the drooping woodland sedge and no-one about. I had lived in the wood for a few months after my marriage break-up. That was 12 years ago. It's always the same picture. I am walking or stepping lightly along a woodland path with sunshine and insects not far away, and the day is before me. It is familiar and unknown. I am on my own. I see old and loved faces and I say their names. They have gone now, our paths go elsewhere. I am sad when I think of this, that somehow this childhood trail – for that wood enclosed without horizons had much of the childhood world within it, unknown and timeless – does not last forever. I mended there. I carved a stone in a shed and put it on a hill near Glastonbury, a phallus stone with little red hearts up one side. It is still there. I remember the excitement I felt venturing farther into the wood, the thrill I experienced leaving the trail, perhaps following the notched ways of deer or the five-padded claws of badger. In this little house with the oak-butt and bramble world, I would sight the ruby-tail wasps or the glint of opal jay feathers. Yes, there was something precious in those moments. I did not look for them. They came to me. While I write this a Bavarian girl talks to her plastic doll and dresses it. 'Tut mir leid,' I say. 'Ich spreche nicht gut Deutsch.'

I was playing at Tellisford, in the best sense, serious play of re-discovery. I went back to simply being, like these words. I found the pond newly-dug and holding water in spring. Alongside it grew a young oak tree, just taller than myself. I often sat there with my back to this tree doing nothing at all. I loved this tree. I trimmed the stubs left by grazing cattle. I burnt sage for this tree and wished it well. From here I looked out onto an open field with two veteran oaks photographed by Ken Day in spring, summer, autumn and winter. Sometimes I walked slowly around the field margins throwing spears at the hay-bales or just enjoying the panorama of trees billowing to the edge of Salisbury Plain. I was happy because I did not want anything.

I am always saying that I should write about being middle-aged. I never do. I never know how to start. This man playing, this man being a child, this self-healing, this private zone, this man sitting by the oak tree, by the water, is a picture I like at this moment. I am middle-aged but it is not a line with young at one end and old at the other. It is a place also, by this pool, this oak tree. It is a place with a view. It is a dream for myself.   (Deggendorf, May 16, 1998)

PATCH OF EARTH IN THE SUN

I smile at this foolishness half-kneeling to tower over this stone and a few fallen leaves, and a single seedling of Dog's Mercury. A sudden breeze gusts with tidal water over my head. I listen to sound droplets like pebbles sucked by a wave. I feel silly setting this up, putting myself on the spot. What is there to say? I look again at the capsized leaves, red-stalked, green blotches on yellow with inscrutable veins, rich browns of mining insects. This red is startling against the anonymous grey lumps of earth all weathered to crumble. Leaf shadows cut the sunlight into continents... suddenly Sammy the Border terrier finds me and tramples this little world I am entering.

I breathe out slowly. I smile each time the sun warms my cheeks. I always notice the exception: the straight line of a plant stalk, the gloss of browns, the tip of reds, a fly polishing its back legs on this page and tilting carefully forwards to keep balance. The seedling has lost half a leaf, perhaps to a slug. It trembles in the breeze, not like the fallen leaves which curl and rock sideways or turn completely over and cartwheel the span of my hand. I notice that which moves. As I look carefully, I listen better. The quick burst of a drone fly startles me; a ground-hugging car hurtles by. The golden metallic sheen of a hoverfly showing iridescent green on the wings lures my attention as it sunbathes. I return to my little world. Two leaves are leaning on the seedling tilting it farther towards the stone. A faded blow-fly showing barred white along its thorax, circles slowly in the sun keeping close to earth. I relax as I write. I feel almost like a child, not having to prove anything. Sammy returns, friends from puppyhood, and licks happily my dirty hands. He tramples the seedling and scatters the leaves. It still trembles in the wind, just. I feel the unknown of

146

myself going at this speed, in this moment. I am inside myself and, para-
doxically, with other things outside. Already we are connected. I notice that the
seedling has been gobbled from the top too. It will become squatter, more
crabbed in growth, perhaps better able to withstand cold winds. I will not make
a parable out of you; enough to say that I appreciate your struggle.

I move positions crunching a gladioli. I dither. I think about looking at that
which does not move: the stone, the earth, the twigs. I imagine the roots...I
smell for the first time! Smooth, rounded, mellow and satisfying. Something is
at work...The smell goes and I cannot reclaim it. Here one moment and then
it's gone. Not like touch. Clittle-clattle, dry shake, murmurs and roars, sounds
sieved into fine particles. The wind cools, the sun warms. I return to my
seedling. Everything is in contact with the earth, fatally attracted, except the
seedling pushing upwards. I will remember its struggle against slugs, dogs, wind
and leaves, the way it has to give. It is part of me now.

I quite happily sat on the gladioli without remorse; somehow it was not part of
me. I feel more self-acceptance and calmer after sitting half-an-hour beside this
stone. I smile at the thought that it is virtually certain that this moment is
unique. It is unique as it is both anonymous and highly personal.

(Upton Cheney.)

Halfway down was a much smaller canvas hut with a hole dug inside, and
beside that was a wooden seat and a tin of white powder. A trodden path
led into the clearing where we had a clear view of the steam rising from the
canvas, especially around the chimney. Thin ice filled the ditch dug around
the house; wooden plates and black pots were turned upside down on
planks outside and set beside a fire-pit circled with stones; green hazel poles
lay beside that. I should have walked away, some instinct told me this was
none of my business. I kept seeing granny, her face tilting and her eyes
staring up and praying to Jesus; and Jesus' eyes were big and red and staring
at me. They followed me. I whistled softly by the flap. I whistled louder. I
lifted the heavy canvas. The warm air flapped against my cold cheeks; light
glowed on the back wall. I squatted by the slippers with sequins, and a
bundle of kindling; poles crossed each other. I could see shelves with clothes
and books and glass jars. Wood smoke and something lemony tickled my
nose. I crawled in. Jo butted me with his head.

PETER STAG

I see him inside the blanket and asleep in his chair, still counting his blessings
after being kicked by a horse a few weeks earlier. A few inches higher or lower
and it might have been curtains. On a rainy day in Machynlleth – the sus-
tainable capital of Wales – he walks red-hooded and there is something of the

gravity stillness in his face and bearing, an acceptance of the warpy wefts in his life. Peter Stag speaks with his nose; it trembles as he thinks, a long face, a long nose, eyes slightly set back and with the habit of switching sideways when thinking. Out come the words from the mirror of his face. This story is characteristic of him and it's about his cat Lily. 'She looks after me,' he says. One day he is sitting in his caravan off a mountain road when he hears a car pull up. He's not expecting visitors and so his ears are on full alert. It's an official car without any mud, and there's a man in a suit and with a briefcase and a brief face. He knocks on the door. Peter opens it dressed in his baggy jumper and loose trousers.

'You live here?' asks the man.

'Yes.'

'Not much longer. You've got to go. This caravan is illegal.' He reads out the rules: the caravan has no licence. It's there in black and white. His face is expressionless, wired for confrontation.

Peter says: 'This caravan has been here for 25 years. I'll apply for a right of lawful purpose.' The man nods knowingly. 'You know the rules. It's true we cannot tow the caravan away, but do you have a residential licence?'

'No.'

'Then you'll have to go.'

'I'll apply.'

'I can assure you, you will not get it. And who owns this land?'

'The farmer.'

'We'll investigate him too.' The tension drips between them. And here it might have ended, except enter Lily, Peter's Irish cat. She leaps from the floor and crawls up the sleeve to peep out from his shoulder. She starts purring and Peter strokes her. The man puts down his briefcase.

'I'm sorry I've been so officious. I really thought you were going to hit me.'

'Me, hit you,' laughs Peter. 'I'm not the type.'

'What a lovely cat,' says the man. He strokes her while Lily purrs. They talk of this and that, but still the rules are rules, you understand. But the tension evaporates. After that Peter never hears anything more about the matter.

(Chipping Sodbury, January 8, 1999)

I was on a platform floor built from pallets with carpets and piles of cushions. A tilly lamp glowed in the middle space, hanging from a wire and flaring shadows across the canvas. There were pots and pans, jars packed into boxes, and more boxes stacked on each other. A kettle simmered on a rusty black stove with four legs. The heat had melted Jack Frost from the windows but not the picture of frozen grasses like an old-fashioned

148

Christmas card, icy on the outside with fire within. A piece of glass dangled by the window, and the slowly spinning rainbow circling the canvas wall belonged to it.

I watched its progress until Tugger leaped up yelping from the shadows. I held him tight. I clipped on the chain. 'Got you! You won't get away from me now.'

'That's mine.'

I said nothing.

'That's my rainbow.' Her face emerged from the smoke, a girl surrounded by cushions all prettily patterned and made from patchwork.

'I'm sorry, I should have knocked.'

'You can't touch a rainbow. You have to go under it. Nobody can own a rainbow.'

She sat propped inside a chair of three cushions with a board across her lap. On it were a wooden bowl and cup, and two packets wrapped in Father Christmas paper. She patted them.

'I mustn't open them until Christmas. I promised.' She had big eyes and there were holes in her jumper. Her hair was tied into several plaits and they were joined by a red and yellow ribbons. 'I don't know what's inside.'

'I like surprises,' said Jo, now perched inside on his hands and knees like some gigantic armadillo. 'It's nice in here.' She put her hand over her mouth.

'You!...You got my letter?' And in a higher voice. 'It's *you*!'

'I like biscuits best.'

'It really is.'

'Ginger biscuits.'

'I don't believe it.'

'Like teddy bears.'

'How did you find me? Where are the reindeer?'

'But without any arms or legs.'

I said quickly: 'Father Christmas visits all the children who write to him. Don't you?... Your hat is falling off, Father Christmas.' I adjusted his red bobbly hat. 'Please come in, Father Christmas.' A smile went round his face.

'Me...Father Christmas.'

'You mustn't tell anyone,' I said to the girl. 'It's our secret.' She tilted her head. She was thinking.

'You're early. It's still two days to Christmas.'

'I love Christmas.'

'You must be busy.'

'All the cakes...'

'He starts early. He has to see everybody.'

'Who writes him a letter?'

I knew what she was thinking. 'He can't do it all himself. That's why I help him.'

'But where's your sack?'

'He's left it in the woods.'

'In the woods...' repeated Jo.

'I'll cry if you go.'

'We've got to get back.'

'To the reindeer?'

'The reindeer...'

'It's very cold in snowland.'

'In the woods...'

'They're tired and need biscuits.'

Jo pulled a ginger biscuit from his pocket and gave it to the girl.

'It's got a sad face and no arms. It doesn't want to get eaten.'

She leaned forward. 'I've seen your friends. They come when I'm sleeping and that's why nobody thinks they're there. They're shy. One scratched her little fingers at the flap last night. Dad said it was a badger looking for the oat-flakes, but I knew.'

She pulled the blanket over her shoulders and pulled a serious face.

'Are you all right?'

She said nothing.

'You're not, are you?'

'I'm sick.' She coughed a nasty rattling cough. 'My doll beat me at draughts today.'

I didn't believe her.

DUTCH NIGHTINGALES

Everywhere you go in Holland, if you listen carefully, you will hear the twanging laughter beside the road, down in the ditch and in the wet, still places. It's the golluping gurglers, fat green frogs hanging in the clear water, blowing bubbles or staring at the roots glittering in the sunlight. Or just sunbathing with their backs clear of the water, perhaps with one eye on the road or other frogs. Sometimes they stretch out their legs and float closer together. Then one croons and croaks and the others laugh a little meanly. Perhaps they are telling another bad, toady joke.

'Did you hear the one about the wide-mouth toad?'

'All toads are big mouths.'

'Ha ha ha hee hee hee yacketty yak!'

'He puffs up and says in a deep voice, "I'm the wide-mouth toad." He says that to everyone he meets.'

'That's a toad for you. Talk talk talk and they never say anything.'

'Ha ha ha hee hee hee yacketty yak!'

'One day he meets a heron. He puffs himself up, "I'm the wide-mouth toad," he says in his deep voice.'

'I like fat and juicy wide-mouth toads,' says the heron.

'The toad screws up his mouth. He squeaks, "You don't see many of those around here.'

'Ha ha ha hee hee hee yacketty yak!'   (Groningen, May 16, 1997)

THE PIKE

The pike surfaced in my thoughts in Friesland. Two years previously I had shared, for one night, a camping barn in Yorkshire with twenty teenagers, all apprentice gamekeepers. The evening unwound to a melody of emptying beer cans, expletives and farts and stories free-falling from one girlfriend to another through a fog of tobacco. I'm exaggerating but not much. I listened, as I had to. There wouldn't be a moment's silence, but I was wrong. The biggest bloke, best at the manly bluff and guff, started talking about the lake they had just visited and speculated about the trout, the tench, the pike...yes, the pike. His voice dropped, and they listened. He had heard stories about the old pike in the blue claypit at home and how big it was. He baited a corner for a week without taking his rod. He knew how to wait. We could see him creeping along the bank, sliding silently against the willow and concealed in khaki by the reeds. Time and again he trailed his spinner backwards and forwards, effortlessly tracing his words before us. The mosquitoes began to bite, but he didn't move. Backwards and forwards, again and again. Something nudged his spinner, mouthed it thoughtfully. He sensed it. He hardly dared to breathe. His hand stayed steady. He felt the resistance. Wait for it. They understood this hunting game. They respected the gaps in his words. The camping barn became a deep pool of silence. He struck! The tremors ran through us. Nothing happened. Then a single ripple travelled across the pool. Our mouths opened. The line went dead. He wound it in. The metal trace had gone, and so had the pike.   (Groningen, May 15, 1997)

OFF MY ROCKER

The Frenchman was drunk. Once out of the bottle his words boomed over the small talk of the restaurant in Sigmaringen subduing the Germans eating

151

dennetle, a Swabian version of pizza. 'Vive La France!' he shouted and said
it again. Once he must have been a handsome man, full mettled in the arms
and legs, and long in his face and also in his hair. He could have been a
Viking chieftain but alcohol had puffed out his cheeks and reddened his eyes.
They had a wandering intensity, on the bottle, on the waiter, anything which
caught his attention. 'Liberte, Fraternite, Egalite!' I kept my head down,
English phlegm or is it cowardice? I heard the high-pitched laughter, saw the
knowing winks among the other customers. He heard my English accent.
'Anglais! A Good Place!' He staggered over to my table cradling his beer. I
collapsed with my smile, the first line of defence. The owner intervened and his
words were firm as his feet. The Frenchman challenged me to a 30-kilometre
race. 'You will win,' I said. 'There is no contest.' He swayed on his legs and
out came more gibberish French. I offered my hand. He gripped it as if he were
drowning. The associations come easily: the barricades, a man out of his depth,
and me too. What could I say to bridge these worlds? I'm off my rocker, again.

'It's Krakenfartus!'
'What?'
'I don't believe it! Krakenfartus is here. Krakenfartus! Krakenfartus! You've
come to save us. Ring out the bells!'
'But...'
'The Most Holy Fart. The scriptures said: 'He will arrive on a great puff of
wind...'
'But, but...'
'On his back will be three yellow crosses... He will come on burning wheels.'
'That's my day-glo jacket. The idea is to be a big insect and...'
'Krakenfartus! Bless us with the holy wind. It is said: 'Who knows where the
wind comes from, and where it goes?'
'But, but, but...'
'Krakenfartus! Speak to us!'
'You've asked for it. On your knees you sinners. I'll blast you to eternity.'

* * *

'And is it true that Transdanubians eat grasshoppers for breakfast?
– Wear red knickers on Sundays?
– Make drums out of their grandmother's skin?
– Drink blood instead of coffee?
– Loan their wives to honoured guests?
(He smiled at this one.)
– Balance knives on their tongues?'
'But there must be some mistake.

We thought the English did this.'

* * *

'Hello Mr Racing cyclist.'
'You microbe on wheels. Say hello to me? What's the weather like down there? Can't you see this lycra? Do you know how much it cost? You can't think. I can see that. This stuff's expensive, more than you can dream...You're with Triceratops, ankle clips and cap. I was like you, once. A long time ago. I can't stop. Can't you see? I'm going somewhere.'

* * *

'Hey you cyclo freaks! No more adrenaline wipe-outs. Erase those traffic queues. Fast-wind those mind-bending hills. Eliminate zero brain-cell drivers. Teach them respect. Be in charge with Proton Dissembler. Laser-beam technology helping you to get ahead. Guaranteed karma free.
Simple as abc. Load alpha trance rays. Systems GO! Wait for that hill. Search target. Steady. Let those tracer lights converge. Fire! Miss? Try again. Hit? Locks on. Relax, enjoy the views. Let them pull you up the hill. When host is exhausted, disengage and search new one. Have a good day.'

* * *

Don't let motorists get up your nose. Beam that smug arse to Uranus. Reassemble that bimbo on Stratofartus — the galactic centre for fungus production. Hot heads? Cool them off on Icebergus-3 (average rush hour temperatures -47C). Send them to asteroid delta Z31762 smack in that 10 mile jam, average temperatures 65C. Simple as ABC. Select planet of your choice — 10 to choose from — with Proton Dissembler. Load alpha trance rays in Real Time. Choose target. Evaluate options, select planet of your choice. Choose delay function for a discreet getaway. They won't know what zapped them!

* * *

At night I lie in bed. I can see you smiling, grossen fartenbugger. I can see them coming. Their hairy legs and sharpened teeth. It wasn't me. I didn't do it. I'm not smiling. They creep up the blanket. They can't fool me. Wait for it. Let me see their eyes, damn them. Yes here's the big gun grossenrottenbürgerenfarten! They put on their gas masks. Too late. I blast them off the edge.
I'm off my rocker again.

She whistled through her teeth. 'You're a silly Father Christmas. No wonder it takes you yonks.' She was practical. 'Pour me tea and we'll think where you left it.' She broke off the head. 'Where then?'
'By the railings.'

153

She pretended to write it down. 'Before or after?'

'After what?'

'After!'

'Before?'

'Yes.' She closed her hands, nodding her head firmly. She informed Father Christmas of the names of her friends. Then a terrible thought clouded her eyes. 'But you MUST find it. We're going on Christmas Day. To says it will be quiet then.'

'To?'

'My dad. The only one I've got.' She pointed to a rolled bundle of matting. 'He sleeps there. He's gone to fetch medicine. Do you like porridge? To makes porridge every day whether I like it or not.'

'I love apples, biscuits and cheese. I can live off that my whole life. I'm very hungry.'

She pulled the corners of her blanket tightly across her shoulders, saying nothing, just staring out.

'You ARE sick.'

'You don't go to school?'

She whistled long and slow. The flap opened and a ginger ball of fluff crept in, rearing up at the sight of Tugger. 'Here beaut.' The cotton tail wriggled over the cushions and disappeared under the cover to reappear inside her jumper and beside her neck.

'Dad likes ginger cats,' said Jo. 'He gave me one as a present.'

'Is he an old Father Christmas?'

'He's a long way away. Granny says we'll all meet again one day.'

The girl turned her face so the kitten could only lick her ear. Their faces were side by side. They both had blue eyes.

GRANADA

I had a premonition about cats and Granada. I had no reason for it; every-where in Andalucia I had encountered dogs, little tigers dozing on doorsteps, brow-beaten street dogs, wild dogs (and they like chasing cyclists), demented ones on chains inside fenced compounds. I disliked their owners. But Granada was different; in Sacramonte the fat cats sat patiently outside the fish shop; people left plates of food by tumbledown houses. In the Alhambra gardens a posse of stray cats posed for tourists and picked out the soft touches. Two trailed me through the rose walks, taking short cuts to suddenly appear two steps above me. Another dropped down from a persimmon tree and brazenly blocked my way; expertly they prized crumbs from my fingers. The Moors came and went but the cats stayed. They are the inheritors of the palace; they drink from the patio pools, slink in and out without glancing at the famous craftsmanship in plaster, pebble and clay brick. They know the right steps along the monumental ramparts and delicate interiors, past the fountains, ignore no-entry signs and take their private walk around the Generalife Palace. They walk past the four-star visitors in fur coats and a personal interpreter. They are nothing compared to a sardine boccadillo. I gave one to a cat and she separated out the vertebrae and thanked me by rolling on her back. This is what she wants.

(Granada, February 2, 1996)

'Sparkler's not frightened is he?' The rainbow moved slowly across the dark side of the canvas and onto her blanket. Jo tried to touch it but it slid through his fingers. 'To says that the road we're travelling goes under a rainbow even if we can't see what's on the other side.'

'Father lived in a house like this, sand, water in buckets, and you could see the stars outside. You have to enjoy your life, take things as they come. He's always thinking about me. There will be two big rooms, one for him and one for me. I can go there anytime I want. Biscuits?'

'You've eaten them all.'

'I liked the balloons best. The big table with jellies and biscuits. The best presents were at the bottom of the sand.' A sudden clockwork noise whirred inside a fold of canvas and then scuttled over our heads. Another one followed quickly.

'Mice,' she said without looking up.

'Mice don't come indoors.'

'They're short-tailed voles. They haven't got a tail.'

'Do they get presents?'

'Only if they write a letter,' I said. 'Father Christmas is very busy. We must go.'

She changed her thoughts like Sarah changes her dresses. 'They say that the dead wood will fall but we'll be all right. The wind will blow it away. The trees will stand. They say that we'll be going soon and we are. They don't like us here. A man told us to go. He thinks we'll steal his land but no-one can steal land, can they? We'll go in the night and only the owls will know.'

'Aren't you afraid,' I said, 'to go somewhere and not know where it is? You might get lost.'

'Silly! We can't get lost. All roads lead back home, that's what To says.'

'I've heard of a ladybird but I've never heard of a manly bird.'

'I live too near a wood to be scared by owls.'

'I like parakeets. They look at life with a good attitude, think about things logically, you can see that.'

'Where do you live?'

'It's a secret. Father Christmas doesn't tell anyone, do you?'

Jo pressed his finger to his lips.

'I'll visit you.'

'You have to write a letter first.'

She jumped up, the cat leaped up screeching. 'Tiger's got me! Tiger's got me!'

'I'm not frightened of tigers. GRRRRR,' said Jo.

'They do rolypoly backwards. I got no more kisses.'

I squatted half in, half out.

'Do owls say what's at the end of roads?'

She switched her eyes left and right. 'That's what the owls say.'

She didn't say goodbye, neither did we.

The Glasshouse

"Outside is a silver stick stuck into the ground, and holding the silver stick . . . is Shiva."

I've promised myself that if a car goes by I'll go outside and light a fire below the embankment. One Christmas I did just that and had the fright of my life. A ball of flame wider than my outstretched arms rolled down the lane and suddenly came through the hedge on this side of the field. I wanted to run but I walked towards it. I knew I would be more scared if I ran away. Fire. That's the baby! I am frightened of fire. [In fact it was the Jack-o'-lantern, the spontaneous combustion of marsh gas.] Every time I leave my house I think: have I turned everything off, is a flame burning? Fire is the missing element in my life. I am scared of starting something. It's safer not to be seen, to stay on the inside.

SCHIERMONNIKOOG

The dolls are here beside my bed, all kinds from ragged teddy bears to little girls with flaxen locks and blue eyes, neat fringes and pigtails plaited to meet at the back. A mother's collection, and she had to point out the two dolls with the white pinafores and long-sleeved dresses without decoration. They had no faces, that's why I hadn't seen them. They were the Mennonite girls, The Plain People from the States, radical Protestants who believed, among other things, in house churches and baptism later in life. Their dolls were not allowed faces as only God could give a face. They were beside my bed because this village – Ieslumbuorren in Friesland – is only a few kilometres from Witmarsum and Pingjum where Menno Simons, a one-time Catholic priest, was born and where he had preached. In 1536 he joined the Anabaptists (The Re-baptisers) in Holland, and he ranted so well against the follies of the Mother church that other Protestants called themselves by his name. I know the face of a Mennonite, a courageous woman who found a new life for herself by marrying a Senegalese, a million miles away from her home in the Mid-West. She wrote me this poem:

> Nectar of love
> Nectar on the wind

Pulls the bees
Overflowing sweet colour.
Harvest of pollen
The seeds of life are created;
Plants cover the earth
So I may inhale the nectar of life.

I put away this doll and let the island of Shiermonnikoog come into view, a silver sand dune 15 kilometres long, five at the widest. It's one of the Wadden islands off North Holland. I went there with the De Ymkers – Frisian for beekeepers – a company of grandfathers, silver hair to match the sand, laughter and wrinkles, and still with sturdy legs – Gerrit, Jaap, Bram, Germ; from Leeuwarden, Dokkum and Harlingen. For a day they accepted me into their secret world of breeding Carneolian queen bees, a gentle bee from the mountains of Montenegro. That isolation has bred tolerance into their nature, unlike African bees which sting freely as they have to fight for survival. No other bees are allowed on Shiermonnikoog, so the strain can breed true; the island is too far for stranger drones.

Early in the morning they lead me along a path into a hollow ringed by dunes and sea buckthorn. The 36 hives in the corrugated shed – the bee stable – are silent. They open the hatches, don their white overalls and work from behind, silently together. They work in slow motion, brief and dextrous movements, breaking waxy bonds and easing off the sections, puffing a cheroot or smoking pendulous pipes to announce their arrival. Their bare fingers examine the combs, each one a ripening sunflower of bees. The queens are easy to see by the number painted onto their head. They pick up bees by their wings, skills a thousand years old. Still there are unanswered questions: Who decides when the Queen will swarm? Or when to fertilise a female worker?

The men transfer combs from busy hives, putting newspapers between the combs so they have to chew through them, so the smells can intermingle. 'But there are some papers the bees don't like,' says Bram knowingly. His shirt pocket buzzes with a queen in a bee cage and a dab of honey, behind a sliding glass door. 'Sometimes I sleep with the Queen,' he tells us, and we laugh at that. All the time they make notes on small white cards. If the Queen is dead or missing then the hive will die in a month or two. 'At one time some beekeepers said: "We should have Dutch bees." This is how Mr Hitler thinks. It will take us back 50 years.'

At tea break Bram identifies a nightingale singing in a bush; the steady trills and ricocheting note is the rare Icterine warbler. The grandfathers listen. I listen to the monstrous humming of some half-a-million bees on the move, each one on razor-line trajectories in and out of the hives. It's a bee storm. The men change and pack their bags. The path out is on the other side of the bees. I will have to go that way. I am terrified, but I have no choice. I walk very slowly through them, the bees miraculously getting out of my way.

I walked alone to the Bad Strand and entered the world of sea mist and silver sand, a gigantic illusion where perspectives fail; a few sticks ten metres away could be a family group with toddlers. I remembered the faces of my paternal, British grandparents; their hard lives, lines set by necessity, a rocky earthiness in their speech and affections. Perhaps it is dangerous to show needs or feelings, perhaps there is a great silence. The other side of my grandparents must be an exaggerated tenderness, an exaggerated longing...For what? All my life I have lived with these extremes. This is my world. What is my true face, the one that is Given?   *(Ieslumbuorren, May 16, 1997)*

TALBOT HOUSE, POPERINGE

The white doves step down the branches of the copper beech, soft and pink lights in their eyes, on the silver bark, everywhere this late spring afternoon. They are sturdy doves nosing the earth and disdain my proffered hand. At the back of the lawn is the big white house with shuttered windows, a colonial sense of quieter, more spacious days. I had wanted to visit Poperinge, 'Old Pop' to the quarter of a million soldiers billeted in this part of Flanders in the First World War. I wanted to see what my grandparents' generation had lived through. Slim hopes of that. The Flander's mud is famous for its cereals.

It would be futile to use words to stretch that nightmare. They would not help me to see the faces, mainly young faces like my eldest son. I cannot walk away when I see his face. I'm involved now. I want to understand.

Providence brought me to Talbot House, and I was grateful. Once inside I stepped back to 1918, an aunty's nest of brocades and flowers, reassuring interiors of thick carpets or terracotta tiles; hand-painted signs say, 'Come upstairs and risk meeting the chaplain', or 'Be reasonable, do it my way'. Slowly some pieces of a jigsaw fit. On the walls are water-colours, moon craters filled with mist as far as you can see. It's Passchendaele Ridge 1918; there are sketches of gunners lighting a fag in the trenches; going over the top was like falling over a precipice, someone said.

This house had been Everyman's Club in Poperinge, the nearest safe town to Ypres's Salient battles. 'Tubby' Clayton, an army chaplain, had set up this club as an alternative to the booze and prostitutes. Life expectancy on the front line was only three days. This home from home for the soldiers was popular; in one ten-minute period a hundred soldiers were clicked in; the lawn by the copper beech would be covered with khaki, the men lounging like lizards in the shelter of high walls. They could 'Come into the garden and forget the war' as the sign says. They must have worshipped this garden as their heaven.

The magic touched me too; the same piano in the corner, the huddle of figures in the painting around the pianist, the gleaming eyes and moustaches beneath the caps, an intense camaraderie, a terrifying consciousness of life fleeting and beautiful as mayflies. I accepted like a child that this experience of camaraderie – Talbot House uniquely defied the rigid class structure of the Army – would be the inspiration for the Toc H movement after the war, peace and reconciliation cutting across society. Those who survived would count these moments in the garden or a silent prayer in the improvised chapel in the attic as the unconditional acceptance of a human being regardless of rank. It would be the golden thread from a war which had destroyed their idealism, shattered their homes and families.

I cycled to Passchendaele on wheels of expectation, as if by visiting the craters where the 'Burnley Masher Boys' counted their lives in minutes I would exorcise a grieving, uncomprehending part of me. I lost my way among the cereals and glasshouses, wandered with a few living figures at the surreal garden cemeteries for the many who had died. Slowly the energy drained from my limbs until I was held by an immense futility. What could I say? What could give any meaning to this? Troubled sleep, troubled digestion and then the boar arrived in my dreams, the classic signal of descent. I perspired with images. One kept returning, the image of being underground, hidden where no-one can see me. 'I am safe' is the thought. I can peer out through a little hole and see long distances. The enemy is out there. If I stay still they might not even know I am here. At least I am alive, I think so. I have returned to this place in my life, dreamed myself there in times of danger. Protection, this is a dark thread with my grandparents. It's dangerous to stand up, you're a target.

Jacques Ryckebosch is the amiable guide at Talbot House who uses words so they stick to your ears. 'People think the Great War was eighty years ago. We saw it three years ago in Bosnia. A woman from Sarajevo visited. She could not take the tour of the battlefields but she found hope in the pictures of Ypres. If they can rebuild that, she told me, then they can rebuild Sarajevo. I could not tell her that they very nearly did not rebuild Ypres.' He talks to a group of Belgian schoolchildren. He makes them laugh, there are silences as they listen. Yes, they listen. In a bombardment during the 3rd Battle of Ypres four million shells were fired in a matter of weeks. 'There were young German students facing professional soldiers from Australia and South Africa. They survived like rats dug in 12 metres under the clay, sometimes 120 to a small hole. There are some mass graves with 9000 German soldiers in them.'

Did they know that they were pawns in the greater, imperial power game of Germany, France, Italy, Britain, the USA? 'This made the war inevitable.' Then there was the shame and revenge of the French after their Franco-Prussian defeat. The same story with Germany after the First World War.

'The War destroyed the old aristocracy, helped women into work — for many were on their own — and after working in the munitions' factories they wanted a career. The war taught people basic humanity. They're the same stories of comradeship in the techno Gulf war.' Ignorance, greed ('a lot of people make money out of wars') and naïvety are causes of wars, says Jacques. 'We need to listen to each other. I am Belgian, Flemish with my own mentality, and I can still have an open mind to others.'

I want to take the wrappers off my mind. I want to see the doves step down the branches, the soft and pink lights in their eyes, their sturdy feet on the ground as they nose the soil. (Poperinge, May 6, 1997)

You pay for everything of course. I should have kept my big mouth shout, and who could keep the words in granny's mouth? 'You promised, and don't blame Tugger. He's only a dog. He might have been run over like your badger.' We had no answer to that, and it was no use arguing. 'It's too fantastic, a girl living in the wood under a canvas, and at Christmas. It's like a fairy story. She'll die of cold. It's true what the Colonel says about these gypsies, they have no sense of responsibility.'

She fetched a small white box from her bag, saying it was time for his iron pills. 'He gets tired so easily. And he needs his extra vitamin supplements and charcoal tablets for down there — but we won't talk about that.'

'That's not me,' said Jo, 'that's the Crackalump. I'll catch him if it's the last thing I do.' He peered under the table, behind the door, winking at us. 'He's crafty, he is.' Jo opened his mouth while granny popped in the tablets.

It's hard telling this story because of the things I have to leave out. Little things seem important, the way he watched the balloons with his mouth open and rolling his eyes, his neck full of creases, not a boy's neck; the way he looked down at the floor when he was thinking or rubbed his hands together when excited; or how he flicked back his eyes when surprised. It's the little things I remember, the fragments of conversations. Once Sarah opened the bathroom door and saw him standing in the airing cupboard with his back to her. 'What are you doing?'

'I'm seeing what's inside.'

'But why did you shut the door?'

'That's what you do with doors. You shut them.'

'Silly!' said Sarah. 'You open them too.'

In front of the full-length mirror, Jo stepped between us, standing taller and staring straight ahead as if we were in a photograph I had never seen before. 'My big ears. I don't like them. They stick out.'

'They're composer's ears.'

'Mine are titchy.'

'They can see in the dark.'

'Like an owl.'

Jo had to bend double to climb the narrow staircase to our bedroom. Halfway up he got stuck and my stomach ballooned as if I were trapped too and there was no way out of this. I always felt trapped in narrow places. This time I knew what to do and I picked up a foot. Jo said the steps would fall away if I let go. I put his foot onto the next step and the one after that until he got going. He was a giant in that top room, his head scraping the ceiling; he could almost touch both walls with his hands. It's how I saw him, stuck in his small room. First he tapped the mattresses as if he were looking for money and then he stroked his finger through the dustline on the wall. To our amazement, he found an earwig. He scooped it expertly into one hand and then opened one finger at a time. The earwig reared its pinchers aggressively at him.

'It's a very little earwig,' said Sarah. 'It must be a baby.'

'It can't be a baby,' I said. 'There aren't any babies here.'

Jo balanced it on his finger. 'Earwigs look after their babies. They take them for walks. The mother earwig will attack anything which comes near.' Sarah wiggled a finger on each side of her head and pretended to attack something. Then she exclaimed, 'But there was an earwig in your card.'

'You saw him.'

'With a golden helmet.'

'That's His messenger. He finds out what's happening and reports back.'

'His messenger?'

'To Shiva,' said granny entering the room. 'Isn't that so?' She had crept in like a mouse. 'Shiva comes in like that so that no-one can hear him. He's got lots of arms so he can do things at the same time. That's right, isn't it?'

'He combs out his rat tails with twelve of his fingers while his two left eyes look at the sky. He can spin those arms, like an engine, then raise them above his head and fly away. It's true.'

'He lives in a desert, with red sand...'

'Nothing except stones and sand, a blue sky.'

'In the middle of the desert...'

'In a glass house. He sits on a chair.'

'With his silver listening stick.'

'He can see for miles. He puts it in the ground. If it hums he knows someone's coming. He lives a long way away but I only have to whistle and he'll come. That's what he said.'

164

'Go on then,' said Sarah, sticking two fingers into her mouth. Out came nothing.

'It's a secret. I can only do it when I need him.'

'You remember everything,' said granny. 'J.P. repeater, says the same thing at least twice.'

'I just have to whistle.'

Straightaway she saw the picture against the wall, and she turned it the right way up and hung it properly. 'She can't hurt you, she's been dead a hundred years. I have never been good at throwing things away.'

'Who is she?'

'The Grand Gala Ball, by Invitation only. Introducing Bella, Queen for one night. I feel so old sometimes, I do. Perhaps it's her wedding dress. Perhaps she had been born below and wanted to live upstairs like a lady. We'll never know. What the eye doesn't see, the heart won't fret over.' She sank onto the bottom bunk and signalled us to do the same. 'This is what we wanted, to be together.'

'Like sardines.'

'In the sea! Shiva likes the seaside.'

Granny had that contented look of knowing what to do. 'One day Shiva walked along the beach. He took his swimming trunks, three pairs of goggles, eight flippers and four pairs of sand shoes. He wore his brightest orange shorts and put on three pairs of sunglasses so no-one would recognise him. He had the beach to himself. He made forty-eight sand castle at the same time and paddled all his legs in the sea. There were lots of crabs. They followed him everywhere.

'Did they keep saying, "Dada" and blowing big bubbles?'

'When he sat down there wasn't enough ice-cream to go round. The bubbles, millions of them, were very hungry so they followed him along the pier. The people at the end kept diving off the sides. He wondered why, especially as there was no sea, only thick black mud. They were stuck in this mud waving their hands and legs. It must be a game thought Shiva and he dived off too. So did all the crabs. The people suddenly found their legs. Amazing! They were making the same high-pitched noise. How peculiar. They can dangle in the mud and then fly off. Perhaps they're feeding, thought Shiva. Then he had a kind thought. His 148 long skinny fingers, each with a sharp nail, dug into the mud and pulled out a wriggling sea worm. The crabs did the same. Then he ran after the people waving all his arms. His eight tongues – as long as red boot-laces – shouted, "Dinner!

Dinner!" The crabs did the same, "Dada Dada". The people ran very fast. He had no idea why. He wondered where they were going. It must be somewhere interesting.

'Shiva ran very fast, and so did the crabs and so did the people. They were very excited. Some ran out to sea, most ran to the end of the beach and onto the pier. They jumped off that when they saw Shiva coming. It must be a game, he thought. Others climbed over a high wall. 'I'll climb that too.' The crabs thought the same, 'Dada Dada.' Lots of people, very kindly, had made themselves into steps. Others scrambled up the wall onto the street. The street was deserted but the shops were full of people. How strange, and it's such a nice day outside. Shiva banged on the doors of four shops, all at once. 'Come out to play.' But no-one opened the doors or came out to play. Very odd. He thought he'd go for a bus ride, but the drivers had gone. Their buses were empty. "Never mind," thought Shiva. "I do like being by the seaside, don't you?"'

Once more the radiators broke into the silence and frozen lights appeared on the window. Winter was the shield, and here, on the inside, we were safe. Her words, spoken to nobody, brought us closer. 'There are stories and stories, and the best are the ones you never know if they're true or not. Sometimes we can see outside but we can't touch it. The glass is in the way but it keeps out the wind as well as the rain. What would we do without that? Once there was a boy who had the longest nails in the world. They curled over so far that they he could scratch his own wrist, if he had wanted to, or he could pick up coins from the cracks of floorboards. He had been lying in his bed so long that his hair had grown down his back, and he never washed it so it was always green and things grew in it. There was a skylight in his room and he could see a blue patch of sky. He could be anything he wanted, just by thinking about it: a bird, a greyhound or a sloth bear hanging upside down in a tree.'

'I've seen one in the zoo,' said Sarah. 'It looked like grandad.'

'Grandad wasn't a sloth.'

'Sometimes he balanced upside-down at the bottom of his bed. You or I would have died, but he could live on very little. His parents didn't know what to do. They paid a nurse to cook his meals, change his sheets and read him stories. He was alone a lot. Sometimes the walls and ceiling wobbled like fresh pastry. Nothing stayed still except a spider on a web by the window. The first day it sat there and never caught a fly. Then it crawled back into the corner. It crawled out the next morning and sat in the centre of the web all day. At night it climbed back slowly into its corner without catching a fly. He saw that. It did this day after day until one morning it didn't come out of its corner. The boy thought that it was dead until he saw the spider crawl out. He wanted that spider to live. So he got up and hunted for a fly to give to the spider, and from that moment he got better. He learnt to walk again and never looked back.'

'I like happy endings,' said Jo, 'I do.'

DANUBE WATERS

I am in this now beside the Danube where the evening songs swoop down to glassy water along with a single swallow. I wanted to find water, to settle this stirred-up part I name me, to find some peace and gravity at the end of this day. I fear I will try too hard to make sense and I will lose my way. A swan, with one foot sunbathing, sails into view. The Danube is out of a picture book, a blue line wiggling its way through Europe: Germany, Austria, Hungary, Yugoslavia, Romania, Bulgaria are tied to this line as are the coots, white spots moving in the shadows. Will that bit of wood end up in the Black Sea? Where will I end up? A mallard flies by, going somewhere. I want to be going somewhere. Last night I dreamed : 'I am at Auschwitz again. I have made a fruitcake but the Germans are trying to take it away from me. I ranted at my parents because they wouldn't let me eat the fruitcake.' *I make little sense of it. With every preen and paddled turn of the swan, perfect circles travel across the water. Is it possible (and I wish it is) that with every touch and strange turn of living there will be these perfect ripples? The water understands. Here in this domain everything finds its place.*

Happiness cycled with me out of Tuttlingen. A thousand scents and sounds and play of weather and none could I name or point to. I looked out of the Dark Ages in black shorts and shoes and dayglo orange jacket and my white baseball cap. Everyone — and the cyclists appeared miraculously on this Danube cycleway — were out in a rash of lycra. I could see the hush patrolling their faces, the sideways look of the eyes said it all. Is it possible that what I see is true? Like the alsations they looked through me and past me to some secret place in the jutting outcliffs of limestone. With this middle-aged face, with lines sometimes strained or laughing, with my green-blue eyes, I am coming home into the world. I am always saying there is a lot of fruitcake in Bath. Today, for the first time, I say: 'I am fruitcake.' *I like the sound of that, for fruits are at the end of journeys.*

The missel thrushes strike their ratchets, the lone swan still makes ripples. I am fruitcake. Why else would I be sitting here and alone with these words? There is a bell chiming at Sigmaringen, the missel thrushes hammer out their notes, small birds come into my ears along with children's voices speaking German. This is a strange language, I can't follow it.

(Sigmaringen, May 9, 1998)

EXCUSE ME

A woman – with the basket over her shoulder – appeared at the top of the steps. Behind her trailed an older woman clutching her arm, then two middle-aged men holding each other's hands. They sat beside me in the thatched hut to enjoy the shade and a clear view of the alpine waterfall. Years ago I had called them mongoloid. The minder passed a hot drink to the older man with the Michael Jackson T-shirt. He put out his hand but the woman behind him took it first. He stared at his empty hand, clutched the air and pretended to drink. No-one noticed, except me. The minder passed a tin of cakes. The old man rattled the tin. The girl took the tin and passed it back. He shook the tin and listened. There was no sound. Not once did anyone look at me. But I understood. They were just ordinary people.

(Botanska Traigard, Goteborg, June 6, 1997)

TOO GOOD TO BE TRUE (A Cautionary Tale)

Too Good To be True wanted a man but no man wanted her. That was what her neighbours called her: 'She's nice but too good to be true.' That's what they said behind her back.

Picture a forest beside a white house and a terracotta roof. Across both ends are ladders to stop the snow falling onto the path. Here lives a woman by herself, not young or yet old, but in those middle years. She draws pictures to make a living. Her favourite subjects are the elves and goblins and old hags and wizards and cherubic dragons and baby mice. It is a world of dark woods and short days where vegetables are hard to grow and where wolves and bears and worse are never far away in your mind. Perhaps, she thinks sometimes, that's why she likes the forest.

She is careful about what she eats: no beans ('Do you really need to know?'); no sugar ('bad for her teeth'); or meat ('How can anyone eat a dead animal?'); or drink tea ('It's a stimulant'); no onions or mushrooms ('They give me bad thoughts'), and alcohol is out. She drinks only mineral water and flower teas ('preferably weak'), and eats dry black bread with every meal of boiled vegetables.

White is her favourite colour: the curtains are white, the carpets are white and so are the plates and the dried flowers in the vase. No TV or radio disturbs her peace, or polluted city air. To tell the truth, she is afraid of cities, the noise, all those people. If her neighbours are conservative and family-minded, at least she is glad of her privacy. Her main vices are butter and cream and home-made bread she makes each evening for the yeast to rise overnight.

Every day after breakfast of muesili and dark bread and honey, she cleans the corners of her home, polishes the plates, stacks them in the fly-proof cupboard. Her house is spotless. A pin could see its reflection; flies landing on the polished table skid and fall over the side. But the more beautiful her house looks, the heavier she feels. She does not know why. Sometimes she has no energy to climb up the stairs or to fetch a log from the back of the house. No man could love her like this. How she wanted to be held! She longed for a man to love her but he would have to be strong to lift her. A BIG man she could lean against, who would never let her down. Each night she took Miss Bear to bed with her; though she is big and bear is small, in the darkness it did not matter. For three years she lived alone with her work, her beautiful house and sometimes she dreamed. It was always the same dream, standing by the door of a castle, in a long white dress with flowers on it and a little boy is by her side. Her husband arrives in a large car. He is a tall, strong man and puts his arms around her. She wants someone who can hold her as if she is light, as light as a feather or a mouse.

Now one day she finds a dark grain on Miss Bear's pinafore. She knows immediately. Mouse shit! She throws Miss Bear against the wall and stamps the floorboards until her breath becomes hot and full of thoughts, and they are not nice. The following day she sees a mouse boldly cross the floor while she is busy at her desk. It stops and combs its whiskers. She stamps her feet again and this time out comes roaring. That scares her. She sits trembling on the edge of her seat holding Miss Bear. Next morning she drives to the city and buys a trap, one which catches the mice alive, and she puts it beside the floorboard. Crack!! The mouse is busy eating the pumpkin seeds. She releases it into the forest behind her house. The next evening she catches two more but one is a baby lying in a nest of hair and droppings and dust. She cannot tip it into the forest, so she makes a home from a shoebox and fills it with straw, food and an egg-cup of water. First she keeps it in her wood-shed, then in the hall and finally in her bedroom. She notices how attached they become to their home, running back into the box if she places them outside. She talks to the mouse, 'No man wants me'. It twiddles its whiskers as if thinking. This makes her laugh, and she likes that. She sings them a song:

'Three little angels all dressed in white
Tried to get to heaven on the end of a kite
But the kite end was broken
Down they all fell,
Instead of going to heaven
They all went to hell.'

And so we make connections: it was granny who told the stories, peopled Jo's mind with the strange characters which he believed walked or flew by his side. But how can a silver earwig and a monster who could come at a moment's notice be important? There's a big rabbit on the wall. I can move it with my fingers, make it say 'Hello' or 'I'm watching you'. A shadow follows it whichever way it goes. That's what happens when it's in front of a light. I have to face up to it. I am on my own. I never thought I would grow up like this, be talking to myself in the top room of an old signal box. They say every man needs protection. Protection from what? I would like to fall back to the comfort of family life. I would like my wounds attended to by a woman, but I would just be part of a long sorrowing line of men. I am out here now. Sometimes the way forwards is hard to see even when you know the right direction. I am sitting in the bend of a road and if I look left I know where I've come from but I can't see very far. And there's a bend ahead and I can't see around that. That's what this road is like. I have to walk it to find out.

In the evening Sarah sat in the high-backed chair sharing it with the basket and the balls of wool she unravelled to finish a jumper. Slowly and rhythmically she knitted like granny does, not looking at it but over the top as if she were really thinking about something else. *Are there more earwigs than stones, more stones than bananas, more bananas than monkeys?* Questions you could never answer. Jo kept touching the kindling and taking away his hand as if it were alight. He said he had never lit a fire by himself or struck a match as it was forbidden. Mr Jackson, the gardener, had to light the fires outside. Sometimes on wet days he got stuck by bending down and the nurses had to carry him back to the house, two at each end. We rolled up the newspaper like granny had showed us – granny's firelighters – and you had to fold them into long strips and plait them together to make these paper crackers which burnt the kindling. Then I showed him how to split the wood with the cleaver and keep your fingers. I remembered grand-father's words. 'Don't put on too much wood or the air can't get in. Little by little, small burns big; a fire needs lots of air. You build it bit by bit, nothing is wasted, and on top of that you put the coal. If you can see the flames then the heat is escaping; it's got to go into the coal. And don't stare into the fire too long, you might forget who you are or where you are going.' Jo's fingers quivered excitedly, his mouth dropped open and nothing, nothing could keep his eyes from the match. One he struck, then twice and nothing happened. I slipped my hand onto his and we held the match together, his fingers gripping mine as if it were his life. I felt so much older and yet he was old enough to be my father. The third time the match flickered into flame and I steered his hand onto the paper.

'*I did it!*'

Whenever I was with Jo I felt free to speak what was in my mind, to laugh out loud and not care if it made sense. I could walk slowly, stop and stare with my mouth open or say boo to a fly, or say nothing. The fire could burn freely when he was with me. This is still a mystery. When we were together it was as if I were by myself, that he was me too, an impossible thing.

ONLY KNEELING IN MY MIND

I know where to start. Characteristically – on my way to the Tortworth Chestnut – I kept thinking of the candle which I had lit earlier this morning. The flame might be spreading, a conflagration out of control. It's all in my mind. This fear of fire which burns, gives heat, is here beside me. It is a fear of action, of being seen by others, to see the world through my eyes. I am perched under the cliff of this chestnut said to be ancient in the 12th century. A motorway drones over the hill. Underfoot the tips of snowdrops congregate, arums in small companies spread their sails. I wanted to come here, to this auspicious place, a place without signposts, in the far corner of a field beside the Church of St Leonard, and in the first part of the year. Leo the lion, the fire – is that what I am looking for? In fact this grove is one tree, old age reclining, leviathan seeking earth, submitting to gravity; and so slowly do the branches lean over. The mother tree rises above a thousand winters, twisting round, leaning on great elbows to see her offspring. They go in full motion, a youthful canopy to shelter their parent. There, I have said it. I am here now.

I wonder who planted this tree? Chestnuts came with the Romans. (The oldest trees in Britain are said to be coppiced chestnuts in Sussex with stools five metres across.) It is not a pretty tree; no-one, thankfully, tidies it up. Rains, winds and fungi dismember the old branches; antique moulds and grotesque outgrowths mock time. I wanted to see the bones, to come in mid-winter without dappled shade or kind lights. It matches how I am now, exposed and frightened of a candle flame. I tried to glimpse the faces behind my parents' faces, the many many winters of my maternal and paternal ancestors, marking time, as this tree does now.

This tree feeds itself from its leaves, the fallen branches; a cosmos of bacteria and fungi with impossible names does the rest. I cannot comprehend this activity, enclose it in my thoughts. I prefer to sit beside this tree. I am only kneeling in my mind.

'May Man Still Guard thy Venerable form
From the Nude blasts and Tempestuous Storm.
Till mayest thou Flourish through Succeeding Time
And Last, Long Last, the Wonder of the Clime.' *(Entrance plaque to grove)*
(Tortworth Chestnut, January 5, 1999)

He wanted to know more about the dead badger. 'At the beginning.'

I told him again what I knew. 'It's was a dead badger. You see them beside busy roads. I couldn't just walk away. It wasn't the badger's fault he couldn't look left or right.'

'Don't leave anything out.'

'I buried it under the willows, below the embankment. I covered it in leaves. I said: "Goodnight badger". That's all.'

'You didn't say that before,' said Sarah.

'I don't tell you everything.'

'You've left out things.'

'Saying goodnight to a dead badger?'

'That's important.'

'The little owl,' said Jo, 'did he say: "Out hunting?"' He tilted his head like a little owl does, and that made us laugh. He fingered the corners of his mouth: 'KKeeeeEE KKeeeeeEEEEEee!'

'It's like someone blowing fast through a comb.'

'Do it again.'

'KKeeeeEE KKeeeeeEEEEEee! When he's tired he sits in a tree, and the friend sits on his shoulders. He can see in the dark. Did Father Christmas point into the wood and say, "That's the way the badger went. Follow him".'

'I told you it was Father Christmas.'

'He was dressed in black.'

'It was night-time. And you can't follow him as you promised to be back for tea.'

'You keep saying that.'

'A promise is a promise. What would you do?'

'I don't know.'

'We should keep our promises otherwise no-one will believe us.'

'But sometimes you promise and it's not the right thing. You can change your mind. You might only have one chance.'

'Who says that?'

'That's the point! You don't know. And you still must make up your mind.'

'I'd go back home.'

'This might be your only chance.'

'You're breaking promises. No-one will believe you anymore. They'll call you a liar.'

'There's a right way and a wrong way. There's a reason for everything, even if we don't understand.'

'The trail might not be there tomorrow.'

'Dead badgers can't walk anyway.'

COLUMBE

Everywhere at Le Boistier – a dairy farm at Preaux-du-Perche – go the doves, kneading each other along the gutters or crooning their woody omens of contentment. This was once a manoir from pre-Revolution days but what with requisition and divisions and predatory time, the farmhouse is now modest and homely beside the milking barns and hay barns and animal feed mills. Dominating the main yard is an ancient round tower of squared Caen stone, a glory in its day but now half-tumbled and used as a diesel store. The peasants must have walled it up after the Revolution hoping that this act would cut the chains of a detested past. (Only the nobility could own doves and they fattened on the serf's holdings.) But the birds, I mused, could not forget so easily. Like the rabbits to their warren, it was the only home they knew. The doves still perch along the drip-line courses, cling to the sides where sparrows find homes in cracks. Or they step down the roof to dislodge the ones below, and do this over and over again.   *(Vendôme, April 30, 1998)*

There were no rules to this game; we played it as wild as fire. Jo may have been clumsy with his body but his mind was always ready. 'There were blue eyes and yellow eyes looking at me. "That's the way the badger went," said the old man. And the little owl screeched, "KKeeeeEE KKeeeeeEEEEEee!" '

'I followed the trail twisting under the trees,' I said. 'I had to find out now. I could not see the way. Ivy hung down from the trees, brambles scratched my legs. I came out between two big earth banks with old trees on top. The roots criss-crossed in front of me. I stepped over them and over them. I reached a wall covered in ivy, all that was left of one of the big houses.'

'There was a small door and light around it. It was. The badger's prints went under it. I touched the handle to stop my hand from trembling. I turned it open. I got down on my knees and crawled through.'

'And...'

'I saw light on grasses, going backwards and forwards. No-one had been here for a long time. I crawled through and stood up. I looked to my right. The light came from a funny, round house built onto the back of the wall. From a long narrow window...'

'Like a canary house?'

'Made of stone.'

'With parakeets crawling on the roof?'

'I wanted to run back. I was scared to be alone. Someone coughed behind me. I ducked and turned my head. The same old man! I could see his blue eyes just like you're looking at mine. The yellow eyes of the owl stared into mine.'

'Father Christmas.'

"What do you see?" he said, pointing his hand to the window. His voice was deep. The shadows ran around the walls. On the floor a candle burned, and behind that was the badger lying on its side, the legs turned towards me. Someone had brushed the dirt from the fur and wiped away the blood.'

'What did he say?'

'This badger lived in the wood before the new road. The badger that you found and buried was no ordinary badger. It was The Badger King.'

'Did he say, "Look after the badgers, help them?"'

'He did.'

'How?'

'By going down the road that no-one's been down before and no-one knows where it goes to.'

'But how can you go down a road that no-one's been down before and no-one knows where it goes to?' asked Sarah. 'You'll get lost.'

ARCOS DE LA FRONTERA

The girl hurried down the street with a satchel on her shoulder. I was lost in Arcos so why not follow her. She threaded her way through the maze of the old town to the troglodyte houses dug into the cliff; she closed the door on a house with blue ceramic letters on the wall: La Academia Inglesas. I rang the bell. A man in his late thirties with a candid, humorous face greeted me in impeccable English – David Landfear, the only English resident in Arcos, along with his wife. He had been a primary school teacher in London until he saw an advert for English teachers in Morocco; handsome pay, a two-year contract and no special qualifications apart from a university degree. He flew into Morocco with eighty other disaffected British teachers. After two week's paid holiday they were sent to Casablanca; others disappeared into remote town-

ships in the desert and were never seen again. The two years came and went, and he couldn't face England and the weather. The ferry dropped them off in Spain. That day he searched the yellow pages and was offered a job teaching English in Cadiz. Two years came and went and he thought: Why not take the plunge? Set up my own language school and get all the money? He hired a car and travelled north with two questions: 'Is there an English language school here?' If yes, 'What's the quickest way out?' Arcos was the first town which said 'No'. That was eight years ago and now, he and his wife, run La Academia Inglesas, a quietly prospering venture. When he's not teaching he's looking after his orange trees. He's concerned about the drought and the leaf miners, and understands the intricacies of their life cycle. We chatted about English places and people, nearly knew someone he knew; sometimes he forgot the technical English word such as 'pruning', but knew the Spanish equivalent. His daughter speaks fluent Spanish. Once or twice he replied in Spanish even though I'm an Espanol ignoramus. When the time came to go, he put on his flat cap, scarf and cord jacket. I hardly recognised him, the transformation was complete: El nuevo Espanol.

(Carmona, January 30, 1996)

JUAN BAENA – NEO RURAL

This elegant man was propped at the bar at the Alma Alpujarras. Unlike most Spanish men his jacket was neither cord nor leather, but cotton in flamboyant pastel shades. We talked in pidgin Espanol mixing French, English and Spanish to make some sense. He reminded me of an English friend, Paul Cheshire, tall and skinny with a curious mix of innocence and hard-headed thinking. I liked Juan from the start, a native of the Alpujarras dividing his time between his farm on the edge of the winter snowfields and studying regional tourism at Orgiva and Granada. In his hand was a book he had written about the Alpujarras emphasising the necessity for both a rural and urban mentality. I had not met anyone like him in Andalucia. His brother was a driver in road construction, his sister in discotheque management but he – like many women in Andalucia – appreciated the value of education. His future, he predicted, included more ecological farming and initiatives which linked him with cities. When I mentioned the colourful travellers of Orgiva he shrugged his shoulders; if they stayed ten years they would become rural people. He wanted the Internet and his olive trees.

'I'm a techno-peasant,' I said.

'I'm a neo-rural,' said Juan.   *(Orgiva, February 8, 1996)*

* * *

Where wheatears skid-dive their white rumps among boulders, where meadow pipits absail to earth, where herons outstare their shadows in rock pools, where the sea is zipped with sunshine and diamonds, where the bumblebee patrols wayside anemones, where the golden eagle steps of the Cliff of Gribun, where sensation eclipses thoughts and childhood memories are stirred, where the hard winter shows in people's faces, where a polytunnel clings to a mountainside, where the nearest shop is ten miles away, where the lava flows can be climbed as steps up a mountain, where the bog myrtle rises from its winter ashes – there you will find a small green caravan, light and white and airy inside, where the south is a distant dream, where the world comes in on the screen, where a fence keeps out the red deer, where older age is expanding the horizon, where new foundations are being dug, life is being re-invented on Mull.

(Kinloch, Scotland, May 2, 1999)

CONKER SHOES

Andy Longford stretches out his arms, one high, the other low. 'This is how my life is, these two levels.' One plodding around in his back yard, living on small earned incomes, tending his salad garden, buying local produce, supporting the community development trust, the other contributing to the city decision-making centres. This is why he moved up to Oxford from rural Devon where he helped set up Conker Shoes, a pioneering, small shoe-making business to emerge in the mid-seventies, a David among the Goliaths. Originally he had worked on the shoe factory production line but he could see that the graduate entries were in the fast lane, so he studied at college for a diploma in management studies and later for an MSc in organisational analysis and development. During this period he twigged that the factory system churning out 1000 shoes a day did not cater for exact fits. Why not tailor shoes individually for customers? So he returned to his roots in Devon and experimented in his front room.

'Everyone thought I was mad. Shoes could only be made profitably on a factory system.' He practised cutting patterns and developing an alternative system. With a small team, they rotated the production work avoiding isolation and the repetitive strain injuries where people could take an hour to stop jiggling after work. Cutting out on Monday; closing on Tuesday; sole stitching on Wednesday; lasting and side-edge grinding on Thursday and finishing off on Friday. Conker shoes in Totnes and Exeter still flourishes and prides itself on their individual touch. 'We showed that you can reverse the mass scale. It's not inevitable.'

(Bath, June 25, 1997)

NATIVES

The lush lands of Schleswig-Holstein concealed their natives well. Rain, rain, five sombre days on cycleways; the fretting and drooling skies kept everyone inside their red-brick homes, except the red cattle lying in protective circles in the meadows. Closer to the Danish border – a moveable feast in these parts –

176

real woods, hedgerows, farm ponds, gardens with vegetable plots appeared, but still no pigs or free-range chickens or small flocks of geese. Who lives here?

'I do,' says Monica Angermann smiling with her whole body, Saxon blue eyes beneath a fringe circling her head. She is small and compact, a pint in a half pot, I think. She lives down a rural lane near Grobsolt, her husband Dirk needing the clean air to ward off allergies. They had always wanted a small house in the country after another life in Hanover and the Ruhr conurbations. They buy beef from their neighbouring farmer, chop wood in the backyard, even cultivate vegetables. 'We are not typical Germans,' she says. 'We don't do more work than is necessary.'

They have restored their home themselves but kept the simple rooms, the homely furniture, built a fireplace with an internal chimney stack. It radiates heat as we eat their neighbour's boiled beef with cauliflower and potatoes and horse-radish sauce. I am polite and eat all the potatoes, but only one at a time. 'It's how the English do it.' They met in the municipal sauna at nearby Flensburg where Monica teaches. They married seven years ago, late in their lives. It's a change Monica likes. Before that she had lived with Friedlin, her cat. Now she has also Benjamin, an Irish bloodhound and German sheepdog cross they found in a home for strays. He sleeps on his mat. Cars roar by, doors slam and nothing happens, but crackle a paper and the great mound of ginger hair and huge staring eyes dwarf the table. I give him meat gristle to cement our friendship.

Monica's face is often still, her eyes thoughtful until some new laughter appears in them. In her student days she had no money but somehow there was always enough time for travelling. She hitch-hiked to Alaska by herself. 'I do things if they sound good.' She loves learning something new and says she is unhappy if there are no changes. She thinks she would have been successful managing a company, but she likes her work and being a public servant; she cannot be fired unless she steals the golden spoons. One of her nieces worries her. 'No-one has the courage to give her boundaries and now she just likes her own way. Perhaps I'll go cycling with her. But what can you change in two weeks? It will take a year.'

Dirk is practical and plans to put a toilet on the ground floor for when they are old and cannot climb the stairs. He likes to stay at home with Benjamin when Monica travels; recently she went by boat from Kiel to St Petersburg.

The Luxembourg rosé talks merrily when it is released from the bottle. We exchange prejudices, love stories. 'The English are prudes,' declares Dirk. Monica laughs loudest at my Spanish male joke: 'They keep their hands in their pockets to check everything is still there.' Friedlin is in heaven when stroked by Monica; he lies on his back stretching out all his legs. Benjamin tries to sleep but cannot. 'He is excited that we have a visitor.' Dirk loves

'Queen' and counts his fingers for the Ruhr cities and their live concerts. This stranger on a bicycle feels at ease. Contentment is a favourite word this evening. 'Who wants to live forever?' says Monica, serious again.

At midnight we drink coffee and look at photographs of her cycle ride from Harwich to London. We have nothing more to say. 'We did two days' entertaining in one,' she says smiling around her face again. Perhaps she will come cycling in Somerset. This little link of friendship goes a long way for strangers.   *(Gelting, May 23, 1997)*

'Where does the road go?'

'You must find that out' said the old man. Then he pulled an acorn from his pocket and held it in his hand. "Plant it, and when it is taller than you, you will go down the road that no-one has been down before and no-one knows where it goes to".'

'My fist squeezed the acorn but when I looked back up he had gone. I ducked through the door. He had gone, gone completely. The only foot-prints in the mud were large pad marks returning along the track.'

'Is that the end?' said Sarah.

'I don't know.'

'Did he turn into a badger?'

'I don't know.'

'I like that story,' said Jo, 'I do.'

'But we don't know the ending.'

'That's why I like it.'

TREES FOR LIFE

When I close my eyes I see the room clearly, the motley armchairs in a half circle, the slumped bodies staring into the fire, saying nothing and content to be rocked to peace by half lights; ten people, all strangers from the day before. Here we are at Athnamulloch, the mountain bothy, upstream from the north end of the hunter's road by Glen Affric in Scotland. The bothy is without water or electricity, our simple needs for the week met by mattresses and candles and gas lights; carting water from the river, chopping up lodgepole pines, themselves cut down to allow natural regeneration of birch and Scots pine. Here are our names: Adam Powell, Paul Kendall, Phillippa Scott, Mary Dodds, Peter Gilbert, Ricardo, Ewan Kelly, Peter Please, Guy and Mairi Hands. We are volunteers with Trees For Life, the Scottish charity helping to piece together the historic Caledonian Forest.

The world we left behind at Cannich but not the dungeon undertones of the Kosovo crisis. That came away in a special place, not just in the dozing hours; the image of the refugees was there in the supreme moments of planting young

178

Scots pines below the snowfields in Gleann na Ciche, Valley of the Breast.
What had they in common? I had no answer. All that week I experienced bad
digestion, finding it hard to stomach that undertow of fears, something literally
raw, at war within me. I could not articulate any of this. This writing is the
same: I have no idea how to bring the rich strands and paradoxes into one
page. And there are so many paradoxes: the monumental mountains are full of
details such as the lizard frozen onto its calluna perch; the sluggish adder, a
greenshank skulking on the shore of Loch na Canaig (Curl lake); the chatter of
stonechats; the evasive white rumps of wheatears; the return of a lone swallow,
the cocoons of the Northern eggar moth, tadpoles swimming in puddles. I am in
my nursery picture book of Scottish wilderness and two steps away from Father
Christmas – and it's full of people! I am amazed by the generosity of giving,
the foil of dry American humour, 'Getting a little snippy, are we?'

The day starts, the bothy door opens and the ground stampedes with red deer;
their heart-shaped rumps bound across the rushlands between the two rivers;
trails of young stags step single file through the floodwaters, my idea of
'Monarch of the Glen', a Victorian fantasy of wilderness which led to over-
grazing of the mountains. When a deer fence is put up, the whorled eyes of a
Scots Pine, silver birch, eared willow and alder by the streams can appear
miraculously. Trees For Life works with Forest Enterprise, the National Trust
and the RSPB to create islands of native regeneration in the designated
conservation zones; they stand behind the reintroduction of the wolf, the
beaver, the lynx, but no-one knows how practical this is yet.

Adam Powell, the field officer with TFL, is a gnomic character at the half
century mark and often with a look of fulfilled gentleness in his face. His words
and actions are measured and pithy. The works combines many strands of his
life; rock climbing, the life-long naturalist, the business acumen, visionary,
communicator; an important part of his work is talking to the locals – the
foresters, the farmers, the stalkers, the estate owners, the hunting community,
the ramblers – about their fears that fencing will inhibit the movement of deer,
that the high moorlands will vanish, that wolves will snatch babies from prams.
Dialogue with competing interests, building trust, finding the meeting place is
essential work. The Caledonian Forest had lost the battle with the sheep and
deer interests. How do you redress the balance? Bring the natives back? High
over the glen a golden eagle patrolled the snowfields, and all of us huddled in
the heather conscious that one eagle was enough. The tyranny of numbers did
not matter here. Yet the number of trees needed to make a difference in Glen
Affric is like the number of refugees in Kosovo. This struggle for the forest to
exist, for diverse interests to co-exist, appear linked. And I still had my heart
burn, the pain of trying to be connected, that something is not right, but what?
Dialogue is the only way forward, and it's a struggle the heart knows best. 'It

179

looks hopeless,' says Adam pointing to the tawny calluna as far as the eye, the dappled skin of deer grass and purple moor grass, 'but every tree planted makes a difference.'

We believed him. On our hands and knees we slotted the trees into the mineral earth and into the sphagnum moss as thick as mattresses in places; sometimes looking up at the treeless horizons mirroring the sky and home to the parachuting meadow pipits or a raven grundling to itself. Two thousand trees in two days, a small part of the quarter-of-a-million trees planted by Trees For Life volunteers. Other days we dismantled old deer fences, rolling up the barbed wire and mesh and dumping that onto the forest track. At first we painfully negotiated the slurp and slurry of peat hags, hobbling between the hummocks of cowberry, being lost then finding our way, crossing over our tracks, stopping at a stump where others had stopped, until little by little a trail emerged for us to follow. Is this how connections are made in our mind? The terrain made simple tasks difficult and all breathed lightly when Daphne the wagon took us home along with the rosy glow of larch, calluna, pine bark up to the black and white transfers of the snowfields.

Night brought the deer back to graze the rushes, the banging of the bothy door would stampede them in all directions. The loony calls of the black-throated diver or the drumming of snipe inhabited the night, became phantoms of our own choosing, and some of them had Kosovo faces. Hard on that is the spectre of Russian involvement. The cool out-breath of the snow-fields became a Cold War, something I had lived with most of my life, being a Fifty's child. I remember watching 'Quatermass and The Pit', a Fifty's sci-fi about an alien space capsule from the 13th century found buried in the earth. I vividly recall the eerie stillness on the housing estate every time it was broadcast, a cold fear of fascination and flight impossible to ignore; the blinding light, the burrowing in the ground, the nuclear annihilation only four minutes away.

My heart-burn lasted all week at Glen Affric. I felt that this simple act of planting trees, native trees unique to Caledonia, had put me on the front line. There's a crisis of identity in Kosovo and it belongs here too, in this Scottish wilderness, in the dialogue of competing interests, and in a dream... I am part of it now. I can't walk away. I'm a tree-planting idiot, you're a Kosovo peace idiot.　　　　　　　　　　　　　　　　(Loch Ness/Loch Lochy, April 27/28, 1999)

THE IDIOTS

In the Eighties Renaud Dengreville worked as a plumber, but his passion was always photographing the private lives of insects, flowers and animals in the forests and tumbled granite of the Aubrac. He had lived there since childhood. One day he was pricing up a job to clean a boiler when he noticed, with his artist's eye, something he considered unfinished about a picture. Cheekily he remarked on this but the lady was not amused. 'Art is not within the reach of *a plumber,' she said coldly. He finished the job and nothing more was said about it. Ten years later Renaud completed his magnum opus, the book I was holding in my hands,* **Guetteur de Vie** *(Editions de Rouergue): a song of praise for nature, an exquisite collaboration of words and photographs. Every fine art publisher he tried had turned it down: brilliant but too expensive to produce, they said. In the end he sent it to a publisher in Rodez, on his doorstep. They accepted it straightaway and asked to meet him. He recognised the publisher. She remembered him as the plumber who had fixed her boiler. They eyed each other steadily and in silence.*

'I thought you an idiot that day,' she said.

'I, too, thought you an idiot.' More silence sealed their mouths until the laughter burst out. They shook hands. (Le Moulin d'Ayres, September 21, 1996)

I can hear granny's words floating in from the kitchen. 'It's got to be done if we want that tasty dinner. At least I didn't have to pluck them. The itchy feathers ruin my fingers.' Still wearing her apron, she eased her weight onto her chair crossing her fingers on her lap. In the half-light and the glow of the fire, the slipping coals, the familiarity and strangeness of our togetherness, there was an anticipation, a feeling that at last we were in the same picture and that anything could happen. Her silver hair was bunched over her head and the pins were in place like a big pincushion, a face from the 19th century. 'They lost six turkeys last night, the heads all cut off, and he only took one. Once they get the smell of blood they can't stop. It's in their nature, they can't help themselves. They'll get him on Boxing Day. They'll run him to earth. They'll come across the top of the field below Kings Wood, the drumming of the horses, the red coats, the horns and the hounds. The horns! Watch out Slipperadoo.'

'Slipperadoo?'

'The fox.'

'I don't like hunting,' said Sarah. 'It's cruel. They don't stand a chance.'

'We have to eat, darlings.'

'We don't eat foxes.'

'They eat turkeys.'

'Only if the Colonel is stupid enough to leave the door open.'

'Life is hard, my children. Life feeds on life. *Do you not see that nothing that enters a man from the outside can defile him?* We didn't set it up this way. You either run or get eaten. What else can we do? Someone's got to kill the turkey.'

GOURANGA

I walked past him, a youthful man with chirpy eyes under a base-ball cap; a black satchel hung across his shoulder. He spoke gently while flicking expertly the identity card with the reverse showing him in a saffron monk's robe. 'Hare Krishna', he said, now smiling, and asked for a donation for a book. 'But it's in Hungarian,' he added, 'it's no use. But you can make a contribution for our campaign to stop eating cows.' Quickly he said he was celibate and a vegetarian for five years, no fish or eggs. 'No' was his opening line. He lived in a van with two other monks – I could see the same white caps bobbing on strategic corners in the main street in Esztergom, the Danube crossing from Slovakia.

'Will you support this?' he asked directly.

'I cannot support this,' and now I had to say why.

I am on my hobby horse. Shopping in supermarkets is a passive experience, good for factory, intensive farms but the scale is wrong. It splits people from the producers, city from the country. Organic farming relies on the fertility of animals, not the chemicals which only improve the pump. What we need are more local producers selling variety for a local market. Food has a face, not just a shelf number. I respected his choice, the differences, and I sneakily thought it was good for the meat-loving Hungarians to listen to this message. For generations, he said, people in India had been vegetarians.

'You eat vegetables. Traditionally they are grown with the fertility of animals on small mixed farms. Everything has to be used.'

He said they had cows on a farm by Lake Balaton, and they drank the milk. 'The cow is like our mother who gives us milk and we cannot kill our mother.'

'But a farm is a business too,' I said. 'The small organic farms live on a knife-edge. The cows are part of this economy. You drink milk, but what happens to the male cows? It is only because some people eat meat that you can be a vegetarian.' He said he did not understand this. I did not want an argument with him. 'I like differences. Perhaps it's only because of differences that everything fits.'

He agreed that taking the life of plants was a sin, a small sin necessary to survive. I told him that he was talking to the wrong person. I was passionately against factory farming of animals, the thoughts of Auschwitz uncomfortably close. 'But do you know who loves cows the best?' I asked. 'It is the small farmer. They give the cows names like 'Ziggy' and 'Willow' and talk to them. They cry in private when they have to send them to the butchers.'

I did not talk about my own ambivalence aroused by his sincerity or tell him that his strident purity tarnished me in some way. 'I'm a discerning omnivore. I like to be connected to the food chains.' He still wanted to give me the address of the vegetarian restaurant in Budapest and their farm where I could ask my questions. I gave him some money, not for his cause I said, but because I was happy to see him in Hungary, the first person I had spoken to.

'Gouranga,' he said. 'Be happy.'

'I wish you well.'

PS: And here, for the first and last time, I honour that which supports me on this journey in Mitteleuropa: pig, wheat, sunflower, cabbage, almonds, hazels, tomatoes, motorways, food transporters, tractors, farmers, processing factories, money, yearning for fulfilment, Holdsworth bicycle circa 1975, air in my tyres and in my lungs, dobra voda, pilsner, open minds, telephone links to loved ones, birdsong, azotobacter crococum, my feet, cherries, receiving letters, prayers, grease, wheels, kindness of strangers, self massage, clean air, wood carving, this pen and ink and paper, hope...   (Esztergom, June 4, 1998)

COLLESSIE TATTIE

I have to touch it, hold the tattie firmly between the fingers and thumb, a wee drum full of water, cool and buoyant. To look at it is strange, no face but eyes growing out from both sides, deep purple and extending into mobile limbs, tufted at every turn and ending in a fist of folded leaves. The warty skin belongs to the earth, cratered, wrinkled, the limbs converging into deltas, to end in bump land and nascent eyes. This is the Collessie tattie, one of three given to me over the garden wall by Bill Rollo, who discovered it in his crop. 'Some tattie misbehaved,' is his explanation, drolled out in Fife tongue, a slow and steady resonance as if someone is pouring out oil. He stoops slightly, an old man in country plaid, his clothes as weathered as his hands. The Collessie tattie has purple flesh, similar to beetroot, and is being trialed at HDRA, and at Highbury. I have three destined for my allotment. It is meant to cook firm for salads. The inscrutable face says nothing. It is on its own journey. I am merely a form of transport.   (St Andrews, May 12, 1999)

GRIPE OR GRAPE?

Heather is a northerner, and with the same north-facing vitality. When she buys vegetables she likes to touch them, to pick out the bad cherries, and she does this with an easy grace — it's part of the way of business. So when she comes south she goes to the supermarket to buy some grapes. She picks one and eats it, to check if she wants to buy it.

A hand descends onto her shoulder. 'Excuse me. What do you think you are doing?'

'I am eating a grape to see if I want to buy it.'

'But you can't just eat the grapes.'

'Would you buy it if it tasted horrible?'

'That's not the point. What happens if everyone did it.'

The assistant takes her to the supervisor. 'She's been eating the grapes.'
Heather sticks to her guns. 'I always try a grape before I buy a bunch.'
'That's not the point,' said the supervisor. 'What happens if everyone did it?'
'Are you going to arrest me then?'
'Are you going to buy the grapes?'
'No. They are not sweet enough.' (Bath, February 6, 1999)

FOOD

There was a man who ate anything and said he felt fine. His niece suffered
from eczema with rashes over most of her neck and back. She went on a raw
food diet and so did he to give her some moral support. Two weeks later spots
erupted everywhere on his face, his back, legs and arms. Her rashes disappeared. (Stoke Mandeville, June, 1997)

HIDEG GYUMOLCS LEVES Cold cherry soup, a Hungarian speciality.

   3 cups of sweet cherries
   3 cups sour cherries
   2 tablespoons of flour
   1.5 litres of water
   2 tablespoons of sour cream
   half lemon (don't peel it)
   4 cloves

Put the fruit, sugar, cloves, lemon with water into a pot. Cook for ten minutes
– the fruit will be above the water level. Mix the flour with the sour cream and
put into the soup. Cook for five minutes. Add sugar or lemon to sweeten.
Store in fridge. An old recipe from Rose Arvai who learnt it from her own
mother. (Esztergom, Hungary, June 4, 1998)

KVETAK JAKOMOZECEK (Cauliflower-in-the-way-of-brains)

Put cauliflower into boiling and salted water. Take out when cooked and cut
into small pieces. Drain. Put oil in frying pan and fry small pieces of onion.
Mix in cauliflower and stir-fry a little. Mix in one egg per person and cook
until just done. Serve with boiled potatoes cut into small pieces. Add margarine and salt. (From Eva Packova, Ostrava-Poruba, May 26, 1998)

NAUTILUS

In Flevoland I landed at the bottom of the ocean – Holland's youngest
province. Before the war this land – three to five metres below sea level – was
washed by the tidal North Sea but now a straight-line dyke holds back the
sea; to my left a heron joins seagulls mobbing a trawler, to my right are the
plattelands, fat polders for cereals and cows, or black Friesian horses. Clouds of
itching flies luxuriate in the damp air; a gang of spoonbills trail each other in

the brackish waters, heads down sifting debris by their long legs. I can see the feather-back poplars of Lelystad city, but all I hear are the churring chuttering reed buntings playing the oldest mating game. They chase each other up and down the reeds, each time pulling themselves up with their beaks to signal from the top, 'Here, I am! Come and get me.'

Lelystad is a purpose-built city with cycle lanes from the future and a glass-tec railway station where the cathedral would be. Some say Lelystad is dreary and full of commuter widows. I liked the pine trees and this pioneer's dream of space in a small country. The best thing is the Centrum Biologische Landbouw – perhaps the largest demonstration of organic farming in Europe. In 1985, Lelystad – interested in its green image – gave 300 hectares of the deep shelly soil for organic farming. Now there are over 4,000 hectares, the farmers marketing their organic grain and vegetables through the Nautilus Cooperative. Emma Shotveld from the Centre of Information on Agriculture says that the benefits are clear now to everyone, in health for the land, animals and people. She has just shown around an Austrian group of farmers' wives. 'It's the women who often inspire the changes. They question the use of herbicides, the safety for their children. We are confident for the future.'

(Lelystad, May 14, 1997)

She kissed our foreheads goodnight and Jo supported her hand until the landing. I sat by the fire again and I kept thinking of Jessy. I had never met anyone like her before, serious, gullible, unpredictable, irritating and unafraid to make a fool out of me. Her eyes always followed mine, big and unblinking. A little owl's eyes! Where would she go? These thoughts foreshadowed Christmas Eve as the clouds covered the moon. Perhaps she was like the Jack O'Lantern which comes and goes without warning, and has no home. The freezing mists had travelled somewhere else, and now it was warmer. Perhaps we would be snowified and we would be stuck here for Christmas. I prayed hard that it would be so. I saw the hounds running and the red horse chasing after them, or else I saw her rolling up the canvas on Christmas Day and she was coughing and going away. Absurdly I kept thinking of Father Christmas. I wanted him to help us. I would never see her again. The sound of droning words came down from below. I recognised the muffled donkey laughter, the same silences. A light came out of his bedroom zigzagging across the landing. I crept up the stairs on the sides of my feet pretending I wanted the toilet, if anybody asked. I left the door slightly open.

Jo sat at the end of her bed, wearing stripy pink pyjamas, like the ones my father had, and those were probably war rations.

'You haven't worn those in years.'

'...He went to his mother and asked her to play.
"I'm cooking," she said and told him to go away.'

'He went to find his daddy but he wasn't there.'

'He had no-one to play with, so he took teddy and rabbit and crawled under the blankets. That's what he liked best, pulling the blankets over his head so it was warm and dark. And then he heard a noise at the bottom of the bed, someone tapping.'

'A crackalump!'

'He saw a little door with light around the edges. He turned the wooden handle. "Hurry up! Hurry up!" said an enormous green frog with black trousers and a black cap. "I've been waiting here for one hundred years." He was leaning out of a red train. He blew the whistle.

'Will all passengers taking the fast train to Cricklecrackle please take your seats.'

'The boy climbed into the train just as the frog blew the whistle. Over the bridges and down to the sea. They came to another station.'

'All passengers for Cricklecrackle.'

'In came a crocodile with a crocodile bag, a top hat and a newspaper stuffed under his arm. He opened his paper and didn't say another word. Over the bridges and across to the sea. And who was there at the end of the end of the tunnel?'

'Father Christmas!'

He clicked his thumb and fingers. 'Tickets please.'

'It's a long way. Over the sea, down through the forests, up over mountains where the ice bears live.'

'I like ice bears.'

'The snow is thick on the track. The train can't go any farther. I can see a light in the forests, reindeer outside a wooden shack, and they're eating grass from nosebags. Can it be...?'

Father Christmas's station!'

'Father Christmas opened the door. He was wearing slippers and holding half a cup of chocolate. He wore braces and his shirt was sticking out. He had bread-crumbs in his beard. 'I've been waiting for you. It's getting very busy. I have to be away tomorrow.'

'He's not expecting visitors. There's a fire burning, a kettle on. He's sorting out the letters. There's one from Jessy. 'Dear Father Christmas, What's been born today? I'd like a chew stick for sparkler, and a watch for my dad. He's always burning the porridge. What am I going to do about him? I'll leave bread and biscuits out for you. There's grass in the bag I'll leave outside for the reindeer.'

'This is the last train to Christmas. Children are on the bridge waving! The moon! It's smiling. *Chicketty can chikketty*.' He pretended to shoulder a large sack. One of Jo's pictures had come to life. It was as if he wanted us to be in his own pictures.

'Christmas!' Jo pretended to be hard of hearing, just like granny does sometimes.

'I beg your pardon.'

'Only if you're good,' said granny 'and do as you're told. Father Christmas knows what every child loves. He has presents for everybody.'

'There's so much snow this year.'

'You'll have to get through.'

'I've got a helicopter in the barn.'

'He's got presents for everyone, even the canaries and Tugger.'

'They don't get old.'

'Nothing changes, not really.'

'He's waiting for him.'

'Longing to see his son, to say that he loves him, and will never leave him again.'

'He'll come back.'

'He will. One day he'll come through the door when your back is turned. When you least expect it.'

'It's a secret.'

'Our secret.'

I tiptoed back upstairs.

They say there is a woman behind every man, not **woman** but a woman, a wooing woman tu wit to woo. She knows the way. Eve wanted the apple, this dream of knowledge. I can't blame her. She wanted a way out, we all do. I wanted to trust this woman, to work in her garden and hear the sea and the magical sound of rattle pine cones. But something keeps getting in the way, the lines of mutilated men being ministered to by woman. Where did they come from? I dream *I am pressing young women to me for sexual rendezvous. I am shagging my mother, of battles with spider woman, 'I want you to be my ally not my representative.' Another woman keeps taking off her negligee and saying with tears, 'I am nobody's slave.'* The night after deciding not to fantasise sexually about women, I dreamed: '*I am with Helen who is a bit* *skinny but OK. We are walking by the shore, a wooded, sheltered place and looking for somewhere to sleep. I say to her: 'Come and sleep with me, I won't seduce you.' She comes in. Then I see the most fantastic display of shooting stars. I wake up Helen and we watch it together. Then my brother John appears. He is very gentle-looking. I touch his head and ask if he is all right. He peers at us and he is quite beautiful and gentle. He goes away.'*

Into what abyss had I fallen? I buried the ring in this garden, between the two apple trees, and I buried it with a little ceremony, to return to the earth the promises I had made. They would keep best there.

CHANTAL ALLAIRE

Chantal Allaire lives twelve storeys high in the banlieue of Rennes. From her window the monolith of the Citroën factory dominates the rural north; the city at night is a constellation to the south, east and west. She is very French; elegant yet simply dressed, straight blond hair cut neatly onto her shoulders, confidential yet vivacious, slight with finely made features; altogether an impression of intention, a quiet strength. She is a teacher and likes her work, a professional woman in her late forties and a place in the world. Never once could I have doubted this. She drinks a huge bowl of coffee each morning while the video recorder blinks in the corner. She tells me about her summer holiday at the New Age centre in La Lande — drawing, sculpture and massage. I like her straightaway, her kindness in making room for a Servas traveller while her own daughter is moving out.

The first day back from school she returns with a cold; five of the children have serious problems and now she has to teach an autistic child who will not even look at her. Sometimes she is unhappy about being a teacher. 'Education,' she says, 'does not work for everybody.' Her own daughter studied business management for four years but could not find the job she wanted. 'She wants to go to the country, but how?' The students stay on, live at home and study more and more. She does not know what will become of them. 'This is a consumer society,' she says, 'you must have money. You must have a job.' People are ashamed to wear 'le bleu du travail', she says. The parents want their children to wear white collars but it's not possible. She is still thinking of the autistic child. 'I will have to tell the parents, no?'

First thing in the morning she likes to see the trees. Chantal is the youngest of ten children. She shows me a plate her mother had made, with a family tree painted on and a heart at the base with these words: 1928 Francois and Thérèse, and the names of the children: Marie Joseph, Thérèse, Agnes, François, Jean Claude, Bernadette, Jean Marie, Yves, Marie France, Chantal. She takes her name from the De Sévigné family, a fashion in the late 1940's. She is the only child to go to university; her brothers and sisters are butchers and grocers and traders. *She was born at Loublande — 'A very little village near Cholet in La Vendée' — onto a family farm with cart-horses for power, some cereals, some cows. Her father made baskets from the withies. (She has one in the cellar, another stores her bread.) In death he is a picture of serenity with a rosary entwined around his fingers. There is a family portrait taken when she was two, a rural world in black and white realism, honest and hardworking, puritan Catholic, horizons drawn by necessity and tradition — a closed, peasant world. She still misses the tranquillity but not the draughty damp rooms, her cold fingers feeding oats to the horses before going to school on her bicycle. (A sepia print in the kitchen shows a bicycle with weeds growing up it.) It's only when we say goodbye that I remember her showing me pictures of the churches of La Vendée, her knowledge delighting in the saints and devils, the bestiary of soulful animals. 'History is my passion,' she says, 'the story of the stones' — the Romanesque language of the peasant, of blood and roses, a short hard life of epidemics, famine and wars. 'Can I write about you?' I ask. She looks steadily at me as she does at life's problems. She smiles.*

(Le Vitré, September 4, 1996)

LONE AS IN LUNA

In her garage is a giant oil colour of a tiger, another of a whale's flipper disappearing into the depths. Beside them, where a car should be, is a washing line with socks. 'It would make a good picture,' I say, 'lots of colours.' Lone peers steadily at it through her neat round glasses below a fringe of red hair; reds and browns and soft blues are in her clothes. She likes colours. She shows me photographs of the docks in Frederikshavn, slabs of recycled cardboard, a cliff of oil drums, juxtapositions of oil tankers with tugboats. She is trying to float an alternative guide book for the city but she cannot afford to do it herself. Her fifteen-year-old marriage ended three years ago and now she has to watch her pennies. 'At first I was angry then I realised I was relieved. I like the freedom of doing things in my own time.' But she would like a friend. 'Not a husband, but who can say?' She lives in the spacious designer-built bungalow with her teenage son. Her neighbours wonder how she can afford to stay there. 'I manage,' she says simply.

Her face reflects her clear thinking, a teacher in adult education; a determined chin and unblinking blue eyes. 'I manage but I don't like having to always think about money.'

Her paintings decorate the walls, pure abstracts to still-life oranges, giant birds and labyrinthine landscapes. A panelled ceiling reflects an immaculate wooden floor with tasselled carpets and clean lines to the minimalist furniture. A well-ordered space full of light and big windows, designer chairs and hi-tec lighting. Lone contradicts this. She chuckles easily, a little gravel in her throat. Her mobile ears listen to what she says.

She has another son who lives in a sheltered residential home. 'Do you know the expression: 'Fire in your arse?' He has it! He likes it where he lives. After two hours here he wants to go back.' In photographs I see a happy, full-mouthed, slightly askew face, laughing in the corners. The younger son helps him to climb to the top of a wooden hut. 'He loves swimming. Whenever the sun shines he says: "It's a good day for a swim." Now he can ride the bus alone into Frederikshavn and can ring his father by himself. He rings each morning at 6am. He shuts himself up in the booth and presses the numbers. I can see him thinking: "This is a very important thing."' Lone is sceptical about experts. 'A parent of a three-year-old mongoloid boy was once having her son assessed by a specialist. "For example," he said, "your son will never be able to dress himself." Behind his back the child was busy putting on his jacket!' Her other son now lives without his father. 'At first it was terrible. He would cry for days before he had to visit him in his new home.'

Her son returns with a friend. She pumps up the cycle tyres and wags her finger, negotiating the time they must be back. She is slightly anxious for them. 'This friend is in a home because his parents had no time for him. So this boy built a shelter around him to survive. At school he had no friends and so is teased by others. My son always defends him. He has had this experience with his brother. This night, his friend is staying over for the first time. They told me that everybody at the home clapped when they made this arrangement. This was a big moment for him.' One time, her son goes to the home but his friend has already gone to bed. "Quick, quick get up," the staff said. "Your friend has come." No-one had ever come for him before.'
Once she toyed with being a politician. 'The Common Market is too big, too bureaucratic.' Integration with Germany? 'It's important to keep the differences.' A man complained to her about the Sri Lankans. '"They're taking away our money," he said. He had a big car, a big house, a big cabin cruiser. No-one had taken anything from him. It makes me so mad.' She would like to return to adult education. 'I'm from Copenhagen. I take risks. If it works we learn something, if it doesn't we still learn something. 'Wait and see', 'Perhaps', 'Who knows', 'Let's go slowly' – I have no patience for this.' But she likes the quieter life in North Jutland, the spaces, the big lights. 'Look at the tree. It's a green woodpecker, the first one in this garden.' She writes it down in her bird book.
'Thank you for having me,' I say.
'It's a pleasure,' she sings back.   (Frederikshavn, June 6, 1997)

EVA WIRENHED – HOW DO YOU LEARN?
'See my face,' she says smoothing her cheeks. 'I think I have Sami blood.' Her cheeks are broad and flat, her nose short and neat, her eyes a little close

together, her hair cut neatly below the ears. A practical face; knowing eyes. When she smiles she confounds all her lines and her small mouth; she is surprisingly young and expansive. She can trace her family history for four hundred years, and she tells me some of it and I remember only a patchwork: a Siegfried, a pony trap plunging through thin ice (the voluminous petticoats saved one of her maternal ancestors; her grandfather survived because he was still in the cradle at home); long wagon journeys, cement factories, the house that burnt down, hard times and new lives. And not necessarily in this order. She wears with pride the silver jewellery she made of the Midgard serpent and the Hallristnings figures from the Swedish Bronze Age; the silver torc on her wrist was a gift to her father for giving a hanky to a Moroccan grandmother. It is old and worn and she loves this one the best.

She still enjoys teaching and is setting up video links with schools in England and Denmark. She believes children learn best when they discover for themselves, when they are happy. 'How can unhappy children learn?' She tries to learn from life: drawing shadows by noticing how they change on the wall; the children make a model of the local chrome-plating factory; the boys find out about drainage by digging holes like the workmen. 'After that they dug holes everywhere looking for pipes. Working with the problem kids has taught me a lot about making things concrete.' One boy had no co-ordination so she got him to draw himself on the blackboard. 'He discovered he had a stomach.' Another boy feared failure, so she got him to use a puppet. 'It was the puppet who talked, who made the mistakes, and so the boy learned.' She shows me some eggs. 'How do you find out which ones are hard-boiled and which are not?' I bluff my way, futilely. She spins them, the uncooked hardly turn, the others spin as if on skates. 'This is how I like it.'

She wants to travel when she retires and 'make new experiences'. She is one-sixth owner of an eight-metre sailing boat. On her 50th birthday the other part owners — all men — dressed in straw skirts in sub-zero temperatures and showed slides of their pranks. Whenever a particularly silly one appeared, they said: 'Eva is somewhere else'.

'Those silly men. How we laughed.'   (Åmal, Sweden)

BERIT BRUNSGAARD

She speaks in the rural Jutland accent, slow wide vowels, lots of pauses, a slightly sing-song voice with a bronky drongen baseline. A mass of red curly locks offset her even-tempered face full of freckles and a smile showing all her teeth and her changing lines. She is a farmer's daughter. Her home farm near Hobro is a patch of woodland and a chicken run and outbuildings, set in an ocean of wheat, a gently undulating land never quite big enough to call hills. Pine plantations shelter lanes with sandy waysides of sea pink and hedgerows of whitebeam or lilac. Her parents Karen and Niels are retired and rent out the *land. They travel out of a red-brick bungalow full of comfortable chairs, pictures of flowers and children and collector's plates, a happy home of ease and memories from a lifetime of hard work. Berit is their youngest; she has just graduated from Århus university with a Master of Arts, having studied art history and modern literature. She never regrets this journey into mind. Her father doesn't understand all of it but is proud of her achievement. Her brother is an engineer, another sister is an architect.*

Now she dreams off going back to her family roots on Salling far from the fashionable Fyn where most of her university friends want to live. She dreams of her aunt's small farm and the fat lands up from the fjord with the horse-chestnut, red brick and wooden chalet and wide verandah; the glasshouse, and a massive peach tree planted from a pip. She would like to live there with a milk cow, some chickens and ducks, and work as a teacher at the Folkehojskole at nearby Skive. No-one really wants to live in Skive, so that is on her side, she says. She knows farming is a hard life, with its tidal uncertainty, the long hours, doing other jobs to pay the bills. She worries sometimes what her parents think. Her brother and sisters are settled with their big loves, and she would like a husband and children, and thirty is getting on. The coming year is going to be full of change, like most of her life so far, one of detours; an old derivation for the word 'Viking'; more to integrate, more possibilities.

At nineteen she worked on the Scandinavian ferries then travelled a year in Australia. She came back to the Folk High School in Skive, the adult education movement started in Denmark by N.F.S. Grundtvig in 1844. A bit of religion, history, literature, and art, a school where you could go at any age and discover something new. 'No-one had ever thought of a school for adults and personal development. It was a glorious moment in Danish history,' says Berit. 'I discovered drawing and art, that I shouldn't be afraid of learning new skills. Three months there was like a long journey abroad. It was education for life.

'When my parents were young they dreamed of having money, but now they want time. I think in the future to have time will be valued more highly than money.' (Orris, Jutland, June 2, 1997)

Now I have to bring back the two women in white and their peaked hats I saw sitting on the remote Scottish wayside; and the figure of a man wrapped in a Middle-Eastern shroud who I saw in a reverie on Iona, and the dove a bird of peace coming out of his chest. So I think of him as a man of peace.

Here there is a difficulty. The women I saw with my own eyes, such vivid flesh and blood, yet her transcendental tranquillity hardly belonged to this world – yet she was as real to me as my hands. I do not know her name. I do know she is Middle-Eastern and that is why I linked her with the man.

The shawl around his face hinted that he came from a hot climate, where they needed to temper the sun. And now it is a dangerous game, delusion in full measure and what is real. A voice says: I could be of service to them. But what do I have to offer? If they had a past together, perhaps they have a present? I like this notion, and I do not know why. Is there an easy way to understand? Nothing can be the same the moment when we catch sight of our quarry. There are moments like that when the going back stops, when there are no more crossroads. Every time I close my eyes and think of his face, I see the man and the woman together. He has his arm around the woman, and I can see her face from the side. She is standing by his side. He pulls her towards him as if they are going to kiss, but that's as far as I see. At last they are together.

I did return to Glen Lyon, feeling a fool by studying the verges, and after much coming and going I found the grassy place where they had sat motionless with their backs to the roaring river below. I sat in the same bend of the road; the Range Rovers went by, two friendly cyclists. I fished out my piece of white Iona marble to sit on, but it was too small. Then I noticed that it was heart-shaped and immediately I associated it with the two figures, as if they were lovers. What did it matter? I could walk away from this fantasy, this fugitive sense of significance. I wanted to give the marble to this place, a tangible token of this connection. I dismissed throwing it into the river, that would make it disappear. I did not want that. I placed the marble in the roots of a young growing beech tree, in the shelter but not overcast by an older Queen of the Forest, as they say down South. It felt like planting a seed, bringing the two together in one place. I was happy with that. A red squirrel scampered into view circling under the drip-line of the tree. It didn't look back.

And neither did I.

PIPSQUEAK IN THE MEZQUITA

I smile at this moment, foolish with this pen and loose ends of the night and before this millennium of Islamic eternity. I will not be able to express what's in me, so this will be my glorious failure. I'm glad I cycled to Córdoba, a dot in the never-ending green downlands engulfing Medina Sidonia, Arcos de la Frontera and Carmona, a single line drawn between the land and the sky, no trees apart from orchards, no birds, no animals except for black bulls, no song nor insects or people for that matter. I could have been the only person alive. Here in the Mezquita, the great Islamic oratory of the Western Caliph, I find the same sense of space, the same aloneness.

I try to imagine the hundreds of oil lamps glowing on the red-stained plaster floor and the red bricks in the distinctive tiers of horseshoe arches set in neat lines on Roman and Visigothic columns everywhere I look. History is there in books but some of these columns have been standing for two thousand years recycled by Christians and Muslims. How many thousands of believers have leaned against them, wandered praying around them? This is the stillness I have been missing in Andalucia, space with people and without interruptions. People are dwarves beside these columns and that's exactly how I feel: poignant, a little foolish.

The Mezquita is impersonal, very strange, a primordial creature I have never seen before. I feel my folly, this pipsqueak from Streatham Common before the jewel of Córdoba, The City of the West in the 10th century, the city of the three religions, the peoples of The Book. I very nearly felt ashamed of my shyness with silence, impossible lust, trying to order everything around me when I am tired or lonely. What place is there in eternity for this foolishness? Then I saw the Capilla Royal, the cruciform Baroque cathedral built over several centuries out of the heart of the Mezquita. In parts it mimics the horseshoe arches so the eye can look and see through and make believe there is nothing there. But it is there, and in my mind it is a kind of conquistadorial fury of ornamentation, carvings exquisite in detail but there are no breathing spaces or surfaces left plain so the overall effect totters on the edge of madness for God.

Strangely I felt no sense of outrage; after all the Arabs had demolished the earlier Visigothic cathedral on part of the present site. I experienced an inarticulate sense that they are not at war with each other. I liked to be reminded of the little lights burning briefly against the immensity of eternity, and somehow lighting it up to see; it's the peace I find watching waves in the sea, ripples in sand. The flawed sincerity of the Capilla Royal is there; the tortured piety, faces of children, animals, brothers and sisters in oil and stone, of everything we love; how sad are the names of the sponsors, heady with reconquest and will to immortalise themselves, as no doubt the will to demonstrate their religious piety motivated the earlier Arabic lords. The Christian church is Time itself; how foolish time appears besides this ageless eternal spirit! The follies of its makers are there in big letters to see. I, for one, am glad of that.

Time and eternity are in my heart, and the pipsqueak is there too. Here they are still two worlds, aliens forced to share the same bed. I long for a religion of space and time, an Islamic prince wedded to a Christian princess. The pipsqueak is tapping my shoulder; he wants to play hide and seek behind the columns, but the patrolling guards would chuck me out... An electronic jingle plays over and over again. I don't know why. Japanese tourists take flash *pictures of gilded Madonnas in the chain of chapels... The Mezquita is a museum, but it comes away with me in a special place.*

(The Mezquita, Córdoba, February 1, 1996)

BLACK VIRGIN

Le Puy-en-Velay is made of dark volcanic rock fissured by steam. They built it into the medieval lanes, cut it sober for the Sixth century Notre-Dame-du-Puy cathedral, a great cavern and fittingly the home to the Black Virgin. She is the Queen of earth and sky, the Mother of God, and on her lap is the Christ child. It is said the Crusaders brought her back from the Middle East, and there are earlier echoes of Isis and her beloved son, Horus. I thought of Mabon, the beloved son of the Goddess in the Celtic tradition. The Christian madonnas are exquisitely carved, both slender and robust, or as humorous or pious maidens holding their son; the tenderness of the embrace is always stressed. Nearby is the plug of an extinct volcano which makes Le Puy famous on postcards: the 10th century Chapelle of St Michelle d'Aiguilhe. Here was once a temple of Mercury for the Romans, and long before that a sacred enclosure with dolmens. All traces of this past have been extinguished by Roman and Christian zealots, as the Revolutionaries burnt the original Black Virgin. They could not destroy the magic of this place. The chapel has a door of red, white and black lozenges dancing with Islamic eternal flow and the Velay Romanesque down-to-earth intimacy. I like these connections, this bringing together of light from the celestial night, young and old, male and female, earth and sky, Christianity and Islam.

I am glad the pig with the golden digestion, the brute guardian dogs and the badger with the eliminator nose are going to Santiago. I am going with them.

(Le Puy-en-Velay, September 18, 1996)

SANTIAGO DE COMPOSTELA

The shrine of St James is the nearest thing to an Aladdin's cave I have seen. There is a golden silhouette of the saint in glory, and, without my glasses, the angelic aureole is like a turban wrapped around his head. It is a treasure house of winged phantasmagoria and cunningly lit to throw dark reliefs onto the Infantas holding up His crowning dome. The electric candles are static below the great chandelier; two real candles interrupt this flamboyant solidity with sparkling haloes. Waves of people appear before the shrine...but only for a moment. They are swept away. Sudden flashlights illuminate the arms appearing behind the saint and embracing his neck, adding a surreal touch to this already overloaded theatre stage. For what else can it be? This is drama at The Most High Altar.

Here I remember the grave eternity of the Mezquita at Córdoba, the Islamic peace and certainty, no stage whatsoever; The Void, the Unknowable Will of

Allah. Time and space are made for each other. In an alcove where the candles burn brightest, Santiago Matamoros, the Moor Slayer, hacks off another head of the infidel. On another portal St James is dressed as a gentle pilgrim with his wide-brimmed hat, cloak and pouch. A score of other sculptures show the peace and determination etched into their faces. Only here in Santiago am I reminded of the real reason for the pilgrimage route – to rout the Moors from Spain. Not once across Northern Spain has anyone mentioned the Moors; they have spoken about homelessness, the conflict of time and money, the lack of jobs, the search for new horizons, a belief in something superior. But who knows the Will of The Most High?

All agree that wine is a saint of the Camino.

Here in Santiago I remember the oxen supporting the main entrance of San Martin at Carrion de los Condes. The land had long ago surrendered to the maize, but the Church still remembered that it once depended on animals. I fulfilled two promises to myself; the first to place a feather of a little owl I had found on the wayside near Conques, one that I gave to the homeless man at Moissac. One that is also for me, that I may find a way in the world. This bird of the night is no stranger to dreams. I placed this feather behind a column supporting the chapel of St Joseph; a child sits on his shoulder, a positive picture of mankind. Outside the church, in the middle of the monumental square, I placed the red, heart-shaped stone I had found at the southern tip of Europe, Zahara de los Atunes. This gesture fulfilled my desire to bring something tangible from the heartland of the old Caliphate to the Christian heartland of Spain.

I thought this would be the symbolic end to this journey but when I received my Compostela, I was asked to read something at the pilgrim's mass that morning. Tigger the badger and the golden pig came with me. I said: I pray for the many different peoples, all going in the same direction, for many different reasons.

May the power to love, the heart of faith, bring fulfilment to our lives. May this love show us how to respect other lives; animals, birds, plants, the earth.

(Santiago de Compostela, October 18, 1996)

Emergence

"It's a wise son who knows his own father."
Athene to Telemachus, *Odyssey*, Homer

Christmas Eve arrived out of silence. The whole world was asleep in some special time zone. And just for a moment, that delicious childhood moment of going into a wood for the first time, it seemed as if it could last forever, and that only the striking of timely bells and their solemn silences would break the spell. The door to the bedroom barged open and in boomed a voice kicking out sleep. 'Look! See!' Curtains were pulled back and in poured grey light around his feet, then more silence, and there was Jo bending by the window with his mouth open and a lush grin over his face. Around his head was wrapped a towel as if it were perfectly normal. He must have been up for an hour already but had been as quiet as a mouse. His finger pointed outside, his face ready to burst with the word. 'Snow!' Outside, the snow kept falling, falling, falling. There seemed no end to the millions of soft feathers out of battleship clouds. BIG had answered our prayers, he had got it right at last. Or was it Father Christmas? Someone had answered, someone had listened. The snowflakes abseiled to earth, every thing in slow motion, fatally attracted to our eyes, the hill, the branches, to our fingers. Each one landed out of slate blue clouds, yet already, from a gap of blue sky, luminous light beaconed onto the pines of King's Wood. I could hear my heart beating. Yes! This is it. Then something brained him and he became a statue with a question mark. He saluted the window and did a slow about turn. Sarah tapped her head, he winked and I winked back. He marched on the spot, backwards, forwards, and I returned the salute. I wanted him to be BIG. Some back-room theatre took us over, and we loved him for it. Sarah walked like a frog, crouching down in her night-dress and waddling, while I sang nonsense from the edge of the bunk bed, 'Sinky woopee pee pow!' Then we marched single file onto the landing, keeping the same pace, down the stairs, and nothing mattered until that first touch, as sure as grey ashes, the assurance, the delicious

199

mouth-balling touch of snow giving way to a white world, a blank piece of paper. A whole day, unknown, the day we had wanted.

Our hearts were on fire.

REFLECTIONS

After the storm the Aubrac blossoms. The sun reclaims inches of rain; mist spills out of the earth and the sky inhales it; pine needles dangle with pure colours; butterflies creep out of thistles; even big-backed violet beetles plod across the road. Well-being sweeps me along. A solitary figure looms beside the high-banked verge, snailing under an enormous pack; he is literally dripping and he holds a notebook in his left hand. 'Lars Overby,' he says, smiling out of brown eyes and a long-boned Danish face. He is in his mid-thirties and soaking after a night on the mountain. At Aumont-Aubrac the community radio welcomes us with piped Spanish rhythms. 'If I had a gun I would shoot the speakers down,' he says. At the fountain we share tea and chocolate, discover a mutual interest in cycling. He used to write poetry until he realised he wanted to make people laugh. For five years he had worked as a stand-up comic and he was now looking for the writer in him. He holds up his notebook, 'I walk for inspiration'.

I show him mine, 'So do I'. We see a true reflection and laugh.

Lars tells me this story:

Once while walking in Corsica he became depressed by the sight of rubbish tips at the exit of each village. Why don't they bury it? he thinks. Then he sees a spanking new rubbish collecting van, progress at last. The next day he rounds a corner and sees the van tipping shite onto the mountainside.

(St Côme d'Olt, September 20, 1996)

Granny's interventions were aimed at our stomach and, unknown to us, she had fried the eggs, lined out the bacon with the beans and the toast, and placed that beside the tin-foil turkey with its legs sticking out. It dominated the kitchen like a trophy from a battle. She was always one step ahead, like the mouse which escaped by using its head; granny with her benign smile, the knowing in her eyes, her wisdom dispensed by the teaspoonful. Was she the cat and we the mice? 'His stomach is the best watch. He always has breakfast at eight.' Jo stumbled into the kitchen rubbing his eyes and stooping to miss the ceiling beam. He had cut his hair! So that was it. The long strands had gone from his eyes.

'We'll chop you up, tasty boy, fry you with dumplings. Mmmm you'll taste nice.' Granny licked her fingers. Sarah made a funny face behind her back, pulling her lower lip to show two incisors. Jo laughed and his hands instinctively touched mine. They were plump and warm, I remember that.

200

'I'm older today. I got down every step.'

'Manners!'

His fingers stopped short of the plate, his shoulders stiffened as if he were standing to attention. This was a game which had rules; he was always playing a game when our backs were turned. From one side of his plate he worked methodically, bean by bean, until he reached the other, then he placed his knife and fork perfectly straight in the middle. Yet once away from the table he would start in the middle of sentences, not finish them or go from one thing to another like one of his canaries.

I never knew what he would do next.

There was drama in the air, the morning glowed, dogwoods on the railway embankment blinked warmly red, and there were holly berries and bottle greens and cold lights and blue shadows and silence roaring out of fleecy woodlands. Christmas Eve was a card waiting to be opened. No-one had been here before, the snow said so, pressing its cold lips to our faces, melting on hot cheeks, the soft feather fall bringing silence, interning small birds, making fugitives of voles and shrews, darkening the trees, making ghosts out of birds. I stared at the snow until my eyes became dizzy. The snowflakes were separate and in their own worlds until they landed to become one. I had a delicious expectancy of intimacy, now we could talk, say the things which had been left unsaid.

'It's like magic.'

'I want it to last forever.'

'But it's only magic because it doesn't last.'

The world started here, in the beginning. Everything was sleeping, hidden in the ground. There were no signposts or paths to follow, only the ones we made. Once again he got stuck climbing over the fence but this time he had no hair to flick away from his eyes; he leaned over by himself, swung his weight onto his other leg and sprung up sharply on his heels. 'I did it!'

'YOU DID!'

Halfway up King's Hill Jo waved his arm and so did the blue shadow behind him, but twice as big. He stuck out his leg and it stretched down the hill almost to granny's cottage. 'Attack of the forty foot giants!' Our arms waved, our bodies swayed, our legs kicked out until we were a long-legged bird trying to fly over the cottage – but we couldn't step over our shoelaces, even if we had any. Or was it BIG coming up behind us, and we had to follow that blue bird? Jo kept stamping the snow, a slow beat with a gap where he dragged his right foot. 'Snowman patrol!'

'SNOWMAN PATROL!' came the echoes. He circled around his feet peering up at the sky as if a pterodactyl was overhead, knew we were there. Soon the snowballs rolled down the hill, little ones becoming masters, then tyrants to flatten all before them. 'Bombs away. Boom! Boom! Boom!' They got as far as the stream and stopped; they had run out of breath. Higher up, below King's Wood, a trail of easy slots crossed our path.

'It's a deer.'

'Following us.'

'From King's Wood.'

'It's probably a veggie lion, eats potatoes.'

'There aren't any lions.'

'People put their heads in his mouth to see if he's friendly.' That silenced him for five seconds.

'How big is a lion's mouth?' He opened his hands, 'This big? Bigger?'

'It's in a hurry.'

'It knows.'

'The hunt is coming. It's getting out while it can.'

'Snowman patrol. Forward march.'

'SNOWMAN PATROL, FORWARD MARCH.'

The saddle creak of boots in the snow reminded us that we were going somewhere. The deer's tracks led downhill through a gap in the hedge to the stream bordering a small wood, in fact they were rows of match-sticks below the railway embankment. They pulped these trees for paper and one day granny would lose this woodland. It would go in a day when giant caterpillars cut a way across the field. A hundred miles of blue sky would vanish too. A gravity stillness had the wood by its throat, made a wall on our feet to keep us hidden. A single leaf floated down against the sky, the only thing which moved. Our eyes grew bigger where snow hampered twig and branch, fattening the winter silhouettes, putting white feathers on the outside. But they couldn't fly away. We squinted at the icy shoulders of the field, clouds on the ground; our breath steamed above us. Then Jo doubled back alongside the poplars. I stepped into Jo's giant strides, but they were twice as big as mine.

'What is it?' He pointed into the trees where a wire gate was hanging from its hinge. A grey transfer loomed out of the wood, making us see where the poplars ended and evergreen laurel decked with snow took over. It was the wire we noticed, the chainlink supported by posts and a roof bulging dangerously from leaves and snow. Inside was a dirty carpet of snow that someone had thrown away, and through it poked grass, rolls of wire, corners of corrugated sheeting. From the roof were suspended metal feeders, heading out to Jones's as dad would say; icicles hung from their bases. There were hoops of iron and barrels suspended on wooden tripods with hosepipes sticking out like broken antennae. Single bird tracks skimmed the snow, mice trails spiralled out below the feeders; on the other side of the wire was a mad flurry of tracks and shitty stains.

'Something's lost.'

'This place gives me the creeps.'

Sarah spat out the words, 'It's a turkey factory.'

'They're kept in barns.' Suddenly – and from behind us – a laurel bush exploded. The tension of wires startled us, then something big and rusty crashed into the sky. Snow fell around us, we toppled back. A cock pheasant! Immediately answered by the upturned bow of a female dashing inside the fence, criss-crossing tracks and the stains in the snow. We understood: something beautiful was trapped inside the prison greys.

'Pheasants!'

The bird panicked at our voices. She repeatedly barged into the fence as if brawn could defeat malicious wire.

'The gate's open.'

'OUT! THIS WAY!'

We rattled the wire to make the pheasant understand. It flew to the corner where snow submerged rings of nettles.

'STUPID!'

'This way!'

'We won't eat you.'

THE CHICKEN

The farm had an intelligent chicken. It was the only one to find a way past the electric fencing encircling the five mobile hen homes. To begin with it was rounded up and returned each night to the communal perch but the next morning it escaped again until, by squatter's rights, it was allowed its head. At night it roosted in the barn with Shakuntla, the massive old sow named after an Indian princess, the last place a fox would venture. When Shakuntla was moved to the field, the chicken attached itself to the small flock of Christmas turkeys foraging on the lawn, walking along the edges of hay bales or hunting spiders in the wood shed. Though dwarfed by its exotic sisters, it had the charming habit of approaching stealthily behind a turkey fanning its tail feathers, then pecking – in the middle where it hurt! The feathers dropped, but the chicken always side-stepped the rebuke. It was only a game. Each night it allowed itself to be rounded up with the turkeys and locked up in the fox-proof pen. Of course this strange relationship could not last and, one by one, the turkeys disappeared until the only bird let out in the morning was the chicken. It never went back to that pen. It roosted in the cattle byre above the posse of black cats waiting for the twice daily hand-milking. I didn't see it for a week and wondered if the fox had cornered it. Then one day I helped to move the calves from one pen to another, and there was the little hen trailing behind to be safely locked up – except it could get past the bars anytime it wanted to. Clever hen!

PS: Three months later some men came to build a barn and one said that he had worked at a farm where thousands of cockerels were held in pens before being shipped to France to make coq-au-vin. One particular cockerel always managed to escape the final rounding up and would only allow itself to be caught after the wagons had left. It had done this so many times that the men left it alone. I wish that I could unite this chicken and cockerel, and from this union more intelligent chickens would appear in the world.

(Dunsford Farm, Somerset, 1996)

* * *

In the drooling rain outside Le Puy, I glimpsed in the distance a solitary figure inside a shell of a poncho. William again. We tramped up the hill in dripping smiles then sheltered inside a hut before St Privat d'Allier. The 20th century vanished into the storm; in the half-light and sitting on the mud-floor we were in another time zone. He started talking. Once in the 1960's he helped to build a hospital for blind children in Zambia. They made a showcase village from scratch out of the jungle with modern amenities. Years later he saw the village on television, but now the jungle had been cleared for firewood. 'It was no longer the paradise I remembered.'

He talked about his sons. He had advised them to start their own business. 'If they inherit mine it could be too much stress. Everyone has to find their own level. If my sons had to ask me for money to start up the business then they have no right to be a company director.' I confided that writing is a strange way, but I am true to myself.

He tilts his hand, 'Little by little and with success.'

What I liked about William is his directness. He talks to anybody. 'A woman says she is happy. "But your voice isn't happy," I say to her.' He met a 79-year-old Belgium in the Ardennes who knew everything about walking in Europe. 'Go at your own speed, don't give height away, go alongside mountains.'

'But have you walked to Santiago?'

'The old man is shocked, "I am not yet a hundred".' William shudders with laughter, the sweat steams from him.

'You like stories, I'll tell you one.'
Near the Belgium border he meets Miske, a Dutch woman in her forties
walking by herself. 'She is a doctor and is out for a week so she can talk to the
flowers and the trees. We like each other and walk together for a day. "And do
you know," she says, "I talked to a black chicken for half an hour. She listened
to everything I said, even nodding in the right places."' '
'Ah!' says William, 'You met her on a wall?'
'Yes.'
'By a white cottage with a big lime tree?'
'Yes.'
'Next to a bridge?'
'Yes, you must be psychic.'
William smiles. 'I rested on that wall. A black chicken sat next to me and
listened to everything I said.'   *(St-Alban-sur-Limagnole, September 9, 1996)*

Jo ripped the door from its hinges and let it fall where it deserved. He stood in the gap beckoning with his arm.

'You're frightening it.'

He didn't want to hear. He walked slowly into the pen, rubbing his hands in that peculiar singing way I had seen with the canaries, softly, persistently. The pheasant – the rusty eye in the snow – stared back mesmerised, not moving. He came closer, ten yards, five yards; the pheasant craned its neck into a question mark. The eyes twizzled. Sarah kicked the fence. The pheasant ran for its life, head down into the darkest bit.

'Stupid! COME OUT!' The grey eye surfaced like a periscope.

'THIS WAY.' It battled with the wire again. 'It's not using its head.'

'It hasn't got one.'

'It's frightened, can't you see.' Sarah spread out her arms and walked towards it. She's just like Tugger once she starts, she can't let go. She has to knock down locked doors. The bird pinned its eye on her, going backwards at the same pace. It wasn't giving in. 'I'm on your side.' The bird slapped hard into the chainlink ceiling and down rained dollops of snow and fisty ice. It panicked as if a pack of hounds were on its tail.

'COME OUT!' Sarah walked straight to the corrugated hoop where the bird pretended to hide. 'OUT!' Nothing happened. She kicked it. The pheasant screeched out, catching her face with its wing, knocking her down. The bird flew straight into the wire. Jo caught the tip of a wing. It somersaulted over him and back to square one.

'I don't believe it.'

'It doesn't care.' We manoeuvred behind the bird, squawking ten times louder than the pheasant did, scrabbling with our feet, kicking away snow, forcing it back into the open. She hummed over our heads to burrow desperately under the wire – but that was buried deep to keep out foxes. It beat the ground uselessly with its wings; a penitent at its prayers.

'You'll kill it!'

It would never leave this place, never, never, never, and that was it. We had made things worse. It was as far away from us as Venus, and there's no water on Mars. We trooped through the open gate saying nothing, the pheasant still cooped into its corner. Sarah kicked a grassy clump, 'It doesn't want to be free.'

FARE-WELL, MY LOVELY

There is a place where you can look down the main street of Ostrava-Poruba and see past the neo-classical blocks of socialist realism parked on both sides like cliffs. Far in the middle ground are the belching chimneys of Ostrava and behind that are the Beskydy mountains bordering Slovakia. And if you turn just a little to the left there is Poland and the Silesian plains, and I think: I'm really abroad.

Eva Spackova who showed me this had a similar experience when she travelled to Paris after the Velvet Revolution. She is an architect and a devoted mother and dreams of the time when she will be able to work again and to travel. Yes to travel, that's the big thing. Her eyes become larger when she thinks of travel, but not with her two small children. 'Anywhere,' she says simply. Her name Spackova means bird, a common bird which sings and flies; perhaps a starling, but she is not sure. She is a diminutive woman, a delicate, shell-like face with gritty Slovakian traits: striking eyes and dimpled, square chin. She appears resilient yet she is tired; her strong face carries its strain, the downward curving lines are there. For a moment I sense what it must have been like living under a regime where one could not choose a way to live. She tells me (and I am a little flattered) that the Party would have imprisoned or exiled me.

The main street – Hlaunt Trida – was once called Leninova Trida, but that was another lifetime ago. This boulevard is modelled on Les Champs Elysées. The normal head-down facade, clean shaven and private lives are still here along with fashionable mini-skirts or leopard-skin tights, all-in-one plastic, men with long hair or flaunting pony tails. I keep thinking of the Sixties, I have been here before: the ubiquitous cigarettes, posters advertising tours of Joe Cocker or Black Sabbath. Everyone appears to be going somewhere, perhaps they are running their own businesses.

'I have no time,' I hear a lot.

I ask Eva to name one good thing under Communism. She thinks by wrinkling her nose, nodding her head. 'Nothing,' she says twice and adding, 'perhaps I'm not typical.' Under Communism everyone worked eight hours a day and child-care was a state business. 'This is a country of extremes. Then the women went to work and now they all stay at home.' There are no easy answers, perhaps job-sharing or flexible hours might help. 'You have had 200 years of free markets – we have had only eight years.' I understand, I need to put myself in their shoes. Of her parents' generation she says: 'They were in the cellars trembling before the Nazi bombs. Who would not dream of the Communists as saviours?'

The Communists won the free elections in 1948 and then came the restrictions. 'Soon every thing came in certain sizes. There was no more china, the glass came in fixed sizes and everything had to fit them. We could not travel to the West, censorship ruled. You could not even take copies of things. We can't go back to this. Now I have the freedom to draw a curve.' I laugh, and she puts her finger to her lips. 'We cannot laugh. There are some now who say that life was not so bad under the Communists, the rents were little, and if they had to queue for half the day at least the food was cheap.' Now she smiles, 'At twenty if you are not a Communist you have no heart; at 40 if you are a Communist you have no brain.'

Halfway down the main street she points out how the socialist realism (and optimism) of the Fifties with the neo-classical bits and fine craftsmanship deteriorated in the Sixties and Seventies. The statues become reliefs, a functional modernism rules. 'After Stalin died the buildings became more fabricated. They did not have the craftsmen to repair these older buildings. It became an industrial process with fixed-size panels.'

'They put up these in England too,' I say. 'They're pulling them down now.'

The statue makers have been busy along with the sign writers recording the changes. Statues of Lenin have gone – many have been bought by Western museums. 'First there were the monarchist statues, then Masaryk of the first Czech Republic, then the Nazis, then the Communists, and now the free world. When the Communists came the patriots buried the Masaryk statues, now they're digging them up again.'

One third of a million people live in Ostrava-Poruba, a huge complex sprawling over 214 square kilometres, much of it straightjacketed by unfettered industrialisation: colossal gas tubing at street corners, overhead grid-lines, a rusting hulk of a railway station. The potential of transformation is the dream. 'But where is the money?' asks Eva. In her flat are red chairs and a table with red flowers. 'I want some colour in my home. Sometimes when the two children are crying, the phone rings and the dishes are falling over, I fear I go a little crazy.' She pats her washing machine. 'The end of socialism was getting

*rid of my Slovakian machine, a horrible thing I had in this house. I had to
hold it all the time to stop it vibrating. And it was a privilege to have one! My
German one is quiet, so quiet.'*   (Turza Slaska, Poland, May 28, 1998)

IVAN VALCOLVIC

*Ivan Valcolvic met his wife Miriam on a skiing holiday in the High Tatras. 'I
was the leader and I think she liked that. But then she found out the truth
after we were married, and it is too late.'*

*'I heard that,' says Miriam from the bedroom where she is setting up the
pagemaker programme on her computer. Miriam is stylish (trained as an art
teacher) blond hair with highlights and sleekly short, her face a little severe
until she smiles. At 40 she did not think she could understand computers then
taught herself after a woman friend said it was easy. She designs the books that
her husband translates into Slovak, pioneering books in psychology: Carl
Rogers, 'A way of Being' (Sposon Bytia), 'Freedom To Learn' (Sloboda Ucit
Sa). It's expensive by Slovak standards, £1,000 to buy the rights and then a
percentage on sales. There seems no way it will pay for itself in the short term,
but Ivan believes that the work of this pioneer of humanistic psychology should
be available to his co-workers.*

*In the sultry heat of a Galanta evening, Ivan walks around the small kitchen
bare-chested, the day's long work with counselling clients showing in his tired
eyes, yet his buoyant humour and twisting ears are always on alert. Dominic,
his youngest son, is under the kitchen table pretending to be a dog and eating
peoples' legs. 'He has no problem expressing himself,' says Ivan. The younger
Ivan is in the cellar (where it's cooler) studying for his exams. Their daughter
has blue ties in her hair and glitter, and she dreams of travelling.*

*'I don't want to travel,' says Miriam emphatically. 'I like to stay at home.'
She's a part-time teacher. She likes spaces in her life. I tell him that
counselling in England is the new profession; people go to counsellors like they
might visit their dentists. His face listens, not many words or much expression
until he smiles or opens his mouth in surprise. In Slovakia – in 1998 – people
will visit him and then go out by the cellar so no-one will see them. Perhaps in
20 years there will a new attitude, the same amount of time, Ivan predicts, for
political democracy to emerge. Before the Velvet Revolution, Ivan remembers it
took him eight years to get the Party's permission to publish a book on divorce.
'Everyone had to give their approval, right down to the local Communist
official. The only brakes now is lack of money.'*

*Ivan recalls that before the revolution, the church collection plates always had
paper money. 'Now it is only small change, 10 kronors.' The gap between the
haves and have-nots is growing daily, a consequence of the free market. He
talks of the Gypsies, the Poles, the Hungarians, the Russians, how they have*

to co-exist together, just like the different lives of his children and his wife in their flat. I am impressed by that. He shows me SME, the Slovakian opposition national paper, and one of the middle pages is in English. I am amazed. 'You would never see this in England.' And he asks: 'Why not?' Why not, indeed. This is a European dialogue.

Each evening I help them in their allotment garden – 'therapy and economics' – with blocks of potatoes, peas, carrots, tomatoes and paprikas (everyone grows paprikas). I pump up the water into the barrel, help hand-weed the strawberries and pick ripe sour cherries. Miriam uses a mattock. 'And do you know the expression, 'The Self' asks Ivan. 'I'm having problems finding a Slovakian idiom...self-concept, ego, me...'

'What about the 'I am centre?' I like that, direct and more concrete. He rubs his hair, short and silvery black, thinking with his alert eyes. I ask him another question: 'Do you think of yourself as a European?'

He answers straightaway, 'I'm Slovak, and I'm cosmopolitan.'

I'm glad the Internet's arrived. Now everyone can travel at home.

(Galanta, Slovakia, 1998)

BOHEMIAN WAYS

Sumperk in North Moravia was once part of the Sudetenland where three million Germans had co-existed in the former Czechoslovakia. The town sits easily among the forested foothills of Jeseniky; to the north is a mist of Polish plains, to the south, the Byskydy mountains. On people's tongues I hear about upper and lower Silesia, Ukrainian grandparents, mothers from Cracow, uncles in Slovakia. I think this must be Mitteleuropa, but I'm not sure. It's not on the map. Everyone else calls it home.

Yet everyone over the age of 60 was not born in Sumperk.

Sumperk was settled by German colonists. They built the 12th century churches, piled up the medieval walls, set out the broad shopping town streets and decorated their buildings with the distinctive neo-classical curves, the baroque floral effects, a restrained exuberance. They called Sumperk, Mayr Shönberg, something like 'Beautiful hill'. When the Czechs settled there, they called their part of town Ceski.

Today in Sumperk there are very few Germans left, and even fewer Jews. They have become tiny minorities, and both left the town in the same way, by cattle-trucks. The Germans sent the Jews to concentration camps, the Czechs sent the Germans back to Germany. (At Yalta, Churchill and Roosevelt agreed with Stalin to forcibly repatriate the Germans who had built Sumperk.) Each German was allowed 7 kilos of luggage when forced out of their homes and histories. To fill the vacuum, exiled Czech communities in Poland, Ukraine, Rumania and nearer home took over the empty properties. (Sign-painters have done good business in Sumperk; the German signs came down, up went the Czech; the streets were renamed, then the Russians came and the communist slogans and Russian signs appeared, and now everything is back into Czech.) Many of the Germans went to Bad Hersfeld or Wurzberg and lived for years in tent camps while rebuilding the cities after the Allied bombings.

Meanwhile the Communists plastered over the sculptured reliefs and carved the muscle-bound heroes of socialist realism into the corners of buildings. Since the Velvet Revolution, Sumperk is changing her face again or reclaiming it. The grey renderings are being removed revealing Baroque curves, and these are repainted in creams and blues and warm yellows; granite setts are replacing the communist tarmac in the historic centre, Namesti Miru, The Square of the Peace. Nearby is the European Friendship House, another cultural initiative, as well as the town's twinning with Maarsen in Holland, Bad Hersfeld in Germany.

Jan Pavlicek is responsible for the tourist development and renovation. With true Bohemian flair he contradicts silly municipal stereotypes; his curly black hair is groomed over his shoulders, a tight red tie sets off a blue floral shirt and maroon suit. He furrows his head when thinking and moves his hands a lot. He is 33 and responsible for the town's historic renovation. He is also a local state representative and visits the minority Czech communities in Romania to see what practical help they need.

'They are living in conditions of 100 years ago,' he says. He shows me a crumbling grey facade in the town centre. 'Before the Velvet Revolution everything looked like this.' He raises his shoulders when talking about the future to emphasise the uncertainty. 'The economy then was good for Russia and now we have to face West. It's hard for us. Our goods are cheap, but so is the quality.'

Recently he visited Wurzburg where many Sumperk German refugees went after the war. 'I feel sad about this history. The Germans from Sumperk lost everything.

'After the Revolution the Catholic priests talked to one another and some Germans returned to visit, others from Sumperk were invited back. And out of this has grown some co-operation. In the recent floods many of the Germans helped financially with the repairs. We are trying to understand our history. This is a start.'

And I wanted to say I saw such a tender kiss between himself and his wife – I still remember it.   (Ostrava, Czech, May 26, 1998)

SCHAATSEN – SKATING ON ICE
Somewhere in Zeeland, I stopped on the sand dunes and beside the triffid-like sea walls taming the ocean. Past the chokkablock camper vans was the open sea

and the coruscating flags of wind surfers, silently, all gleefully on the move. I was in love with this picture, the ocean tranquillity, the changing lights, the Dutch enjoying themselves on a Saturday afternoon. I watched the sail-boards until I was unsure where the sea ended or the sky began. The wind-surfers had turned into swallows on a summer's day, the sails had become bird's wings; the sea, the blue sky.

* * *

At Delft, Hans Bruckers, the physicist, shows me his three Elfsteden Kruisjes, small silver crosses awarded for completing the Elfstedentocht, the 11-city skating tour in Friesland – the Holy Grail for skaters. Already his blue eyes are twinkling, raking lights to his wispy beard, laughter attending lines in an otherwise smooth face. In his eyes he remembers the 16,000 participants in 1985 as comet trails of ants on a sea of ice, cracked and frozen again. It's a 24-hour race, 100 kilometres in the dark; a challenge to the fit, an obsession for everyone. There is a long waiting list for his coveted membership. His father taught him skating on the old-fashioned wooden boards; he learnt how to klunen, walking on his heels between ice, and tasted the pea soup and hot chocolate at the koek-en-zoopie. Every winter he takes his rope (for pulling people out of ice-holes), his screwdriver (for pulling himself out) and ventures slowly out, studying the reflections to spot thin ice or cracks, and sometimes in the sunlight the ice is thick enough to sparkle sand-grains and roots at the bottom. 'You look at the world from another perspective, like sitting on your knees.'

Hans loves skating and knows the names of all the Big Race winners, especially 1963, the fabulously hard winter. He dresses in old clothes when he skates, and secretly enjoys the inverted snobbery of sailing head down past skaters in their techno gear. 'When we were children our mothers said "Don't go on the ice. It's dangerous." So there is this element of danger. Some winters I skate out of the old harbours and it's like skating out to sea. There are no traffic lights or white lines or policemen. I go wherever I want to go. I could be with The Bontekoe Tasman, the 17th century sailors to Surinam and Indonesia. I feel so free.'

Once he cycled to Moscow with other cyclists, a three-week ride of endurance from Warsaw. Even with Russian guides, food was hard to find; the few restaurants had their quota of customers, and that was that. In Moscow he missed the last tram back to his hotel and had to share a taxi. That went past his hotel. The men tried to grab him, and he remembers being chased across urban wasteland in the small hours. Sometime later, he met Natasha at The Hermitage in St Petersburg. They became friends. They exchanged letters, the early ones had half-rouble stamps, the recent ones were worth hundreds of roubles. She visited him in Holland and she painted the dykes and cattle and windmills. 'She is studying icon painting. She lives with her Russian child in a small flat. In two years she will have exhausted her savings. She does not know what she will do then.'

In his house is a painting of a vase of flowers: expressionistic blues, stillness, depth and tranquillity. It is her gift.   *(Amsterdam, May 12, 1997)*

Our happy mood was broken. Stamping the ice in the rutted trackway relieved some of the frustration for Sarah, and so did the snowballs smashing into trees. We stayed single file, keeping Jo in the middle to stop him picking up useless things or touching every squiggle and hole in the snow. The path led out of the wood into a great, white saucer, a pool hidden by osiers and alders, one of the secret places I had wanted Jo to see. But not like this. The willows glowed orangey-red. No-one came here, the snow said so; only broken shafts of bulrushes stuck up their elbows. The path kept to a raised bank where water from a sluice gate dripped into a metal trough full of stinking black leaves. I think a witch put it there and every leaf is a child with a spell on it. Sarah stood on the wall with her hands on her hips, her blond hair cut to her shoulder as sharp as her eyes and the frozen grasses. A stick skidded across the pool, then a bigger one cracked the ice. I chucked in a rock, the echoes splintered around us. More stones followed, the high octane of crackling ice made us smile, switched on a current deep in the ground. Jo rammed a stick into the ice until bubbles burst to the surface.

'It's farting.'

'You're disgusting.'

Winter lights and the earth-bound chill squeezed our throats as if they were hands. He poked the mud harder until a dirty, foul smelling liquid spread over the snow and a wound that wouldn't mend. The mud came up his hand and, by mistake, he dabbed some onto his nose. At once he was so comical in his brown coat covering him like a sack. He tried to brush it off but it spread over his cheeks, and our laughter made it worse. He waddled along the wall as if he were a big duck or a clown in a circus. 'Watch out for the lion,' said Sarah spitefully. She knew where it hurt. He spun round, nearly falling backwards, and just managed to balance himself by holding onto an elder tree – then he fell off! His feet dangled two feet from the ground.

'Lions climb trees. That's where they put the deer kills.'

His face burned red and he wouldn't let go, still swinging on the branch.

'It's not real. There's no lion,' I said.

212

Something brushed Sarah's face, she pushed it away. For a moment she tottered on the wall, flailing her arms and out of reach of the branches. She turned like a big top in slow motion, lost her footing, slid towards the black snow. She fell onto her hands but they kept going until they dipped into the hole. Black hands! The corners of her mouth were held down, holding back her tears. 'STOP!' She refused all help. Her legs carried her over the mound, past the sluice gate and out of our sight. I panicked too, I ran. Jo dropped from the tree. 'Wait !' I ran faster, hearing his feet scramble, his breath, gasping. Our frightened feet had run away from us and we did not know why. We ran from that place, from the coldness clinging to our chest, the mud sticking to our feet. I skidded on the snow, twice fell and clawed my way back up, not daring to look back. The fear that had possessed Sarah, possessed us all. Wait for me! It carried us back into the poplars, along the side of the embankment to a small clearing I had seen before. I rested my hands on my knees. I saw them, they were still here. The wind had blown the snow up the sides of the straight-lined thistles, hung their arms with icy tatters. They were in my way. I told them to move but they wouldn't. It's not my fault, you'll pay for this. I pushed them away. They did not bend, they snapped. I broke their arms and legs. They deserved it, the way they just stood there. They scratched my hands and face. I knocked them down. They poked my shins, butted my arms. I smashed them with my feet. I ran faster, I could not stop myself.

I DON'T UNDERSTAND
The clouds are blowing away from me, so the wind will be at the back. On the bike, the wind is in my face. I don't understand.

In Picardy I see huge billboards of beautiful women, slinking, bending over, lying down and staring at the cars. Beside them are oceans of wheat, a regimented land, not a bird in sight. I don't understand.

It's misty. I want to switch on my halogen bike dynamo, just press and turn. I have been shown it a dozen times. Can I do it? Impossible. I don't understand.

I cycle past a dead hedgehog, turn back and place it in the hairline ditch of wild grass. How can it live here, in this ditch? I don't understand.

In gardens I see windmills, elves and goblins, plastic cauldrons and boundary fences with neatly-sprayed edges. I don't understand.

The little boy wraps a sugar-beet sticker onto my bike, it's a smiling red sweetheart. I would like a sweetheart. I never said that to his parents, by omission I suggested that I was still married. I wanted them to think that I was a good person. I don't understand.

The Austrian woman had a plain face with spots, and she was a bit skinny.
Yet she was a goddess in her eyes and in her words. I don't understand.
She said, 'You have to win integrity.' She frowned a lot. Her husband, whom
she loved, was still dependent on his family; she wanted him to be his own
man. 'The way ahead is so uncertain. I don't understand.'
Dozens of frogs chorused by the lake shore, their roundabout laughter eluding
my ears. One stops, they all stop. I don't understand.
The architect lives in the old Normandy farmhouse. He visits Chicago and is
amazed by the world of Frank Lloyd Wright, the design details right down to
the ash-trays. He visits Ladakh. 'The first time everybody wanted to know
me, the second time they asked if I were an American. I don't understand.'
'I don't understand,' I say, 'how you can admire Chicago and love Ladakh.'
'That's easy,' he says. 'I sponsor a little Tibetan girl, Tsering Pelmo.'
I understand.   (Poperinge, May 4, 1997)

AUSTRIAN DESCENT

I saw a hoopoe in Austria, a whirring black, long-beaked bird with bars and
wings curved in white stripes. It flew in front of me near Ferlach in the Dau
Valley, a moment or two alongside the solemn, sometimes awesome peaks
marking the border with Slovenia to my left. I took heart from this fleeting
hoopoe, as well as the twigs I saw in its beak. It, too, was thinking of home.
In Austria, for me, anxiety was never far away. I submerged easily into a
darker matrix, something half digested and my fears rose up one by one like
horsemen appearing over a hill. Poor digestion started it off, then came
thunderstorms and soakings. I misjudged my money and went to bed without a
meal after a long day cycling to Murek. On the eve of entering Austria I
dreamed I was making love to a hard-nosed and chubby woman. We did all
the right things but there was no rapport or real contact. And this, perversely, is
exactly how I feel about my short tour of Carinthia — well-cared for rural lands
with chalet farms; blocks of maize and vines and pumpkins, real sub-alpine
meadows for hay, firewood stacked so you can hardly put a knife between the
wood, the fruit orchards pruned, old women sitting in walnut shade, orchards
of elder, field crops of horseradish (both world firsts for me). The small towns —
Ehrenhausen, Bleiburg, Eibiswald — are painted and pretty and loved, and I
waved to shoals of weekend cyclists (all men) and they waved back. It should
have been a kind of paradise, the panoramas at every bend — but I felt a
stranger here. I did not know why.
Yet the hoopoe looked contented finding sustenance.
Perhaps something in me doesn't fit here. I'll admit to my prejudices: Austr-
ians are provincial minded, they value security above all else (and I can see the
30's newsreel of goose-stepping youth in Graz). I have to say Carinthia

214

looked obsessively clean, not a seeding dandelion outside the hay meadows or a stray dog or an old car; the new cars were polished, not a finger-mark of dust was on any of the hands which I saw. In short everything was immaculately in its place, and I did not like this. I felt there was no room for anything new, no cracks for stray flowers to grow.

At every town there was a billboard of a Fifty's man, smoking, eyes behind shades, a taut, expressionless face, a sort of John Wayne or desert cowboy; a handsome, action man but skin deep. To compound this association, I kept hearing Buddy Holly, Paul Anka, Roy Orbison on the radio. What's in the shadow of this man? Feelings are for girls, and so is their expression; physical anxiety, homophobia and wimps (and perhaps they are the same thing); woolly ideas; foreign faces. It's a man's world, the advert says, yet perversely all the time I felt the woman were masters, the ones making the decisions — at the hotels, station queues, at restaurants. A formidable lot. I could not escape this feeling that I was in 1962. I felt inadequate in Carinthia. We would never see eye to eye. It was just a one night stand.

I arrived to catch the early train to Sillian from Villach. I had 12 minutes, and I desperately needed the toilet. I could do it if I were quick. I walked back to the tiled reception area. I needed five groschen to open the toilet door. I had three. I had five minutes to get back to the train. Then I noticed the toilet door still moving towards the lock. I just got my foot in — and made all my connections. *(Fartrezza, Italy, June 16, 1998)*

THE GREY ZONE

'Excuse me, is there a shop here?'

'Now you're asking.'

'A shop, anything will do.'

'You better ask somebody else.'

'But there is nobody else.'

'I don't know. I've only lived here 20 years.'

'You ignorant bastard. That's what's wrong with the world, people don't know where they live.'

'What I mean is, I only live here. I don't work here, you understand?'

'I understand. I'm in the grey zone.'

The epileptic youth at Kalundborg frothed at the wayside while people pushed shopping past him.

'We didn't see anybody.'

'There was nobody there.'

'We're sure of that.'

'We would have seen him otherwise.'

'It's not me you understand.'
'I understand. I'm in the grey zone.'

'If it wasn't like this it would be different
And if it were different, it wouldn't be like this.
You know how it is, I'm lost too.'
'I can see that.'
'We don't talk to strangers.
Don't take it personally, really I'm a friendly person.
I know I am.
Deep down I am.
I know, I've seen it.
Once.
I did or did I? I may have been dreaming.'
'You were.'

We were unable to move. Snow matted our hair and hats, dripped from noses, reefed onto coats and boots. Granny blocked the hallway, her concern transformed into anger. It was the inquisition, and we were the lambs. 'I knew it would happen. Look at that mud. Let them out of my sight, for a minute!' *Baa baa* It was useless. 'How did he get it on him? His trousers? His face? You, too, Sarah. What on earth were you doing?' *Baa baa* 'If the mud gets into the house it gets everywhere.'

Our silence made things worse. Jo spoke, 'The lion chased me.'

'You fill his head with nonsense.'

'I saw it.'

'There's enough there already.'

'It was in the tree, waiting.'

'I don't believe this.'

'It was looking at me.'

'You tell him stories.'

'It's only a story, it doesn't exist. You say as if it's happening. He can't tell the difference.'

'He can,'

'You should know better.'

'He knows there are no lions out there.'

'There are no lions,' repeated Jo.

'See.'

'I'm not frightened of lions.'

'See.'

'It's a veggie lion. I can put my head in its mouth. It won't eat me.'
'You'll be the death of me.'

Every branch of the Christmas tree was alive with silver streamers, coloured bobbins and lights, and lording it was the fairy giving her blessing. She had blue glittering eyes, a pink dress, I think. All that was needed was the manger and the animals, the baby cot, and they were stowed in the coal scuttle beside the America chest granny kept in the cellar. 'The settlers called it their America chest because they were going to a new land. The cottage was our new land.' I showed Jo the secret entrance where you pull back the wooden lever behind the front door curtain. Magic! The middle board comes up and you lift out the adjoining two. Three steps go down into the cellar and, if you turn to the left, there's another secret door leading into the coal shed; so you could get outside without a key. I inherited a picture of grandpa coming up the steps with his beard covered in cobwebs. The key to the America chest was hidden in the grandfather clock behind the clockface. I took it while granny's back was turned; it was a secret I wanted Jo to share.

There was plenty of space, I told Jo, but you had to watch your head. The shadows jumped away from the light. Jo chased them with the torch across the end of a brick wall, behind some bags of coal – which are still there – past the cobwebs hanging from the joists above our heads. A thin crack of light was outlined in the darkness away to our left; the hidden door leading to the coal shed. Jo shuffled on all fours towards it. The shadows bounced off his torch, a cool draught played on our cheeks. 'It's just like in the story,' he whispered. 'You don't know what's on the other side.' He turned the wooden handle but it didn't move. There was a trick to opening it

I showed him: you had to lean against the door – then relax – and it would open. You could crawl through on your belly and go up through the floorboards into the outhouse. But time was running out.

The red Christmas bag containing the figures of Mary and Joseph and the manger animals was beside the chest, where granny had said it would be. I restrained Jo's hand. I listened, not a whisper. At best we had two minutes. The America chest was smaller than I remembered but it was built like Fort Knox with wooden panels bound by two metal hoops. The key slipped in as easily as a hand into a biscuit tin. It had been oiled recently, I noticed. A faded velvet cloth appeared beneath the lid, orange in the torchlight. 'Be careful,' I said, restraining Jo's arm. 'She'll know.' He pulled it back as if it were treasure. Some sequins danced in the light, a dress top as smooth as silk. Other clothes were folded neatly below that: a cravat tie, some handkerchiefs, a pair of silver stockings. Under that was something hard, the lid of a box. Still no sound above, no creaking board or granny's face. His fingers and thumbs prised open the lid, an old-fashioned hat box with silk on the inside. First a silver shoe, a dancing shoe, so small he could fill it with his fingers. He danced it on top of the lid, twizzled it round, clicking his tongue in time as if were a dance that he knew. There were old postcards dating back to the Forties, a battleship card with stamps of kings with bearded faces, ghosts from a world I knew only in history books some ghostly palm trees in Torquay – '*Having a lovely time. Glad you're not here!*' – a view of Oxford steeples in black and white, one of the Eiffel Tower from granny's sister, one showing a donkey on a beach; small black and whites, a memory lane. She kept everything, metal buttons with regimental insignia, some letters tied with ribbon, grandpa's love letters (I found that out afterwards). Then more trinkets and bits of jewellery and, at the bottom, a hat: a few mangy feathers that once may have been blue. There was nothing else, no gold or diamonds or Penny Blacks, so we put everything back the way it came out. I locked the chest. Jo insisted on carrying the Christmas bag and placing back the boards so they fitted perfectly. No stranger would know it was there.

In the corner of the living room stood the tree in a bucket, and it was wedged between two doorstops. Jo emptied the bag of glittering streamers, fold-out crackers and Chinese lanterns, colourful baubles, an old set of electric lights, painted clay cows and sheep, a donkey with a tail missing. But what he picked was a plastic Father Christmas with cheery red cheeks and a great sack spilling out presents. He couldn't put it on the top so he placed it by the roots. To the tips of the branches I tied pine cones sprinkled with glitter. Jo wound the streamers about the tree, balancing silver and golden stars everywhere. For animal mangers he cut sides from cardboard boxes and filled them with strips of newspaper.

'They don't look well.' He fished them back out and found the water-colour paints; he touched up their faces and coats until the colours shined. 'They must have proper eyes and tails you can see.' He held up the donkey and I stuck on a plasticine tail. It was a real manger now, a place of animals.

'Silly!' I said. 'The baby's missing!'

So I modelled it from plasticine while Jo made a crib by painting an empty matchbox. He tucked in the baby with a blanket of cotton wool, the animals on one side, the wise men on the other. The crib went in front of the animals at the foot of the tree.

'You have to make hay while the sun shines. That's the straw...and this is the cow...' He put the donkey in the middle beside a lamb. He stared at them with his chin on his hand.

'Where's Joseph?'

ABANDONED AND HAPPY FATHER

I smile as I write this, a foolish smile which appears when I don't know what to say. With puffed cheeks I wear an idiot smile and out comes 'Hello, hello', deep baby talk such as, 'This is my tea, I like my tea.'

I'm introducing myself, here in Bohemia and in Prague. I don't know what to say. My jaws are tight. I'm holding something back. I start with a dream the night before I went to Prague: 'I'm by a deep pool of water and it'

s full of debris and old drums and gangways. I prepare to dive in and then hesitate. I can see a lot of organic debris floating and some of it is shitty'.

This dream came with me to Prague, a frustrating morning of missed train connections and rain. I was under-dressed, over-dressed when the sun came out. I missed obvious connections. I was not in the mood for Prague. I skimmed over the Baroque waters like a water boatman. Prague is a circus, I kept saying to myself, everybody is selling something. On Charles Bridge (Karliv Most) I was a sprat in a shoal of hustlers with trumpets blaring, processions of painted students banging symbols, a hegemony of portrait sketchers, bangle sellers and all shouting in a dozen languages. I wanted some peace, I wanted space. I could not receive in all this noise and commercial hubbub.

Lukas is a silent, thoughtful man, shy I think, not tall and fond of cottons and mild colours. He is Mr Understatement. His house on the edge of Prague is in genteel disorder; boxes clutter half the floor spaces, his Internet computer sits in a darkened room, the doors neither open or shut completely, the hot water doesn't quite work, there's dust on the bookshelves, outside the weeds grow everywhere.

'I don't have time to read anymore, only computer manuals.' He speaks slowly as if remembering each English word. He was part of the Velvet Revolution – 'a revolution without bloodshed' – and remembers the excitement of joining student marches for change. The political freedoms of speech and travel and access to technology had favoured people like him. 'Under socialism there were no differences between people. People had nowhere to spend their money so they escaped at weekends to their country gardens.' Now the unskilled have a harder time of it and people in the country have lost their cheap rents and guaranteed prices.

'The gaps are showing,' says Lukas without expression. Twice he says he has no time. He had given up his hobby of bee-keeping and hardly visited his parents. 'We Czechs are not morally in good shape at the moment. It's hard to find the tradition.' He talks a lot about his son. It's a complex story, the mother for her own reasons puts obstacles in his way. 'How can I be a father if I cannot see my son?'

There are spaces between these words and out I am with my idiot smile and gratitude for simply being here. 'Hello, hello,' I say softly, 'my name's Peter. What's yours?' I am like this here. I am flush with sensation. I twist my head a little too tightly, my head tilts into sacrificial mode. 'Would you like some tea, it's very nice.' Here I am in the shadow of my intentions, rock solid and cracked. I rescue him. I cry as I open his eyes onto this world. Trouvez votre plaisir, and so I will.

Lukas smiles a little, a rare smile. 'When I was young I thought I would have many wives in a village and I would visit them all on my motorbike.' Then he is serious again, in some silence I do not know. I tell him that I visited the Jewish Museum in Prague. The names of the tens of thousands of Jewish victims are written in tiny red and black letters on plain walls (like the words in this journal). The many names seen together create an astonishing, not-knowable pattern. Lukas says his family name is there. His grandfather Ludwig once traded in Kutna Hora.

He plays with his stubble. 'This is not a problem of place or people. It is a human problem. It could happen again.' He is not a practising Jew, but the names and the history of the patriarchs and their wanderings are at his fingertips. 'Only half the Torah is written, the rest is interpretation.' I tell him I will visit Auschwitz.

'I cannot go there. I will cry too much.' He admits he still has emotional problems with the Germans. Casually he says that there is a STP (the former Czech secret police) file on him, and he intends to read it one day. 'It's because of my grandparents and parents. Under Communism if you own something or are well educated you are an enemy. To be crushed and have nothing is the ideal model.' His grandfather was interned at Terezin, the Jewish ghetto, but survived the war. 'He never talked about it.'

His own father had left his native village for the anonymity of Prague. 'After the war the Communists felt guilty to persecute the Jews openly. They called them "Persons of Jewish origin". They did not like their cosmopolitan attitudes.' He says that Mitteleuropa is not a place but an identity. It is not his own.

I'm warming to Lukas now, understanding some of his isolation. 'The Jews have stories from the Old Testament: when the child is sick his parents will change her name so the angels can't find it and call her back. Jacob fought *against the angels and could not win. He was given the name Israel, one who struggles with God.'*

I like this story of being lost and then found again. That God is some promised land. We say goodbye and Lukas photographs me with his digital camera. I tell him that I am a struggling part-time parent and a full-time father. He smiles showing his teeth, 'I am abandoned and happy father.'

(Kutná Hora, May 23, 1998)

KUTNA HORA

I stumbled into Kutná Hora, the richest, the most significant town in medieval Bohemia, said my guide book. I pushed the bike down an unmade road and there it was – a stage set of painted houses, big squares and narrow cobbled streets with intricate towering sculptures. It was architecturally intact, as if a tide in history had stranded it like a log on a beach. What could I say? I wanted to say something about the 13th century silver mines, that they minted Prague groschens here (I have one); that King Wenceslas IV, the king of Bohemia lived here, that the Jesuits had their powerhouse here, a Baroque edifice long abandoned to more worldly gains. The truth is I had nothing to add to Kutná Hora. Here I received the medieval pace, not just the Baroque frenzy of treadmill showpieces.   *(Kutná Hora, May 23, 1998)*

* * *

First thing on a Saturday morning in Kutná Hora I asked a teenager in a shop for a stamp, 'Do you speak English or German?'

'German,' he almost spat, 'I don't like Germans.'

'But this was your parents' war,' I countered. He shook his head defiantly. He did not know why. Ten minutes later and still musing on this, I suddenly remembered a vivid dream fragment from the night before: 'I feel my nose and it has grown at the end, become upturned and larger. It's a Jewish nose. I'm Jewish, I think. Almost immediately I want to hide this nose, keep it a secret. From whom?'

Granny has a way of saying something, almost as if it didn't matter, and it stays in my head for hours afterwards. 'This is how she liked it, with the Christmas tree in the middle. All standing around it and holding hands. We had to be in bed by seven. Our special treat was real chocolate to drink. You can't imagine how precious that was. I remember the smell in my dreams, luscious, spicy and sweet.' A sad, beautiful smile marked her face. She picked up the silver frame on the sideboard. 'He would have liked this, to be here with you, my dears.' A lump squeezed my throat, emotion always embarrassed me. I never know what to say; or that sometimes a squeeze of the hand or to catch someone's eye and say nothing can be golden.

Granny wiped her eyes and put her arm around Sarah and I. Tugger leaped up and this time she let him. No-one said anything. Granny patted Tugger's attentive face, wiping each of his eyes as if he too had tears. 'You're good.' She held Jo last, and longest. 'He was the best.'

The kitchen was transformed into a fairy grotto with balloons in fives at each corner, paper chains hung across the ceiling in happy loops; there were painted pine cones and sprigs of holly above the door. I was inside a glowing oven and, if I spoke, words would glow in my mouth too. A trio of brass angels circled above the candles on the table, striking the bell with their silver wands. They never missed. Six plates had been laid; there was silver cutlery, cut glasses, a cracker, and our names were written in elegant copperplate on a pink card. Granny had done it beautifully, but still she kept fretting the pins in her bun of silver hairs, retracing her steps, going forwards three paces then back one, like some crone in an ancient dance. Words she repeated as if she were in her sleep or too much sherry had got out of the bottle. 'God knows when they'll arrive. *No-one knows the hour...*' The radio told us that snow-ploughs were struggling to keep the main roads open; people with suitcases on their heads were searching for hotels. They would never reach these back lanes; sooner see an oyster throw a snowball.

I saw the empty plates with the names of my parents. I saw them in the night-time struggling against plate-size snowflakes, with suitcases on their shoulders. I wanted them to struggle to find a room for the night, to know what it's like to be lost, to be on the outside, to be the Christmas child which nobody wanted. I put these darker thoughts aside but they were there in the long-legged shadows of the angels circling the walls. Our secret wish had been fulfilled and, in a way I cannot explain, Father Christmas had become our friend, our intercessor. Had he not granted our wish to be together? Perversely I heard the menacing blades of his helicopter *chopchop chopchop*. I could see his red face beaming at the controls. He would complete his mission. The angels' bells were the church bells ringing out the good news. Nothing would stop Father Christmas, nothing, nothing, nothing. He would get through, whatever the cost.

It was a tradition, said granny, to toast Christmas Eve. Tugger was shut in the kitchen – 'for his own good' – and she unlocked the front door with the key she kept around her neck. It was night-time and breathless in the hollow lane; a white brush had chalked the hedgerows, stars glittered between the clouds. We stood in an embarrassed circle facing each other, warmth and shyness in equal parts, made strange and poignant by this intimacy. We appeared in the light, like fireflies. I could see our faces clearly, yet I was standing in the shadows. I could not see myself. Granny brought out mulled wine and the gingerbread biscuits. 'All's well that ends well.' The lamp fingered the shadows of our long arms holding the glasses. Snow had calmed the gaps in the steep sides of the lane; the wind had piled the snow into flying saucers. 'Stay inside then we can see Father Christmas's footprints coming in,' said granny, winking at me. 'You must wish. *Every seeker finds.*' She spilled wine onto the snow. 'We have to give back a little.' Jo stuck out his tongue to catch the last straggling snowflakes. Others he held on his upturned hand and licked to death. With his red hat pulled over his ears, the long black coat from the trunk – the only one which fitted him – he looked the part except he didn't have a white beard. Meanwhile Tugger attacked the inside of the door as if brute force could open it.

TORE CHRISTMAS

Tore was born on a farm called Naess, twenty hectares along a fjord north of Trondheim. Generations had lived there before memory, but as the youngest son he had to find another way. He didn't want to be a priest or a lawyer, so he chose to be a landscape architect, a city life. He remembered his childhood Christmas, the flat bread, the pony and sledge, and especially lutefisk, the festive meal. There were no reindeers pulling Father Christmas though they did mix up a gruel cake and put it in the barn. 'If you put the food out on a plate the rats would get it, but everyone said the old man, the ghost of the ancestors who lived there, had taken it.'

Christmas Eve started with a cup of black coffee at noon and flat bread dipped into beef soup. In the evening were two dishes, porridge with cream, and lutefisk. 'You either loved it or were disgusted by it.' It was a cod that had been caught by line in the fjord and split from head to tail, then dried out of reach of flies at the beginning of winter. A special sauce was made from the ashes of silver birch, bitter to the taste. 'The twigs are burnt slowly in the oven – weeks before – until the ashes cake the oven floor. It is essential during this period to make the women – but not the grandmother – angry otherwise the sauce will not work. They must stay calm, but my father was an expert. He always made them shout at him.' (Oslo, June, 1998)

Then what I had been dreading happened. She went to the grandfather clock and searched for the key I had put back half an hour before. This time she abandoned any secrecy and openly squeezed her hand through the gap at the back, sensing its way in that confined space. A flicker in her eyes, a slight hesitation, was all that betrayed her thoughts. But it was a different key to unlock the bottom drawer of the sideboard. Out came an old red bag and from it she pulled a tatty wasp with the stuffing showing. It was yellow and brown and furry with metal feelers and tired wings. 'Vespa the wasp. I gave it to you for your second birthday. You pushed it in a shoe-box and pretended it was a train. Everywhere you went, the wasp went to, to the bed, to the toilet. You wouldn't sleep without it.' Jo held it as if it were a tired bird in his hands, twirling it slowly at arm's length. He landed it on his shoulder.

'Like this! *Doo dee tooty dooty tee doo.* They're laughing at you. That's not nice. What do you say? *BZzzzzzz bzzzzzzzzz.*' He cradled Vespa in his arms. 'Nice wasp, Shiva's wasp.'

'I don't know why I keep these things. I must be sentimental. Old people are like this, someone has to.' Out came a small leather box; the clip was broken but inside it was as shiny as a pearl and a gold watch glittered on a chain. Jo received it in the cup of his hands like treasure. 'What is the time?' asked Sarah formally. He palmed the half-hunter to his ear. 'It's 7pm, exactly.'

'Your grandfather loved this half hunter. His parents had saved up the farthings. They were poor in those days. On special occasions they had newspapers for tablecloths. You had to survive, it was hard. Now we've got turkeys – then it was beef dripping on bread or pease pudding with a ham bone. There's nothing glamorous about poverty when you've got mouths to feed. It's like being a sparrow.'

I had heard that before somewhere.

Suddenly she got to her feet and pulled a black waistcoat from the bottom drawer, smoothing out the creases. 'You could be his double.' From the air, it seemed, she produced golden cufflinks, a pair of braces and shoes with stitched white uppers. She placed them beside Jo's feet. 'They were his dancing shoes. They might fit.'

Granny said nothing the way grandparents do, long and slow and holding her bottom lip so everyone could see she was more interested than words could say. Before you could say Big Bertie's batty whiskers Jo walked in creaking on his shoes, transformed by the black waistcoat and buttoned up to his neck with an old-fashioned shirt collar like a butterfly. His hair was oiled back smartly. 'If you could see yourself! Wait!' She led him to the mirror. It was a black and white snapshot with granny's adoring face above Jo's shoulder. He gave nothing away. He saluted and down-marched his arms. He pressed them against his hips. Out came the watch, 'It's 7.15pm, exactly.'

WILLIAM LAMPERT AND ANNA KAISER

'It starts with small things,' says Anna Kaiser. 'You go into a supermarket and the trolleys are catching your heels. Everyone is going too fast, they want to get there first. My mother loved the queues in England, she could relax at last.' The techno pace of modern Germany had a price, they agreed on this. 'I didn't like the person I was becoming,' says William. So they moved to south Holland and rebuilt a small, blue-and-white house, more like a ship's cabin, and made a rambling English garden. Sometimes they go shopping in England and Belgium; Bruges is not far away. Part of each year they return to Germany where they founded the Jüdisches Theater in Deutschland over ten years ago. 'I'm a Holocaust expert,' says Anna.

She wonders whether to have a second cake and decides she deserves it. Their life is one of projects. In their study she translates books while William works on his plays. She is an actress, first of all; her gleaming eyes roam a face extraordinary with changes, sometimes closed and enigmatic then she titters curling her nose. 'I'm the practical one, William is the artist. I blow the whistle when the money is running out.' They met in Bad Hersfeld when she walked onto a stage in a play which William was directing. 'William is very tidy and saw the rusty staples where I had shortened my trousers. "Hey you, fat country egg," said this man with cavalier locks and gravel in his voice and unblinking eyes. No-one talked to me like that.' She listened. 'I was a wild woman then. William tamed me.' She loved this man, but on the last day he disappeared. She found out that he had left his flat, cut his ties with Germany and bought a one-way ticket to Israel. Frantic phone calls later, Anna tracked him to a Viennese hotel, his last night in Europe. 'I knew he was catching the plane at 5.30am. I knew this was my last chance, I had to keep him talking.' They talked for six hours. 'I was at an advantage for he was in a hotel and the waitresses kept bringing him wine.' He missed the plane and two days later returned to Heidelberg carrying his suitcases.

I'm moving in,' he said.

That's fine.'

They were fed up being at the mercy of agents. 'Why don't we set up our own theatre company?'

'Why not?' And so the Jüdisches Theater in Deutschland was born, and they toured Germany and Austria with productions such as 'KANNTEN SIE WALLENBERG', 'ADAM, EVA und die DAMPFWALZE', 'TEIBELE und ihr DAMON', 'PESSACH', 'KAIN 88'. In ten years they only had two negative reviews. 'Before 1968 German history in schools ended at the Weimar Republic. After the 1968 student revolution the new teachers rammed the Holocaust down the pupils' throats and that led to an intense reaction. Now it depends on the individual teacher's outlook...'

William believes there is still silence on the crimes against Jews. 'If I tell a Holocaust joke, it's a joke. But if you say it then you are anti-Semitic. People are frightened to criticise the Jews, but they are human too.'

Time is stretched and bended with William and Anna. They are good at telling stories and I am good at listening. Anna's sister worked with handicapped children, painstaking work to enlarge their lives. They loved her, so when she says she will leave to get married and live in France it is very hard for them. On her last day the children surprise her with a play they have created: it is a trial, and her husband to be is to be judged if he is fit to marry their beloved teacher. With painstaking slowness the children play their parts and decide he can marry her. 'And this is all done with everyone crying for they know she is leaving them.'

William and Anna are looking for new horizons, sometimes dreaming of winning the green card lottery to live and work in America. Already many other Germans have bought holiday homes in their village. 'One of our neighbours was in a German internment camp and escaped back to Holland and lived for two years in hiding. Now he is surrounded literally by Germans. Our friends told him that William is only half German and half Jewish. Now he accepts us because he doesn't have to change his philosophy.'

Meanwhile he sails off Breskens — he is qualified in navigation — and talks of the sea and the changing lights of which he never tires. He shows me a newspaper cutting of two old ladies who met as strangers while watching a documentary at Westerbork — the transit camp for Dutch Jews bound for Auschwitz. 'They recognised themselves as children. They survived because of forged papers. I think this could make a play, yes I do...'

(Delft, May 11th, 1997)

'Lets get on with the show,' said Sarah, managing again to delicately end a scene and allowing us to move onto another. Someone kept knocking at some door and all the while a great expectation grew inside us, the way a breeze appears when a cloud covers the sun or it flickers a dying candle light into life. Even Tugger calmed down, eyeing us from under the table, sensing every movement of our hands and feet, every little bump in our hearts. Christmas is here, Christmas with lights, with fire in our eyes.

> *Oh Christmas tree*
> *Oh Christmas tree!*
> *How lovely are your branches,*
> *In beauty green*
> *They always grow*
> *In summer's sun*
> *And winter's snow.*

Oh Christmas tree!
Oh Christmas tree
You are the most beloved.

He read out our names: 'The Most Honourable', 'Her Right Worthy', 'The Most Distinguished'. Granny flicked her gracious wrist, inviting him to sit beside her on the sofa. Jo kept smiling, a wordless pleasure calmed his face, adding a brilliance to his eyes I had not see before. His hands were folded against each other concealing his cheeks, his happiness. Tears streamed from his eyes.

'Are you all right?'

'He's happy, that's all.'

'*For he's a jolly good fellow...*' sang Sarah. '*And so say all of us.*'

'*And so say all of us. And so say all of us.*' .

We clapped. Tugger raced around the table fit to frighten a squadron of demons. Jo looped his arms over Tugger and lifted him off the ground. The angels tinkled on the hot air roundabout. A faint honeycomb smell came from the kitchen. Outside the snow lay deep and crisp and even.

CHEF'S DELIGHT

He is an old man from Bordeaux, all sinews and hollows in his face and hands, a wiry, bent man with a spring still flowing in his eyes. He is half-Tunisian yet you would never guess that from his French accent and careful manners. All his life he had worked as a chef, 'at the best hotels' he emphasised with a raised finger and a smile, and nodding in that French way which tells you that he knows what he is talking about. 'Then you must cook yourself wonderful meals,' I ventured. He wagged his finger at me, clicking his tongue at my naïvety. 'I always buy ready-made meals in boxes and tins from supermarkets. Now I want to be served.' (Belléme, 1998)

LAST SUPPER AT MANOLO'S

They were celebrating the end of their pilgrim's walk across Spain. The rousing drinking song came from the back room at Manolo's, the budget restaurant in the web of old Santiago. The Swiss Father sat in the centre of four tables pushed together and around him were the dozen male students from the Catholic teacher's training college. They had done justice to the wine and now, once out of the bottle, they let it sing. No longer was I the lone cyclist. We toasted each other, exchanged addresses and waved each other out of our lives.

I had met them first at Roncesvalles; before dawn, in wet clothes without smiles or hot tea, they had dispelled the gloom by singing in a circle a four-part devotional chant. I met them again at Rabanal del Camino; this time there were smiles and nods, but still no conversation. *At dawn they sang, and the English warden was tongue-tied with emotion. He saluted them. I was affected by his tenderness and embarrassment. I said nothing. They were there at Tria-castela in Galicia, and this time we talked about bikes and journals, and played some football. The following morning, after breakfast of hot chocolate, they made their circle in the street. The Gallegos pretended they were not there, but I couldn't. It was raining when they started singing. I could see the gap in their circle. Two steps away, and that was a mile emotionally. I shuffled closer, inched nearer. I stepped through my shyness humming their tune. I completed the circle, and they welcomed me with smiles. They dedicated a verse to me. That morning, this solitary traveller belonged to a male circle, and he liked it.*

(Santiago de Compostela, October 15, 1996)

'Father Christmas is coming. Look at the clock.'

'It's 8.15, exactly.'

'*Tempus fugit*,' said granny, 'and no-one knows where.'

Behind our backs, as if she had had it planned, granny produced a music box painted with three infantas playing trumpets. It hammered out an old waltz tune, scratchy and slow as it came to life. 'We must dance.' Where? 'You children. We danced at the drop of a pin, in the kitchens, between courses...until the birds sang. There was no TV or radio. This hair wasn't always silver... In rings down my shoulders. I dressed in my finery.' More laughter found its way out as she placed Jo's hand onto her waist. He kept smiling in that silly way as if he were out of his depth or had lost his tongue. His miraculously preserved shoes fidgeted. 'Wait for the music.' Jo shifted when she did, peering back, his smile wavering. 'Follow me.' Sarah mimicked the steps by pretending to hold somebody. I watched. Their unlikely shadows spilled onto the walls, angels still in their fruitless pursuit of each other. 'He was so light on his feet...as tall as you. You never forget the steps. I could stand on his shoes, not even reach his chin.' She stretched to appear bigger and nearly lost her footing. 'This way, left. You have to let go.' Her cheeks coloured, she leaned back letting Jo take her weight. 'The night whirled us on.' Her hair slipped onto her shoulder; she let it lie there. Faster and faster they turned. His eyes appealed to us. He clung on as if he were drowning. Perhaps he was, there was nothing we could do. Stop! Granny's ears were elsewhere, so were Jo's feet. He barged into the side-board. The photographs fell down, some onto the floor. Jo stepped on the glass. A rush of cold air brought granny to a standstill. She picked up the corner of a frame.

'Your big feet!'

228

'But...'

'You didn't think.'

'You were going too fast,' said Sarah.

Colour drained from his face, the cravat tie hung limply. He undid the top button of the waistcoat. His mouth opened but out came nothing. He stepped back towards the door, pulling off the waistcoat. It fell to his shoes. The door was behind him, his feet would not move. His arms were crossed against his chest, his eyes kept staring at the floor. Granny held the picture; she poked her little finger through. The broken glass fell out. The whistle came softly, heard in the distance, coming down the track. The glasses in the cabinet rattled in sympathy. Granny looked up, so did we. Signal GO! His arms waved. He whistled sharp, again and again, louder and louder. A hundred stones ricocheted on the ice. His feet drummed. Then silence, just the angels and the slow-down bells, until they stopped too.

MUSSULMAN EUROPA

Please release me, let me go.

I had wanted to write this on the stepped ramp where the railway line ends. Some candles burn there and a small perpetual light, and the European languages are cast in bronze tablets.

I had wanted to talk about the pappus from the poplars floating as so many satellites in a dreamy blue sky and all the while a light breeze filled my ears with the pleasurable sound of the sea.

I had wanted to write about the wild flowers, the forget-me-nots in the drainage ditch beside the railway spur line, a thin blue haze as far as the red-brick arch and watchtowers where the sealed wagons were shunted in from the nearby Auschwitz station. Or talk about the ragged robin and delicate campanulas I could not name, all growing abundantly in the long-haired places, the narrow places, the hollow places, the awkward corners trapped by the concrete and barbed wire fences.

I had wanted to sit in the place facing the narrow strip of tarmac beside the railway and ramps, to try and imagine what it must have been like: the heat burning off the lines and the sheet metal of the wagons; the SS officers, family men with homes and gardens and dogs they gave a name to, facing a sorrowing tide of people carrying their wealth of little hopes bundled in greys and blacks; the shoulder bags of older women; the fathers still combing their children's hair, boys and girls trying to calm the terror in the eyes of their younger brothers' and sisters' eyes.

I had wanted to imagine the unfathomable sound in the hearts of these people faced at last with the truth: the smoking crematorium chimneys to their left and right. The rumours they had heard and pushed away during their long night-journeys sealed in wagons from every part of mainland Europe. Here at Auschwitz-Birkenau is the truth. The lies ended with this railway track.

I could not write about these things then, the silence and sorrow held my pen and hands and feet. I could not speak, swim against this rage and sorrow and hopelessness. I could only carry them along the well-thought out paths with machine gun posts around the perimeter fence, the same posts, the same barbed wire I had seen at the nearby I.G. Farben 'Buna' works, the vital synthetic oil plant of the German war effort. These places are linked, the one needing the other.

All day yesterday I wandered around Auschwitz, in the pleasant green and shaded square of Auschwitz town (modern Oświeçim), at least two times trying to find the 'Buna' works, and twice becoming lost and panicking as if I would never find my way out. I would be trapped here forever. The thrifty Polish workers grow potatoes and cabbages up to the perimeter fence where trees shade the ghosts of the forced labour camps, British among them. I did not go there. Each time I got lost panic surged through me.

Auschwitz One is a model village compared to Auschwitz-Birkenau, sturdy terra cotta brick buildings obeying the same grid-plan of uniformity. I will add little to the mountain of words to describe what I saw. I saw pictures that some-how I had known all my life: the avalanche of children's shoes, long-glassed corridors filled with hair, bleached and prematurely grey from contact with Zyklon B, the cyanide gas. How strange that only a single plaited lock could bring back a woman's face. I attached myself to an English-speaking guide and his tour. Stanislav was his name, an old man, short silver hair, expressive with his hands. 'And let me show you this...', he said. Of all the horrors I saw that day, I remember these best: the mounds of women, children and babies in a trench; the sleeping and the dead how alike they are, I think. The betrayal in the children's faces, this is the hardest to take. I force myself to look. Take them in, I say. And something flowers in me, born of rage, and it is a light to see by, to recognise the signs of truth of what could happen to ordinary people in ordinary places — and Auschwitz is a very ordinary place — railways lines, non-descript homes, boys singing in trees, normal paranoia for security alarms, billboards for cars, Auschwitz and Birkenau beside enterprise business zones. Normal life and so it has to be. Hordes of schoolchildren explored the gas chamber at Auschwitz and I hoped that their teachers had the skills to enable them to digest what they saw. We had the freedom along with the pappus and house-martins to cross the borders, to pass under the gate — Arbeit Macht Frei — to walk down the no-man's land between the electric fences.

Freedom is to open a door, but the doors had closed on the Jews, and the Germans, with their barbed wire minds, had closed the doors on their hearts.

At Auschwitz-Birkenau I fulfilled a promised I made to Thomas who had given me the white peace poppy and a rosary blessed in Hebrew. At the 'selection' on the tarmac platform, a single finger this way or that may result in a reprieve and a tattoo number, or as a signal to join the line stepping down into the concrete bunker; the shaving of the hair, the confusion, the ritual undressing, then 600 at a time would be gassed. The families were the ones holding hands. Another picture I cannot forget is a blow-up of naked Jewish women panicking before the concrete bunker door. The picture taken at enormous risk of waving arms and open mouths has no sound; they are in my head only.

I wondered where to place this poppy and rosary. I wanted somewhere near the ruins of the gas chambers blown up by the Germans believing that dynamite could conceal their crimes. I think of the birch trees. Birkenau is to do with birches, but birches do not live long. I chose the bronze memorial in English asking us to remember. Next to it was a candle flame. It is not the horror I remember best or my reflex rage against the Nazis. I understood dimly that by identifying with this righteous rage I would collude with this darkness. It would have no face, and I would lose mine.

I left granny slumped in her arm-chair, behind the shield of her hands. A low murmuring sound came from her lips. Sarah held her from behind. There was nothing I could say or do to change this situation. I longed for darkness and my pillow, to sink without a trace. I cannot remember when Sarah came to bed. The half-lights felt better than being under my blankets. Silver from the hall-light had crept into the room, up the wall, gilding the frame, mooning the fleshy arms and shoulders where the rings of hair lay. I saw the face and the gay, hard eyes and the hair in ringlets. I imagined them to be snakes, something from the earth I could not hold. Something beyond my reach, before I was born. I wanted to take it down. I turned away and kept turning back.

I climbed down from the bunk. The light played on Sarah's face and her arm dangling over the side. I listened to the squeeze box of her snoring. I hardly dared breathe. I saw it as if I already knew it was there, the plumed hat, the long blue feathers. A dancing hat she wore before her marriage. Thoughts are dangerous. I pushed them away, they shadowed back to the surface, circling me as if I were its prey. I had no escape. I had seen this hat before when I had travelled to a new country. I had held it in my hands. The night agreed, I heard tapping. Her eyes watched, they followed me. I could not move. I was in this now. The canvas moved, I saw it bulge in the same place, balloon out. I could not stop it. The fist broke through, a small fist. A white hand, all fingers clenched. They opened like the petals of a rose. I could reach out, hold one, pull it through. It wanted me to. I reached out, I touched it. It disappeared.

MUSSULMAN-EUROPA

And here I come to the part where I have to feel my way as Max did on his walk from Dijon to his home village. For in a way which I cannot explain, I am looking for the home where I belong. And this light of Auschwitz is side by side with horror and disgust of what ordinary people in ordinary places are capable of doing in exceptional circumstances. And I am connected to this. As Anne Frank wrote in her diary, 'We all wanted this war'.

I am always amazed by the hatred of the Jewish people, especially when it flares up irrationally among people whom I know. And at that precise moment I feel myself shrinking as if somewhere I am on the run, not fully present in this body. These are the people, always men, I am frightened of, and my defences are these: timidity, smiles, compliance, omission. I go out of my body, I betray the fine animal in me. My defence is to become invisible and my revenge is always indirect, understatement to trap their misjudgements and later to birch them with it. In short, to humiliate them. I like low status, the gold in the dirt, Christ as a beggar boy at the gates of Bethlehem. At Auschwitz I had to see through my own eyes, my contribution to world peace.

And I see this. Today cycling along the Vah valley from Zilina I glimpsed myself in a mirror and there I was in my hooded blue goretex suit, and absurdly I thought of the shrouded man, that strange mix of British and Middle-Eastern, of Christian and Muslim. Behind this callus there is a love story. Behind this barbed wire mind, there is a love story. I have always had a picture of a Christian princess in love with an Arabian prince. I know it's not out there. At Auschwitz I asked Stanislav — merciful to us and pitiless for the sake of truth — 'Who were the Mussulmen?'

'They were the ones who had given up control of their lives. They just wanted to die.'

'But why Mussulmen?'

'It was a name they found themselves. They wrapped themselves in blankets. They were like the holy Muslims praying.'

So I found my vital piece of jigsaw. The skeleton in the shawl, the one who had given up his life, is connected for me with this Middle-Eastern prince. As if by finding this skeleton behind the shawl, behind the callus, I will find this dream, this healing picture.

*On the morning I cycled to Auschwitz I woke up singing, '**Please release me, let me go...**' I release the man in the skeleton whoever he is. Several times at Auschwitz, looking at the most terrible blow-ups of mothers and* children thrown into a pit, I felt that by a trick of light they were sleeping. And in a way I cannot explain I thought they might wake one day and claim their freedom, but not in this life. The skeleton man wants to be free. Are the dead at Auschwitz still in limbo? Angels might know.

One and a half million Jews were murdered at Auschwitz, as well as Poles and Gypsies; 40 million dead from the Allied and Axis powers from the war. How many hearts were broken, families broken up? How many souls went to heaven? Angels might know. How many souls are lost? Angels might know.

Three miles out of the death camp, in a pastoral scene of families pitch-forking the hay, I narrowly missed being killed at a poorly-signed junction. Trembling, I stopped. I looked up and saw two storks circle down from the sky, surreally for me a swan's broadside with eagle's wings. I watched them circle lower and lower looking for their home. I took that as a good omen.

(Trenčán, June 1, 1998)

THE WHITE ORCHID

Nowhere across France or Germany, Czech, Slovakia or Hungary did this exquisite ribbon of wild flowers repeat itself. No more did I feast my eyes on orchids or cowslips or lungwort or milkworts. I appreciated how rare this picture had been. Then I thought of it again in a suburb of Hradec Králové in Eastern Czech. I saw the same picture but this time there were no flowers. On one side of the road was a Sixty's dream-block of socialist realism, the same concrete panels you see everywhere without any deviation or pretence of decoration. Had civil engineers designed it? I don't know. On the other side of the road stood a single house, an architect's dream house, compact on three levels with a wooden balcony at the back and a garden level office.

I stood in the garden. I looked back across the road at the flats, a giant chessboard of concrete panels and glass squares with functional balconies and repetitive clothes' lines. These were people's homes, I did not forget that. This is not the best view, said the architect wanting me to see the garden. But I was mesmerised and suddenly I knew why. I had seen the white orchid on the Normandy wayside beside the repetition of charlock and wheat, this vulnerable uniqueness against the fanatical uniformity. And I had the same emotion: sadness. These are people's homes. This is the food we eat. I decided I did not want to be the white orchid or the dream house. Neither did I want the gridlock charlock or flats.

I like the contradictions best.

(Ostrava, Czech, 1998)

The Rainbow City

"Silly! We can't get lost. All roads lead back home."

I can't remember the sequence of events, time concertina'd and so did the house. I remembered the night before, the sudden, sharp whistle like a train in the night, the hand in the wall I had touched. I heard jangling sounds I could not place. I crept onto the landing. I seemed to have lead weights on my feet. I saw granny anchored by the front door, in her slippers and gown, and pushing in her keys. Each time they would not turn she pushed harder, jangling them. She talked to herself, 'I locked all the doors. There's no way out. TUGGER!'

'Father Christmas has come,' shouted Sarah from behind me. Granny faced us, her hair uncombed from the night.

'TUGGER!' There was no answer.

'He's hiding.'

'He's probably in Jo's room, under the bed with a chocolate.'

'You know what he's like.'

Jo's door was shut. Sarah knocked, and did it again. His bed was neatly made with the cover drawn back to allow in the air, the way granny liked it. 'His suitcase is here. He's in the cupboard. We can see you.' Hanging up was a black waistcoat, below it the pair of brogues; and in one was the faded leather box. It was empty. A hundred days might pass in that moment of shock. Jo had gone, cleared out. 'I shut the windows. I locked the door. He couldn't have got out.' Down the stairs we trooped. This time she unlocked the front door. The snow had nearly gone. The last bits were like blossom stuck onto the trees. A crust of snow covered the narrow drive as far as the footprints. They stepped out by the coal shed. The board was propped against the wall. A man's footprints, and beside it were little claw prints following obediently. They were not coming in, but going out. And soon to be ghosts of footprints.

'This is not really happening.'

'He's taken Tugger for a walk.'

'Before breakfast.'

'He'll be back in a minute.'

Nothing could stop granny, not her slippers or her dressing gown. Our combined footprints shattered the crust of the snow. What was left of the trail circled the cottage to the field where the snow lay thickest. It stopped by the apple trees where a gingerbread man balanced in the fork of a branch; little golden eyes stared back at us. How long had he stood there with his bag? Did he hear a train coming? Did the signal say GO? We both held granny's hands.

'He's gone.'

'He'll be back.'

'Gone...'

The footprints crossed over the fence which he had struggled to climb. They followed the field to the hedgerow and thereafter I couldn't see them. Soon they would return to the earth, only a bloodhound could follow that. They would be let off their leads and men with sticks would beat their way up King's Hill, clacking the wood, scaring the birds, driving away the deer. They would not give up, they would hunt for Jo like the fox, up and down the hills and run him to ground. He had walked away in the night-time when our backs were turned. He had had to, to find his way. Granny called out his name again. It was answered by the steady splits and splats dripping from the trees. I wanted him to get away. The thaw had saved him, bought him time. I could see the red bag over his shoulder, his red hat and black coat. Even then I knew where he was going. He had wanted to be Father Christmas. Tugger knew, but he couldn't say anything, and neither did I.

Granny called the police. Didn't they have families? An unmarked van with a dog and four policemen, including a woman, arrived within the hour. The dog mauled one of Jo's old shirts which was being cleaned, and off he went pulling a fat policemen and two others around the cottage and up the hill. When the light failed and he still had not been found, all hell was let loose. Three more vans arrived. Sarah and I promised that we would never ever tell what we knew. He was in the papers with that silly face, and you couldn't tell whether he was laughing or crying. He had finally got away from that place.

CAT'S EYES

He says he belongs to no state or welfare system. Long ago he left the exclusive boarding school in Denmark; later he left the good life in Venezuela, secure work in Houston, Aberdeen, his company car and prospects. With his dark complexion and intent eyes (some Spanish blood from the Napoleonic wars), a Transatlantic accent softly-spoken, he could be from Central America. Except he is Danish. He thinks of himself as European but doesn't know what that means. His parents live in the Middle East. All his life, he says, he has done what is expected of him and done it well. It has stressed him learning about engineering. Now he has handed in his notice as head of a business section and is returning to England to marry his girlfriend. 'I suppose you could say I have had a privileged life.' But every time he returned to Denmark he went into a straight depression; the weather, the planned life, the punctuality. 'The conversation had dried up with his friends. I will not go back to live in Denmark.'

For the first time, he says, he is doing something different, something he has chosen. He plans to travel with his wife to South America and see the native birds and animals. 'I have always loved the cats,' he says. He wants to discover their 'slowliness' and poise in his life. As a child he collected insects and put them into a glass bowl and would watch them for hours. In his youth, for relaxation, he walked about cities watching people in railway stations, just happy to see new things. He believes more in philosophy than God. 'I think I am looking for a new direction. I want to find a way of working with animals. But how?' He doesn't know. He stretches out his arms and raises his fingers. 'I used to catch flies like this. I watch the flies. They have eyes in the back of their heads watching me. I wait until they flick their legs back and then I move my fingers closer together. I do this several times. When it looks up, I stop. Then I move my left hand and catch the fly with my right hand. It always flies in the opposite direction. Two or three times out of ten I'm successful.'

These are the same odds he gives himself to change his life.

(Harwich, June 21, 1997)

I WANT TO SEE THE WORLD COME IN

All through the Transdanubian plains with its pulse of small birds and ricocheting rails, horizons without visible ends, I cycled with a white muslin cloth tucked under my baseball cap. I cycled through the privacy of villages, old couples sorting beans in the shade, their strong backs and dark complexions; I saw church spires with the ghosts of minarets in their slender lines, glimpsed attractive eyes, something hidden or modest in them hinting of more eastern allegiances. Somehow I managed the miracle of staying afloat in this sauna bath.

The sultry weather came with me to Pécs, the old university city where the Turks left their mosques and town plan of narrow streets. Officially it's described as the economic and cultural and spiritual headquarters of southern Transdanubia. It's border country – 20 kilometres from the former Yugoslavia – a city of 170,000, and 60,000 live in suburbs of industrial flats, and most of these are in bad condition. The rise in energy prices has hit the city hard.

The day I arrived clouds stole the light, thunder and lightening ended the heat wave. And down came the rain; narrow streets became torrents, the slow bends caught pebbles. Many locals gave up the struggle to stay dry, abandoning their shoes and socks, pulling up clothes, walking arm in arm through the deepest parts. They were happy, it hadn't rained for weeks.

I watched the storm from a flat on the Mecsek hills overlooking Pécs. Agnes Beata, a young doctor, remembers looking out of this window and hearing the shell-fire during the Yugoslavian conflict. She remembers the fear she experienced that only a line on a map kept the fighting on the other side of the hills. The sky darkened into a real pea-souper; lightning chased its tail, a monstrous son-et-lumière. It passed but not the fear, the tremors remained in my stomach, holding the primal reins between fascination and flight. This night is a danger zone of tingling premonitions and flickering light bulbs. I sensed my fear, the fixed eyes, the involuntary step back. It's here. I want to find a hiding place. From what? This exposure to the elements, I'm vulnerable. The sudden illuminations on the window-panes with the replying thunder stir the dismemberment of Sarajevo...thunder and more shock waves, the hiss of dry earth, sudden arc lamps in the sky and then deliciously cool air.

It is said that the bombardment was a revenge by the rural chetniks on the cosmopolitan city. I want to close the shutters, twist shut the locks in the two windows, pull the curtains tight. Agnes says that recently they found a mass grave on the far side of that hill: a 1000 bodies.

I liked Pécs. It is a cosmopolitan city. In the Mecsek hills I identified the richest wayside flora I had seen anywhere in Europe – dittany, dwarf yellow irises, big campanulas, lilies, exotic salvias etc – yet paradoxically a blanket of polluted air drifted over the city in the early morning. (The local authority is campaigning for direct subsidies to convert cars to gas consumption.) On the streets – and the explosion of renovation after the socialist regime – is a bewildering and handsome mix of people: Slavs, gypsies, Magyars, Germanic Habsburgs. Pécs is twinned with Lathi in Finland, Feldbach in Germany, Cluj in Rumania, Osijek in Croatia.

In Pécs there is local government of ethnic minorities, German, Croatian, Gypsy and Bulgarian. I was not surprised to learn that the Mayor of Pécs, Zsolt Pavahad, received the UNESCO's Cities For Peace Award for Europe in tribute to his struggle against exclusion and discrimination, and especially for helping Hungarian refugees from Rumania and victims from the war in the former Yugoslavia.

I only scratched the surface in Pécs. I visited the two surviving mosques, one converted into a Christian church, the other a museum and still with its minaret. It was once a famous tekke, a monastery linked to the Mevlana order of whirling dervishes in Konya. I lingered in that quiet, intricate silence, still a place of worship for visiting Islamic students. The muezzin's call to prayer has not been heard here for 250 years when the Turks withdrew from the city.

In a side square I stumbled on the old synagogue. The caretaker signalled me to climb up the steps, and so I did. Their memorial tablet for Auschwitz recalls that over 4,000 Jewish people lived here before the war – now only 150 remain. Here on this spiritual stage I felt sad, the lack of people saying everything. The past still had its bridges but there was no traffic anymore. I remembered Cordóba and the Caliphate, and how the peoples of the Book – Christian, Muslim and Jewish – had lived creatively together, influencing each others' architecture, cross-cutting the ideological mind. The empty mosque and synagogue, the memories of Sarajevo mocked these associations. I had seen Auschwitz-Birkenau – I knew the end place of intolerance. And why am I worrying about this?

In Pécs I felt European, perhaps for the first time. Because everyone was so different, my own differentness felt normal. I belonged here because I was different. I had found some of my long-distance aunts and uncles. Here I liked the complexity, the pieces which did not fit, the billboards of history in small squares, down side-streets. This was once Pannonia, a province of Rome like most of Britain. I scratched the exotic and unexplained parts of myself. I saw faces I recognised. All of Europe seemed to be here, including its troubled zones. It's in the wild flowers too. I know them all from English gardens.

I left Pécs with no answers, but I had made some connections.

(Kaposvár, June 10, 1998)

It's Christmas Day and Tugger lies under the Hessle pear tree. The fruit last year were small and sweet, the juice melting in my mouth. He never went on any more travels. They found him ten miles down a lane. He had crossed the new road, so that was a miracle. Granny was right; this was her last stop before the crossing. The thistles have climbed the embankment. She would have liked that, but not the ivy growing back over the windows. I've boarded up the bottom ones. Security is an issue even here. By the stream is the small stone sculpture. The moss has grown over it but I can see the little hearts I carved up the front. The oak tree is growing strongly this side of the stream. Each year I prune off the bottom growths, it's twice my height now.

Things come slowly; light comes creeping through the ivy; the sun lights up this chair, the back wall with the wooden shelf, my tins of food. I had the secret but I did not understand. How could I? I was a child. We were all children, babes in the wood. A lifetime could not fathom such goings on. It's obvious. Some things are so obvious, like the tiny initials J.P. in the back of the watch. They're too close to see, like air or someone's touch or soil. And who knows what's in the soil? It's darker than Mars, that's what they say. Or watching house-martins over a weir, the way they circle backwards as if their courses are purposeful and erratic at the same time. It makes no sense if you look at the birds. You have to see their quarry – the insects – to understand each twist and turn. There's always a story, a dance to follow, if you go slowly enough. It's a question of time.

You know Sarah is practical. She can say things which amaze me. She can say: You're frightened of granny, aren't you? And I'll say 'No' but later I'll think she's right. Granny's ashes are scattered with grandpa's between the two apple trees. In the grass, closeby, is a golden ring. I had put it there in a distant time, returning to the earth promises which I had made, returning it to the darkness. Who was that young man? He's gone, gone completely. There's a road out there and no-one knows where it goes to. This is where it starts. Early this morning I stood with the sun streaming through the branches. Out came a deer and watched me from halfway up the field then it bounded away up King's Hill. Perhaps it already heard the hunter's horn. On this Christmas day I longed to see more light, and so I lit a candle and placed it beneath the apple tree. I remembered the gingerbread man, the teddy bear road which Jo took, a lifetime ago. I bowed to myself, to this day from dawn to dusk, from the infant to old age. You are on your own.

Jo, of course, never did come back. Christmas was his birthday really.

SIXTIETH BIRTHDAY

Joost Sileghem is a Flemish Belgian from Kortrijk. He teaches physics (and still enjoys it) and lives in a house full of books on industrial archaeology, history of art, photography, and literature. The Belgian soberness and twinkle comes on and off in his conversation. He tells me he is 61. I can hardly believe it. Now he is a surrogate father to seven-year-old Florian, and partner to Mia Goutsmet, a music teacher. It is as near, he says, as he will ever get to being married.

He remembers his sixtieth birthday very well. As a treat, Mia says she will drive him over the border to a French restaurant in Lille. She takes a long time to get ready and keeps looking at her watch.

'I have something in my eye,' she says, and five more minutes pass.

'We always have to wait for women,' thinks Joost.

They drive out of town with her sister and husband, but Mia thinks she has forgotten her money. She stops in an empty car park.

'Now what is it?' says Joost.

'I must check my purse.'

The minutes pass. She finds it just as a yellow flashing light comes out of a side-street. Out marches a band, all trombones, clarinets, drums pounding, clashing castanets, and a colourful procession of people dancing and singing. They are wearing masks.

'A fanfare,' exclaims Joost. 'You know I love a fanfare.'

'We really have to go,' says Mia.

Joost bounds out the car. 'It's my birthday,' he shouts, 'just five minutes.'

He joins the back of the procession, Mia walks behind him. They are the only ones without masks. More people appear from side-streets and join the procession. They all wear masks. Every minute Joost expects Mia to tap his shoulder. He looks back, she is always smiling. He can't understand, but it's his birthday and he's enjoying himself. The procession winds slowly and loudly into town. Still more people wave and clap at street corners. They, too, are wearing masks. The band enters a school. Joost vaguely recognises it but not the balloons and ribbons. He tells Mia that they must leave, but the momentum of the crowd carries them into a hall.

Perhaps 150 people are standing in this room. Mia and Joost are the only ones without masks. Once again he tells Mia: 'We must go.' She shrugs her shoulders. He is amazed. He knows she loves French meals. Someone with a brightly-painted face and long nose ushers him into a seat, a big seat. People come up to him and pat him. He can't understand why Mia is laughing. Everyone is laughing. An old man hobbles across and takes off his mask. He recognises the face of Mia's father. 'This is not really happening,' thinks Joost as they sing 'Happy birthday to you...'   (Kortrijk, May 7, 1997)

DAY SIGNS

'And do you know day signs? It's dreaming by day.'

'They did that in the Hebrides. The auguror stood in front of an open window, with a question, and she would notice what appeared.'

'You need to be still to do that.'

'I'm sure it works.'

'There's so much happening around us.'

She showed me around the ruined steading, a woman passionate and articulate about the lost opportunities she saw in each tumbled building. I noticed the bird cherry, the squabbling jackdaws, a wych elm clinging to the first floor, nettles rooting into the debris.

'It such a waste,' she said.

'It's a nature reserve. Nature is the new tenant.'

'Everything struggles,' she says. 'Life's not easy.' Such as juggling work and time to work at her own writing. She has a PhD and insecurity, she says she is content, that life is rich. The vitality of her anger about Western progress had been a passion, and she had worked in social development in Malawi and Zimbabwe; a committed face, wise, at turns girlish, sombre and never far from laughter. She likes the East coast where folks speak to your face, get on with things, are curious and friendly, who have confidence in their lives. She's Scottish first and enjoys the intellectuality of Europe, especially Germany, and sometimes thinks about returning there. The gravitas of the world's problems alternates with her laughter. She likes parrots, their larger than life brightness. They turn up in unlikely places, drop out of trees when she's around. Perhaps it's a message. 'A long-lived bird, very intelligent. They know how to play.'

One evening we sing at Auchtermuchty in a private house, most of us in our forties and fifties; three men and six women, accomplished and novices. There is a place for everybody, songs for everybody: negro spirituals, raunchy doo ron rons, the liquid golds of **'Green Grow The Rushes O'**, songs to remember such as **'The Emerald Stream'**, the companionship of singing together. That night I dream of animals, deer and dogs, swimming to the shore.

The old lady who lives in the gardener's cottage is extending her garden, even though walking is hard for her. The garden is already in her mind; she just has to do it. Her humour is unflagging. A rare orange-tip butterfly lands on sweet woodruff. 'Kill it and press it,' she laughs mischievously.

The American artist lives in a small Fife village. Sometimes she wears a black T shirt emblazoned 'Neighbourhood Witch'. It's an ice breaker.

She shows me the Collessie stone, the Pictish monolith in a field. She points out the shield and weighted spear, the feet, the eye and the prominent nose. Through her enlivening eyes, I see it too. I show her my carved wooden bull roarer with the cow parsley blossoms and St Mark's fly, a love story appearing each spring, the flies attracted to the flowers and going when they go. On the way to the stone I see a few St Mark's flies, their long legs dangling above hairy bodies. I point out some clinging to the stone. I whirl my prayer stick three times. The air hums. The sky above us is visibly dark with coruscating St Mark's fly. Yet one hundred yards away only a few skitter about. That night I dream of my father, and he is seated on the ground.

I see rubbish which is a habitat for natives, orange peel is food for slugs, the discarded concrete pipe a home for shrews.

I sit in the ruined choir chapel at St Andrew's Cathedral, choosing a sheltered spot out of the sun to write. It's hard to imagine what songs gilded these massive pillars brought down at the Reformation. The walls are like the dogmas, they fell down. Now the sun wins through and I can hear the pulse of small birds. Everywhere I look are tombstones, the past, but here it is light and airy. St Rule's tower is both the formal and symbolic end of this journey, and it is fitting that it is beside the sea. The past is a maze, behind me, and now there is a trail, a journey to be made.

(St Andrews, St Rule's Tower, May 16, 1999)

Now I come to the part where I must end this. It's not one of those stories which ends neatly, all the loose ends tied up. From here I can't see where I am going. The roots are here and so are the ties. I can close the door now this story is done. He did go down the road that no-one's been down before and no-one knows where it goes to. From granny's chest (and those letters) I found out that Jo is short for Johannes. His father had been a German tank officer. Granny's sister had fallen in love while nursing him. Is that a crime? He returned to Germany; he never had died. That was just a story, it was like that in those days. Love crosses frontiers. It doesn't bow to flags or the shapes of people's noses. Love is kind. So I have done my bit, Jo. It really is time to say goodbye. I have lingered here too long. I hope you are at peace, wherever you are. It's hard going through this door of saying good-bye. You are so much part of my life now. You showed me the details and I am carried by them. You have your wings, and I have my feet. I will plant them and grow the world around me.

He changed his name back to Johannes Pieter, the name of his father. His hair is grey now, but he still keeps it long, tied loosely. He's gone down the teddy bear road, that's what he said. Not so long ago he was in a newspaper, front page, and in a silly picture of him hanging out of a tree with the other protesters. He had his front tooth missing and that look on his face as if he couldn't make up his mind to laugh or cry. A big yellow balloon inside me wanted to burst with laughter. One last thing, and granny used to say it: *'Why need you look for me? Did you not know that I must be about my Father's business?'*

PEDALLING PAST THE MILLENNIUM —
Caergybi i Gaerdydd

When I close my eyes the silent procession of faces goes the same way: in and out of fence lines, threading the hollows of Welsh mountainsides, shadows in low-lying clouds; all strangers in shouting lycra shades or de-mob shorts; some freewheeling, some upright and sedate, some in love with tandems and each other, some pumping, heads down, dragon-lines of reds, whites and yellows beside grass and sheep, hallucinations for cows. Who brought them here? I can't see where they are going or where they come from, nor the details of the faces. The names matter but not now. Then the procession fades into a ghostly calvacade and I am back with this blessed rain and a calf chewing a bar in a breeze-block byre.

The faces are important. I see them against landscapes: Peter Tocher from Wimblington under a glittering Anglesey sky and an eddy of farm kids. He's a deputy headmaster of a comprehensive and wants to cycle to South Africa when he retires. 'I'll come back to Wales,' he says later, fingering his fag in the cup of his hand, 'Beauootiful. But in my own time.' Brian Brett is in his late seventies, a techno-kid from Sydney, Australia; a retired engineer with smiling eyes above high cheekbones. He stands alone in the fretting rain outside Caernarfon leisure centre. His mission? To bring cycle lanes to Australia. He gives me his card: Bicycle Advocacy Group, Sydney West and N.W. Region. 'You have to win the politicians to change the law.' The unknown grandfather and grandson on the wooden estuary bridge at Barmouth; side by side they listen to the wailing chorus of 180 cyclists filing across the wet beams.

I cycled from Holyhead to Bristol, the Welsh section of Sustran's emerging national cycle network, an extraordinary effort to reconcile private and public interests (a byzantine partnership with 250 local authorities), a one-off comparable to the canal and railway building eras. At Neuadd Dinas Caerdydd, Cardiff City Hall, I stepped back onto the lawn to see how others saw us: a chequerboard of colours, fluorescent tabards, day-glo rucksacks, lycra and muscles; testing brakes and pressures, ticking index gears, packing panniers or staring at the sky, flexsome bodies hooded against rain, a picture of random orderliness, criss-crossing lines, no special focus like watching leaves on a tree. A whistle sucks in the crowd and suddenly the cyclists are beads on a necklace around Isobel Stoddart; conversation dips then laughter drowns the rush-hour traffic. But only for a moment. The talk is of high winds and tail winds. The tintinnabulation of bells is overwhelmed by the police sirens and the honking wave of traffic marshals. I balance and jostle for my place. I like this moment best.

From the outside, we're strangers until they see our faces. Where you going mate? Land's End. Jesus! Did you hear that! Where from? Belfast. For

247

Christ's sake! I wish I had the time. Where do you get it from? Time, after all, is the only thing we inherit at birth. Andy Bakewell, a re-invented production engineer, cycles alongside me. 'I've been thinking about time debts and technology.' He drove his car four miles into work and back but this privilege cost him one third of his net salary, say 15 hours weekly work plus all the time of servicing, chasing tax, insurance, repairs, car thefts etc. 'I realised one day I was on a road to nowhere, nothing was changing in my life but it was costing me my life.' Now as a post-graduate at Bangor University he researches the economic impact of cycle tourism for Wales. Perhaps the brambled beer gardens I saw near Merthyr Tydfil will be transformed into rose beds. Perhaps continental cyclists will roam the Taff trail like coach tours today. Who knows?

There is a yearning for something simpler and modern. The bike embodies the paradox, a child can mend it yet today's cycle is the child of the space and aircraft industry: the alloy frames, aluminium welding, aerodynamic profiles, sexy millennium textiles. 'If you spend £2,000 on a car, so what. £2,000 on a bike, WOW!' says Andy. If the paths are there, people will use them: 1.6 million journeys are made on the Bath-Bristol cycleway annually. Everyone is interested in safe routes to schools and who wants asthma? Eight out of ten children in Dutch and German comprehensives travel by bike; two out of ten in Britain, yet there are five times more accidents here.

In drooling rains, a chain of Mayors, looking well-fed in sober grey suits, greeted these cycling lifelines in the old strongholds of Norman and Welsh castles. Political love-spoons were exchanged. ('An inflatable mayor,' says my son Michael. 'They keep it in the Halford van.')

'We're glad to welcome you today and we hope that this event will lead to ever greater ties…If it wasn't for the rain we'd all be speaking English now… I hear the Millennium fund gave you £42 million to set up these national routes — and we still got to give you tea!'

The riders invent Cro-Magnon man, The Witch, Bio-Wires, Bunter — some notice how many cucumber sandwiches and Welsh cakes they take — but did they see Cro-Magnon strap the rope to his seat and haul bedraggled children up the hills? 'That's what I call a REAL gentleman.' Then Road Rager drives in for the kill. 'Just had my first taste of it. I'm shaking,' says the sweeper. The youth in the Cortina had signalled with his index finger only to submit sheepishly to 180 cyclists around the corner. T-shirts shouted back: One Less Car. He could be the boy next door.

The argument is won. The issue is about safe routes. Where there is real choice people will exercise it. But in this country there is no choice. But what makes people change? Andy again, the only person I've met who wants to see playgrounds for adults. 'I think everyone wants to do something remarkable in their lives. When I'm 80 I want to sit in my rocking chair and think, yes I did that!' Then a doctor admits he was a fast and aggressive driver until his epileptic attack. For three months he apologised riding his bicycle until he realised that he enjoyed cycling. 'It was my road to Damascus.'

STOPPING! ON YER LEFT! CAR! SLOWING! On Drum-dhu, the barrowed hill above Rhayader, the sun overwhelms the clouds and sees off the English rain. The riders are like coloured sugar puffs or rainbow drops carried by ants across this moorland route. I'm full of conversations: the Welsh Eisteddfod and the rumpus when someone suggested selling beer at this traditionally dry festival. Someone else fills my imagination with golden orioles and how to identify a redstart; or else I'm back to the future at the south London workshops of Holdsworth (There are six on the ride and I've got one of them); at glaciers and fragile beaches in North Island, New Zealand ('No dogs on trackways there'); with the BP manager who handles a £20 million budget ('Everyone had to come to me because I didn't have a car'); 'I got a new cycle computer for my birthday,' says Sam, 'and it's got EIGHT functions.'

Ben Hamilton-Baillie from Sustrans, cycles alongside me, a re-incarnated architect. He treads a fine line between a charity, a campaigning group, a public body; private initiatives and public consensus. At times he's serious ('Curtailment of private motoring is on the horizon. There's a snowball effect when 70% of a track is in place. Everyone can see the benefit.') He buffoons soulless efficiency and makes me laugh. He points his finger to infinity. 'And zis machine will spread ze concrete relentlessly.' He defuses tension at another wet luggage-sort: 'There must be some more grumbles around here.' Every mile of new track has to be negotiated. The risk of failure, perhaps, is what makes it real. 'Sustrans is pro-bikes not anti-cars,' he says.' Most cyclists have a car after all.' This captures the spirit of the millennium for me: because everyone is different, I can belong here. I like that. Then somewhere on the Brecon Beacons I remembered the faces that had joined and left since Holyhead. There were so many. One is Geoff Hamilton, the gardener. One moment he was cycling above the Tal y bont reservoir, the next he was dead on the wayside. Earlier in Brecon he had unveiled a bronze sculpture for the Taff Trail linking Brecon and Cardiff. He raised his hand and made us see the hills, the swifts, the moon in the day sky. 'This is what it's all about,' were his last public words.   (Dunsford Farm, August 16, 1996)